12.50
N

# Inalienability of Sovereignty
## in Medieval Political Thought

NUMBER 591
COLUMBIA STUDIES IN THE SOCIAL SCIENCES
EDITED BY
THE FACULTY OF POLITICAL SCIENCE
OF COLUMBIA UNIVERSITY

PETER N. RIESENBERG

# Inalienability of Sovereignty in Medieval Political Thought

AMS PRESS

NEW YORK

COLUMBIA UNIVERSITY
STUDIES IN THE
SOCIAL SCIENCES

591

The series was formerly known as
*Studies in History, Economics and Public Law.*

Reprinted with the permission of Columbia University Press
From the edition of 1956, New York
First AMS EDITION published 1970
Manufactured in the United States of America

Library of Congress Catalog Card Number: 70-120202
International Standard Book Number:
    Complete Set: 0-404-51000-0
    Number 591: 0-404-51591-6

A M S  PRESS, INC.
New York, N.Y. 10003

TO MY PARENTS

# *Preface*

THE EMPHASIS in this study is upon the legal and political aspects of the theory of inalienability, not upon the theological. Hence, with but a few exceptions, no attempt has been made to examine the vast body of medieval theological literature. And, although German private law presents analogies to the concepts developed under Roman law, since we are here concerned with the effect of the theory of inalienability upon the growth of the national monarchies, and since German politics moved rather towards decentralization during the late Middle Ages, the theory of inalienability in German law is not discussed in the present work.

Since 1953, when the research for this book was completed, several works have appeared which touch very closely upon the subject of inalienability. Notable among these are Professor Ernst Kantorowicz's article in *Speculum* to which reference is made in my text, and the work of Professor Marcel David, *La souveraineté et les limites juridiques du pouvoir monarchique du IX<sup>e</sup> au XV<sup>e</sup> siècle* (Paris, 1954). As its title indicates, M. David's book is necessarily concerned with many of the issues treated here. Rather than punctuate my notes with repeated reference to his work, and considering both our substantial agreement and difference in emphasis, I have decided merely to refer to his volume here in this fashion.

Many persons and institutions have been very kind to me during the preparation of this study. Columbia University's grant of a Cutting Traveling Fellowship and the Fulbright Program of the State Department made possible several years' work and travel in Europe. The officials of the Vatican Library, the Bibliothèque Nationale, and the various state libraries in Rome and Florence were at all times most co-operative. In the United States, besides the New York Public Library and the libraries of Columbia University and Union Theological Seminary, I have been fortunate in using the collections at Harvard and Princeton. Long ago Professor Benjamin N. Nelson introduced me to the questions of alienation and renunciation in the civilians. And more recently Professors Austin P. Evans, Gaines Post, Theodore Silverstein, David Smith, and Anne Trinsey, and Mr. Benjamin Linder, read the manuscript at various stages in its preparation and were good enough to put me right on many issues. Throughout my work on the subject Professor Lynn Thorndike has been especially rigorous and thereby helpful. Miss Vergene Leverenz of the Columbia University Press has aided me with both encouraging words and good advice; and my student, Frances King, has devoted much time to the preparation of the index. To all these, and to my wife, whose labors as typist and copyist have been great, my deepest thanks.

PETER N. RIESENBERG

*Swarthmore College*
*March, 1955*

# Contents

*Inalienability of Sovereignty*
*in Medieval Political Thought*

# I

## *The Theory of Inalienability: Its Chronological, Geographical, and Theoretical Limits*

THE PRACTICAL and theoretical influence of the idea of inalienability of sovereignty upon the growth of the national monarchies during the late Middle Ages is the major focus of this study. During the thirteenth century Roman and canon lawyers developed the idea that there were certain rights and functions which a kingdom had to exercise if it was to exist and flourish. Simultaneously they stressed the concept of the king not as *dominus* in the absolute legal sense of the word, but rather as guardian, *curator,* of the office and responsibilities entrusted to him. Since the king was but a temporary official in a position of trust, he might not alienate the essential functions of his office to the prejudice of the state. Gradually other theories, each the result of its own peculiar history, entered into sympathetic relationships with the concept of inalienability. Most important among these were the concept of the Crown, canonist views upon obligation to the public welfare, and civilian private law concepts of an individual's inalienable rights, all of which were applied by publicists to their immediate purpose: the establishment of a sound theoretical basis for the independence and further growth of the national states. The theory of inalienability of sovereignty, however, was not restricted in its use to the nationalist writers. Developed as it was upon the

two great laws of Christendom, it was also claimed by the proponents of the Empire as their own. They, in fact, regarded
the use of the theory of inalienability by the monarchist writers
as an improper arrogation of their own ideas.

In 1275, reports the English lawbook *Fleta,* all the kings of
Christendom met in council at Montpellier, declared prescription to be invalid against royal power, and in another statement
of ecumenical scope, ruled that previous alienations made by
rulers in prejudice of the rights and lands of their Crowns were
initially invalid and must be recalled.[1]  One historian describes
this passing mention of a world conference as a legend,[2] and
this indeed it is—in its reporting of a meeting which never took
place; and also, more loosely but perhaps more importantly, in
the sense that *Fleta* gave dramatic reality and authority to an
idea which had been developing for at least a century: the
theory that the kingdom was dependent for its identity upon
the preservation of certain inalienable rights and privileges
which generally were treated as a theoretical sum and were not

---

[1] This passage is not unfamiliar to historians of English law and constitutional
history, nor to those of medieval political theory. It was first noted in modern
scholarship, I believe, by John Selden, *Ad Fletam dissertatio* (ed. and trans. David
Ogg, Cambridge, 1925), p. 189. He gives other references to such alienations in the
Middle Ages, citing the *Siete partidas,* and the decretal *Intellecto* (X. 2, 24, 33) of
Honorius III, the comments upon which form a major part of medieval thought on
this topic. He does not find mention of the conference in the writings of the
medieval and Renaissance jurists, a finding which I would confirm. What the author
of *Fleta* may have had in mind was the Second Council of Lyons, 1274, to which
were invited all the rulers of Christendom, including Michael Paleologus. Cap. XXII
of the decrees of the council is entitled "De rebus ecclesiae non alienandis," and is
a general prohibition against alienation of church property. For the text, see I. D.
Mansi, *Sacrorum conciliorum nova et amplissima collectio* (31 vols., Florence, 1759–
98), XXIV, 95-96. It was later included by Boniface VIII in the *Liber sextus*
(3, 9, 2), and, according to Hefele-Leclercq, *Histoire des conciles* (Paris, 1914),
VI, i, 199, was directed against the institution of usufructs which placed protection
of ecclesiastical property in lay hands, an action which gradually led to complete
separation.

At the outset it might be well to state that the spelling and punctuation of foreign
language texts will be given as printed in the early editions.

[2] Adhémar Esmein, *Cours élémentaire d'histoire du droit français* (9th ed., Paris,
1908), p. 328.

differentiated.  The ruler was entrusted with the power of office for the span of his life, and had to pass it on undiminished, if not strengthened, to his successor.  Medieval as well as classical Roman law considered the ruler's sum of authority as an abstraction, the *imperium,* and in this was seconded by contemporary philosophical theory which held that the *imperium* had to retain its essential characteristics, if indeed it was to justify its name and definition.  Hence it was the common belief that the ruler should not and could not diminish the effective scope of his office and pass on less than the sum of authority requisite for proper executive action.  The successor had to enjoy the complete *imperium* if he was fully to rule.

Until the time of *Fleta,* probably the early 1290s,[3] the idea had appeared in documents of limited scope, for the most part in commentaries and glosses upon passages in the books of the canon and Roman law.  Although, as will be made clear, it was part of a body of interrelated concepts of public law formulated by the theorists of the two laws, this was the first time that it received anything like dramatic application to all Europe.  That such a statement should have been made is itself surprising, for the conscious application of such an idea implies consciousness of individuality which we hesitate to ascribe to the monarchies of the thirteenth century.  Moreover, this entire pattern, a seamless cloak of interwoven political concepts, is all the more difficult to grasp because it was formulated as public law at a time when the lines of demarcation between the spheres of private and public law, as they are known today, were extremely shadowy and hard to define.

The exact nature of the governmental rights and functions to be protected is likewise vague.  The civilians and canonists to whom we owe the elaboration of a theory of sovereignty were

---

[3] N. Denholm-Young, "Who Wrote *Fleta?*" *English Historical Review,* LVIII (1943), 1-12.  (The *English Historical Review* will hereafter be cited as E.H.R., the *American Historical Review* as A.H.R.)

not always precise on this point. Concerned with high-level abstractions, they did not treat the specific royal or imperial privilege, but rather such generalized phrases as " iura coronae " or " honor coronae." To some extent their imprecision may be explained by the fact that still, in the late thirteenth and throughout the fourteenth century, the legists were in large measure dealing with the rights of a feudal society. Their legal education was in part based upon the *Liber feudorum,* which formed a course of study in the university curriculum; but beyond this, they were bound by a terminology charged with traditional meanings. So, although as servants of the national monarchs or the emperor they were concerned to build a new or protect an old system, they had yet to use words which linked them with the society they were trying to refashion. This vagueness, however, cannot all be ascribed to education and tradition; as we shall see, it was to the advantage of the theorist to keep his terms broad to allow for internal expansion. Basic to our discussion, therefore, must be an attempt to determine just which rights—that is, in essence, functions—were in question.

When the legists used such phrases as *iura coronae* and *iura maiestatis* they did so in more than one sense, and basic to any use was their ultimate reliance upon their conception of the term *iura regalia.* To attempt to define with accuracy the degrees of essentiality of a prince's regalia is a profitless task. Frederick I and his advisers drew up a list at Roncaglia in 1158 which codified for a moment the developments of the preceding centuries. At that moment the *feudisti* and the schools took up the question, and by the end of the Middle Ages commentators agreed on but one point: in placing their estimates of regalian rights in the hundreds.[4] Modern authorities have sought to

---

[4] Georges Blondel, " Etude sur les droits régaliens et la constitution de Roncaglia," *Mélanges Paul Fabre* (Paris, 1902), p. 237; Antonius de Petra compiled a list of 408 *regalia!* See also the gloss of Charondos Le Caron to *La somme rurale* (Paris, 1611),

avoid the problem, tried to fall back upon the selection of Barbarossa, or have attempted to synthesize from the medieval confusion some few essential rights which would add up to sovereignty.[5]

Despite this confusion, a hierarchy is perceivable. Lucas de Penna (ca. 1325–90) listed several very special functions for the emperor: the power to make universal law, to interpret a law equitably, to wage war, to create new taxes, and to sell property in which he had at least a half interest.[6] Most im-

---

p. 658. The proceedings at Roncaglia are themselves found in the *Monumenta Germaniae historica. Legum. Sectio IV. Constitutiones et acta publica Imperatorum et Regum* (Hanover, 1893 *et seq.*), I, 247-48 (hereafter cited by the term *Constitutiones*). Andrea de Isernia, *Constitutiones regni utriusque Siciliae, glossis ordinariis, commentariisque* (Lyons, 1560), lib. III. tit. 1, speaks of the term *regalia* as "nomen generale, fiscalia et patrimonialia comprehendens, quae omnia regis dicuntur."

[5] For various views on the *regalia* see Blondel, "Etude"; F. Olivier-Martin, *Histoire du droit français des origines à la revolution* (Montchrestien, 1951), p. 303; William Newman, *Le domaine royal sous les premiers Capétiens* (Paris, 1937); P. Viollet, *Histoire des institutions politiques et administratives de la France* (3 vols., Paris, 1890–1903), II, 185-86; Walter Ullman, "The Development of the Medieval Idea of Sovereignty," *E.H.R.*, LXIV (1949), 1-34; Samuel Chevallier, *Le pouvoir royal français à la fin du XIII⁰ siècle: Les droits régaliens* (Laval, 1930); H. Koeppler, "Frederick Barbarossa and the Schools of Bologna," *E.H.R.*, LIV (1939), 577-607.

[6] *Lectura* (Lyons, 1586), to C. 12, 35, 14. But even the strongest supporters of the monarchies did not allow, theoretically, all the important privileges to the kings. Paul Fournier writes that in the early years of the fourteenth century even such a monarchist as Petrus Jacobus denied the king the privileges to levy taxes, coin monies, and to revoke concessions of immunities made by the emperor to the clergy in the past: "La 'Monarchia' de Dante et l'opinion française," *Bulletin du jubilé du comité franc. cath. pour la célébration du VI⁰ centenaire de la mort de D.A.*, fasc. III (Paris, 1921), 168-69. It should also be noted that when Lucas speaks here on "universal law" he means it in an already atrophied sense. The emperor was to make universal law for the Empire—what was left of it—and the kings for all subjects in their realm. See, for example, the *Tractatus super feudis et homagiis*, cap. XII, of Johannes Blanosc. This is cited by Francesco Calasso, *I glossatori e la teoria della sovranità* (2d ed., Milan, 1951), pp. 118 *et seq.* Calasso uses this passage to point up the *naturalis jurisdictio* pertaining to the king. This passage deals with the relationship of the inhabitants of the kingdom to the king: "Set quamvis in potestate regis ita quod iure homagii regi non sint astricti, sunt tamen in potestate regis iure naturalis iurisdictionis quam rex habet in regno, nam verbum potestatis pluribus modis accipitur . . . nam in hominibus omnibus regni sui habet imperium . . . . Nam sicut omnia sunt imperatoris quantum ad iurisdictionem, cum sit mundi dominus, sic omnia, que sunt in regno sunt regis quantum ad iurisdictionem . . . ."

portant of these, of course, was the power to make law. Another great privilege ascribed by the medieval lawyers to the highest public authorities was that over life and death . . . the original sense of the *merum imperium.* Obviously, there were certain of the regalia which counted above the others. One historian of the meeting at Roncaglia finds the emperor stressing these rights: the power to appoint local territorial rulers, control of the ways of communication, the exclusive right to coin, control of the mines and the revenues of judicial processes, regulation of loans upon taxes, and the right to command or rebuild a fortress wherever one had existed before.[7] Another historian, writing of sovereignty at the beginning of the fourteenth century, after some century and a half of legal speculation, sees the legal aspects of sovereignty in the imperial or royal ability to enforce the penalty for *crimen leasae majestatis,* issue universally binding laws, create notaries, legitimatize bastards, and, in the case of the emperor, to sit as a court of appeal in judgment on the sentences of kings.[8]

These were the most vital governmental privileges; yet, in particular discussions of inalienability of sovereignty they are rarely specifically mentioned. What the theorists were summoned to protect were *iura, majestas,* or *dignitas* without qualification. Texts in the discussion show that the legal loss of the most important of these functions was invariably denied, or permitted only after the lapse of infinite time or under the most pressing circumstances. In other words, the highest imperial and royal functions were those denied alienation.[9] But there is

---

Unfortunately, Calasso does not go into the reasons for the *iurisdictio* of the king being called *naturalis.* I venture that the explanation will be seen in the concepts of kingship developed in this paper

[7] Blondel, "Etude," pp. 246–47.

[8] Ullman, "Medieval Idea of Sovereignty," p. 3.

[9] See the constitution of Frederick II (1231) reaffirming the law of Rogerius; in Huillard-Bréholles, *Historia diplomatica Frederici secundi sive constitutiones, privilegia mandata . . . et documenta varia* (7 vols. in 12, Paris, 1852–59), IV, 119: " Scire volumus principes nostros, comites, barones, archiepiscopos, universos episcopos,

something more in the very fact that the terminology is invariably both abstract and vague. The legists knew what they were doing when they wrote a blank check, so to speak, for the proponents of centralized government. Not one or even several specific rights were to be protected—though of course these would benefit as the general view was applied to each specific case; rather, the theory was always to stretch to cover newly won powers. So, when viewed by the opponents of centralization, the mantle of protection had a serious defect: once stretched, it never regained its original, theoretical shape. The protection now always remained, to be used by the proper man at the proper moment. Such employment of the theory might be made by a strong king such as Edward I, or by the supporters of a weak one, say, Charles VI. The political results varied, but one effect was common to both: a reassertion of the fundamental theory of inalienability in contemporary terms.

No claim is made, however, that the theory of inalienability is the dominant or uniquely causative factor of any national movement or constitution. It was important primarily in the way it gave strength to and was integrated with other ideas; and it was from these relationships that it developed its own individual significance. Medieval writers related it to the most fundamental concepts of public law: representation and consent, Crown and office, patrimony and fisc, and others. Throughout the thirteenth century they were busy developing a coherent pattern of political theories based upon specific passages in the two laws. Each element, each tradition of commentary upon a single idea, simultaneously reinforced the entire system and gained for itself added weight. The significance of the theory of inalienability lies in its integration in the Romano-

---

et abbates, quod quincunque de regalibus nostris magnum vel parvum quid tenet, (nullo modo, nullo ingenio) possit ad nostra regalia pertinens alienare, donare vel vendere (in totum vel in partem minuere) unde jura nostra regalia minuantur (aut subtrahantur aut damnum aliquod patiantur.)''

canonical system; and the truth of this statement may be illustrated now by an examination of the major theoretical elements of and approaches to the main theme.   In this fashion the chronological and territorial limits of the problem will also be clarified.

Although the full elaboration of the theory came only in the thirteenth and fourteenth centuries through the speculation of civil and canon lawyers, its elements were already germinating during the years before.   Since the new monarchies were feudal states, the theories of the legists and publicists were based as much upon traditional social and political structure and theory as upon the realities of contemporary change and their conceptions of the future.   In this sense the feudal problems faced by Frederick II were somewhat akin to those of Charlemagne. Prohibitions against the alienation of holdings are evident in Carolingian texts, for the basic feudal antagonism between centralized and local power was already manifest.   And, as Dopsch suggests, despite the over-all prohibition against alienation of real property, the king could and did allow it.[10]   The assumption was then what it continued to be, that the ruler had his own best interests at heart and would use his feudal powers for his own, and thus the state's eventual gain.   Nevertheless, throughout the feudal period rulers found it increasingly difficult to maintain effective control over a fief; a system of hereditary fiefs became commonplace; moreover, sales of fiefs took place as early as the tenth century in France and the eleventh in Germany and England.[11]   To be sure, the lords benefited momentarily at the transfer of a fief, but the final result was the acceptance in customary law of the legality of such transfers and the weakening of the personal element in

---

[10] Alfons Dopsch, *The Economic and Social Foundations of European Civilization* (London, 1937), p. 274.   This in turn was dependent on Merovingian ideas.   See also François Ganshof, *Feudalism* (London, 1952), pp. 34 *et seq.*, on the break up of Carolingian feudal ideals.

[11] Ganshof, *Feudalism*, p. 130.

feudalism. This led to unsureness on the part of the lords as to just what resources they could depend on, and to confusion among vassals and feudal theorists as to primacy of obligation.[12]

It is against the background of just such a debilitating state of affairs that Roger II, the Norman state having finally come through a century of violent feudal warfare, issued his assize forbidding alienation of the regalia by any of the great nobles or prelates of the kingdom.[13] Similarly, the constitution of Lothar II [III] of September, 1127, was an attempt by the emperor to strengthen and insure his potential military force relative to the great nobles. A situation had developed in which many knights, having alienated their fiefs in various ways, were no longer liable to military service. The unity of the Empire could not permit fluctuating obligations of military support which perpetually threatened its position of supremacy; so, for

[12] The attempt of national rulers to regularize their vassals' obligations to the throne constitutes a major theme of medieval constitutional history. For certain aspects of this problem, see below, Chapter VI.

[13] Francesco Brandileone, *Il diritto romano nelle leggi normanne e sveve* (Turin, 1884), p. 97. " *De rebus regalibus:* Scire volumus principes nostros, comites, barones universos, archiepiscopos episcopos abbates quicunque de regalibus nostris magnum vel modicum quid tenet, nullo modo nullo ingenio possit ad nostra regalia pertinens alienare, donare, vel vendere, vel in totum vel in partem minuere, unde iura rerum regalium minuantur, aut subvertantur, sive aliquod etiam dampnum patiantur." He develops the theme of Roman law influence on the centralized Norman state, mentioning also Byzantine tradition in this area, and the clerical-centralizing ideas brought by the Normans from their duchy in France (pp. 20-23). F. Chalandon, *Histoire de la domination normande en Italie et en Sicile* (2 vols., Paris, 1907), II, 612, remarks on the glorification of the Norman king in his titles, exalting formulary references in his charters, and in the representations of the king in Norman art. Brandileone assigns the assize to Roger II at Ariano in 1140, an opinion substantiated, finally, by Vito La Mantia, *Cenni storici su le fonti del diritto greco-romano e le assise e leggi dei re de Sicilia* (Palermo, 1887), pp. 63 *et seq.* See also Albert Brachmann, " The Beginnings of the National State in Medieval Germany and the Norman Monarchies," *Medieval Germany* (ed. and trans. G. Barraclough, Oxford, 1948), pp. 281-99. The articles of C. H. Haskins, in Vols. XIV and XX of the *A.H.R.* and in Vols. XXIV, XXVI, XXVII, and XXXI of the *E.H.R.* upon the centralization and administration of Normandy offer an interesting analogy to the Sicilian monarchy—an analogy which Professor Haskins was willing merely to point out. For his reserved conclusions on the reciprocal relations of the two states, see especially his " England and Sicily in the Twelfth Century," *E.H.R.*, XXVI (1911), 433-47, 641-65.

violation of the imperial constitution the vassal was to lose that part of his fief he had alienated, and, if deserved, the entire fief.[14] Edicts which followed upon this extreme position tended to modify the system and make it more workable. Although some freedom of alienation was permitted with the lord's consent, only those arrangements might be made which would increase the value of the fief and insure that no hurt came to the original suzerain.[15] Some three decades later, Frederick I renewed Lothar's prohibitions for identical reasons and in almost identical terms; but he went further in that he imposed the restrictions retroactively and nullified claims based upon prescription because of their initial invalidity.[16] These prohibitions imposed by rulers in the interest of their Crowns indicate only the obligations of lords and vassals. There is no mention of a superior obligation of the ruler not to alienate; yet the need for the preservation of regalia and military support is implied, as is, too, the consciousness of a certain continuity of the state which is supported by these regalia. Late in the thirteenth century the imperial obligation became more formalized, but by then it was too late. In 1276 Rudolph declared that he

[14] *Liber feudorum* (Venice, 1591), lib. II, tit. 52: "nemini licere beneficia, quae a suis senioribus habent, sine ipsorum permissione distrahere, vel aliquod commercium adversus tenorem constitutionis excogitare per quod Imperii, vel dominorum minuatur utilitas." For a medieval discussion of great clarity, see Andrea de Isernia, *In usus feudorum commentaria* (Naples, 1571), fol. 232v. Geoffrey Barraclough, *The Origins of Modern Germany* (Oxford, 1947), pp. 153-62, brings out the hopeless nature of such an edict given the complicated internal history of the Empire at the time. For an analogous situation and decree see the *Usatici Barchinone* (1064), which provided that the lord might do what he wished with a fief whose holder alienated it knowing his lord was opposed to this. The *Usatici* are included in *Cortes de los antiquos reinos de Aragon y de Valencia y principado de Cataluña* (Madrid, 1896), I, 18.

[15] *Liber feudorum*, lib. II, tit. 8, 9.

[16] *Ibid.*, lib. II, tit. 55. But now the notary responsible for the act loses his hand as well as his office. See Constitutiones, I, 247-48. Somewhat later, but identical in intent, is the constitution of Pedro II (1211), which for the good of the realm forbids subinfeudation, alienation, and selling of the rights of the high ecclesiastics and nobles of the kingdom. Appeal is repeatedly to the common good, and "public utility" is mentioned as early as 1173 by Alfonso I of Aragon as a reason for action (*Cortes de Cataluña*, I, 56, 89).

was unable to alienate *imperialia bona* without the consent of the princes. Five years later he announced that donations or other alienations of his predecessors, William and Richard, were to be considered invalid unless they were shown to have been made with the consent of the majority of the prince electors.[17]

These imperial constitutions were issued by authorities who faced feudal society as the reality which their theorists, using concepts of Roman and canon law, were trying to refashion.[18] Two illustrative and significant canonist contributions to this process of elaboration are letters of Innocent III, one to the guardians of the pope's ward, Frederick Hohenstaufen, the other to the protectors of the young King Ladislaus of Hungary. In both cases the pope forbids alienation of the essential sources of authority of the two princes. Frederick's *domanium* is to be preserved for him, and is disposable only in instances of the gravest necessity; and, moreover, any contemplated matrimonial alliances are subject to papal interference.[19] Writing for the protection of the Hungarian prince, Innocent, among other phrases, used the words *iura* and *integra* in apposition, so creating a natural phrase for future discussions of the problem.[20]

---

[17] *Constitutiones*, III, i, 100 (1276) and 290 (1284). See C. Bayley, *The Formation of the German College of Electors in the Mid-Thirteenth Century* (Toronto, 1949, p. 170.

[18] For a statement, perhaps exaggerated, of the influence of early canonist theory upon the development of the national states, see the recent book of Sergio Mochi-Onory, *Fonti canonistiche dell'idea moderna dello stato* (Milan, 1951). The literature on Roman law influence upon medieval theories of empire and central authority is too vast and well known to be detailed here.

[19] Huillard-Bréholles, *Historia diplomatica*, I, 57. "Innocentius etc. . . . . familiaribus regis Siciliae etc. . . . . prohibemus ut domanium regis nullatenus distrahetur nec titulo quolibet obligetur, nisi evidentissima urgente necessitate . . . nisi ex communi omnium voluntate vel ex majori saltem parte consilii sanioris . . . ." I intentionally omit discussion at this point of the decretal *Intellecto* of Honorius III which, incorporated in the *Compilatio quinta* and later the *Decretals*, served as one of the most important elements of the theory, both in itself and as a vehicle for the comments of every medieval canonist.

[20] *Reg.* VIII, 39, April, 1205, in *M.P.L.*, CCXV: "ut igitur eidem regi [Ladislaus] regni iura integra conserventur, nos . . . auctoritate . . . inhibemus ne dum idem rex fuerit in aetate minori, alienentur regalia in detrimentum ipsius." Apropos of this letter, John Figgis wrote that Bartolus developed Innocent's idea "into a general

The pope was no innovator here, for over many centuries the Papacy had developed theories of responsibility and regulation for the alienation of church lands and goods. For the moment, looking at his letters from a purely legal viewpoint, Innocent was merely applying good canon law to major political problems.

England presents both another scene and another element of the theory. The early thirteenth-century compilation known as the *Laws of Edward the Confessor* specifically enjoins the king, if he is properly to justify his title and function, to maintain the lands and honors of his Crown: " Debet vero de iure . . . omnes terras et honores omnes et iura et libertates corone regni huius in integrum cum omni dignitate et sine diminutione observare et defendere, dispersa et dilapidata et amissa regni iura in

---

principle of the inalienability of sovereignty " (Figgis, *Studies of Political Thought from Gerson to Grotius, 1414–1625* [2d ed., Cambridge, 1931], p. 78). The general principle is under discussion about a century before Bartolus.

Another phrase, the ring of which occurs time and again in legal discussions, is the caution that " per hanc concessionem non leditur imperium." The earliest use of it known to me in relation to the problem of inalienability is in the gloss of Cardinalis to *Dist.* LXIII, c. 30, of the *Decretum* which is a grant by the Carolingian emperor, Louis, to the pope of various powers and territories. The gloss, which is a marginal comment on the *Apparatus* of Johannes Teutonicus, is found in Vatican MS lat. 1367, fol. 47v. It was not noticed by Stephan Kuttner, *Repertorium der Kanonistik (1140–1234)* (Vatican City, 1937), pp. 53-54, in his analysis of the MS, and is not to be found in another Vatican gloss of Johannes Teutonicus on the *Decretum,* Pal. lat. 625. Cardinalis (car) writes with reference to the emperor's grant: " Quia imperator potest alienare rem imperii . . . Item quia per hanc concessionem non leditur imperium. ex quo res reddit ad primum statum."

Something must be said with respect to the question of similar phraseology. The Latin vocabulary is limited like that of any language, and so must operate within certain limits in its expression of any single line of thought. There is always the danger, therefore, that one may read influence or relationship into the similarity of two documents, or between members in a chain of texts, which similarity is merely the result of the inherent stringency of the vocabulary. Yet, formalized language met time and again in the same context does indicate what in the present case may be called the traditional statement of a problem. What appears a most natural phrase to the inexperienced will immediately serve warning to the initiated that he is once more facing a known problem. It is on the assumption that such phrase patterns did exist and are detectable, and that the congeries of problems raised about and by the question of inalienability produced such a specific set of terms, that much of the argument of this study rests.

pristinum statum et debitum viribus omnibus revocare." [21] Important here is the concept of the Crown which, as the symbolic creation of the idea of office, perhaps predated the idea of inalienability. Whatever the question of origins, the Crown, as an abstraction, was soon regarded as the symbol of the nation itself. With this symbol the theory of inalienability entered into full contact, empowering and restricting the Crown at the same moment. It strengthened the Crown in the sense that it conceived it as something lasting beyond the lifetime of the individual ruler and therefore above our mortal plane. And while restricting the Crown the theory fortified it in this manner: by circumscribing the freedom of action of both the Crown and king. This the theory did by denying the ruler the freedom to alienate rights which pertained to the Crown, that is, to the state, the presumption being that these were fundamental to the continuity of the state. As we shall see, land alone, the royal demesne, was not the exclusive object of the theory, nor even the regalian and feudal rights which were so essential to military security. Beyond these, which always formed a necessary foundation to the state, the theory aimed to preserve the less tangible but ultimately more powerful assets of the monarchy: its very regality, dignity, freedom and scope of action—those characteristics which the medieval thinkers in the Aristotelian tradition tended to regard as the constituent formal elements of their definitions of a ruler and that abstract of his authority, the *imperium*.

In Spain, as in England, the kings of Castile were often opposed by combinations of feudal nobles. We find in the *Fuero*

[21] F. Lieberman, *Die Gesetze der Angelsachsen* (3 vols., Halle, 1903–16), I, 635-37. H. G. Richardson, "The English Coronation Oath," *Speculum*, XXIV (1949), 44-76, has studied the relationship of this passage to the tradition of the idea in England. See also Gaillard Lapsley, "Bracton and the Authorship of the *Addicio de Cartis*," *E.H.R.*, LXII (1947), 4; he supports the older belief that the *Legis Anglorum saeculo XIII ineunte Londinis collectae*, in which the passage appears, was not widely known in the thirteenth century.

*viejo,* therefore, the idea that certain rights are the natural peculiar perquisites of the kingship, of its *señorio,* and that these must be preserved undiminished. Apart from the suggestion here of some qualitatively different aspects of the royal *señorio,* we find the rights of justice and coining among others reserved to the king.[22] The *Siete partidas* adds to the list of *inalienabilia* the liberty of a free man, sacred objects, public places, royal fountains, and certain feudal benefits.[23] The king may enfeoff and make donations, but no harm may come to him or to the kingdom through succession, use, change, or alienation. If he shares ownership in anything, he may sell his share; later theory limited this freedom to sales exclusively in the public interest.[24] The heart of the theory is the maintenance of the *señorio* which under discussion appears to be more than feudal suzerainty, to have a qualitative difference arising from its association with the king who is unique among nobles. It is this *señorio* which the king's guardians, should he be a minor, must swear to uphold, never dismember, and indeed increase. And the king, for his part, must similarly swear, when of age, that he will never violate the *señorio* entrusted to him. To be definite about the certain attachment of royal rights to the king, the *Siete partidas*

[22] Salvador Minguijón, *Historia del derecho español* (3d ed., Madrid-Barcelona, 1943), p. 97. The *Fuero viejo* (1 del tit. I, lib. 1) states: "Estas quatro cosas son naturales al señorio del Rey, que non las deve dar a ningund omne, nin las partir de si, ca pertenescen a él por razon del señorio natural: Justicia, Moneda, Fonsadera e suos Yantares." He also notes (p. 30) that the kings of Asturias and Léon had both their own property and that belonging to the realm. They could give freely of the former, but the Cortes clamored long and in vain against alienations of the latter. Minguijón claims that the kings were aware that it was to the advantage of the Crown not to alienate, but that they were forced to by the need to secure feudal support.

[23] *Siete partidas,* ed. Antonio San Martin, in *Los codigos españoles concordados y anotados* (2d ed., 12 vols., Madrid, 1872), 5, 15, 5 and 2, 15, 5. Another chapter, 2, 17, 1, threatens banishment for magnates who unjustly deprive the king of his lands or rights.

[24] *Siete partidas,* 2, 18, 1; 5, 5, 53; 5, 4, 9. The gloss also notes that in great feudal grants *jurisdictio* is never included "nisi hoc expresse diceretur in privilegio" (ad. vv. *secund los privilegios,* 2, 1, 12).

goes on to give them a special nature which insures their use by no one other than the king.[25]

The situation was similar in the Aragonese kingdom of Sicily, where the rulers had the long statist tradition of the Normans and Hohenstaufens behind them. In the first year of his reign, 1285, King James II prohibited alienation of still useful royal rights without the consent of his court.[26] Soon the document had its local theorists who arrogated for their king the Roman law concepts and protections that the glossators had developed in support of the emperor.[27] For example, Andrea de Isernia (ca. 1220–1316), while admitting the necessity of alienations in perpetuating feudal society, inveighed against gifts extremely harmful to the Crown (*in grave preiudicium corone*), and held that these might be revoked in every case.[28]

Later and greater Italian jurists discussed inalienability of sovereignty too. Bartolus (1314–57) while making special exception for the Donation of Constantine as did almost all the civilians, yet stated the general rule: " non potest (imperator) minuere Imperium donando vel vendendo." [29]   Baldus (1327–

[25] *Ibid.*, 2, 15, 3; 2, 15, 5. That chroniclers were aware of the obligation of the king to retain all the income of the Crown is indicated by *Los cronicas de los reyes*, cap. XIX, pp. 14-15: " Mas señor, que nos tiredes de la corona de vuestros reynes el tributo que el re de Portugal e su regno son tenudos de vos jacer.  Yo nunca, señor, vos les consejaré."  The statement was made with reference to the renunciation by Alfonso the Wise of tribute due from his grandson, the ruler of Portugal.  Reference is from Gifford Davis, " The Incipient Sentiment in Medieval Castile: the Patrimonial Real," *Speculum*, XII (1937), 354.

[26] The reference to James is in the *Ordonnances des rois de France de la troisième race* (21 vols., Paris, 1723–1849), I, 667.  For a brief statement on the importance of the *Regnum Siciliae* and its lawyer-statesmen in medieval political theory, see Calasso, *I glossatori*, pp. 127-58.

[27] See below, p. 89.

[28] Andrea de Isernia, *Utriusque Siciliae constitutiones* . . . , (Venice, 1590), p. 210, his comment on lib. III, tit. 4.  See also his comment to the constitution of Frederick I, " Imperialem " *In usus feudorum commentaria* (Naples, 1571), p. 270. Here, referring to the problem of royal alienation, he brings up the question of the alienation of the men of the domain.

[29] This gloss of Bartolus appears as a marginal comment ad vv. *semper Augustus* in the *prooem.* of the *Institutes* (Venice, 1591).

1400), too, emphasized the uniqueness of the Donation (*fuit miraculosa*), and condemned other such diminutions of the *imperium* as threats to its very existence.[30] Also, like other commentators, he stressed the position of the emperor as office-holder; albeit *procurator maximus*, yet a temporary public official who might not act against the welfare of the state which was entrusted to him.[31]

In France, one of the most dramatic applications of the doctrine was made by the royal lawyer Pierre de Cuignières (d. 1345) at the Council of Vincennes of 1329. Under discussion here were problems of jurisdiction which long had been troubling ecclesiastical and lay authorities. Church courts had been encroaching upon the justice of the royal courts, and so, to halt this drain upon the government, Pierre denied that royal perquisites might be lost over the years by prescription. Moreover, said the royal spokesman, the king may not alienate jurisdictional rights since they are essential to the Crown, and since, too, he has sworn in his coronation oath never to alienate them, and to revoke the alienations of his predecessors.[32] Once enunciated, the idea became a commonplace for French political theorists over the next two centuries: for example, Philippe de Mézières (ca. 1327–1405), Jean de Terre Rouge (d. 1430–

[30] Baldus de Ubaldi, *Consiliorum sive responsorum . . . Baldi* (5 vols., Frankfort, 1589), III, cons. 159, n. 2: ". . . nisi Rex aliquid ordinaverit in praeiudicium Regni quia talis ordinatio ruit cum concessione si laederet enormiter ipsum Regnum. Nam quicquid dicatur de donatione Constantini quae fuit miraculosa, si similes donationes fierent a regibus non ligarent successores . . ."; and I, cons. 327, n. 6, "Imperator non potest se abdicare imperium quia per minimas particulas perveniretur ad interemptionem totius totum dividendo per frustra [*sic*]."

[31] Baldus, *Super primo . . . codicis . . . commentaria* (Lyons, 1539), fol. 2v, n. 8, to rubr. *De novo codice componendo:* "Quia est officialis et non dominus." And *Consilia*, I, cons. 327, n. 7: "Et quidam Imperator est procurator maximus, tamen non est proprietatis imperii dominus, sed potius officialis ex eius electa industria . . . ."

[32] F. Olivier-Martin, *L'assemblée de Vincennes de 1329 et ses consequences* (Rennes, 1909), pp. 117 *et seq.* Martin is unable to verify Pierre's allegation of the coronation oath (p. 122); it is only at the beginning of the fifteenth century that a specific clause on inalienability appears in the oath. See Esmein, *Cours élémentaire*, p. 329, where he gives the oath; also presented in F. Isambert, *Recueil général des anciennes lois françaises* (29 vols., Paris, 1821–33), V, 240.

35?), and Juvenal des Ursins (1388–1473). As national consciousness grew, the doctrine which proclaimed a sacrosanct
guard about the king's unique position found universal support.[33] Theory was one thing, however, and over the years the
reality of family, politics, and war another. The repeated
ordinances of revocation issued by the French kings until the
final definition of the royal domain in 1566 indicate the hopeless nature of the regal dilemma.[34]

That the imperialist doctrine was stolen for their own use by
the lawyers of the national states did not prevent the emperors'
publicists in the fourteenth century from using the formerly
exclusive theory. As kings were helpless when faced by the
natural demands of feudal inferiors and growing sons, so too
were the emperors when confronted with national defections
from their universal *imperium*. To no avail did Ockham weave
the twin concepts of the indestructability of the Empire and the
inviolability of the emperor throughout all his political works.[35]

[33] Philippe de Mézières, *Somnium Viridarii*, in Melchior Goldast, *De monarchia
Romani sive tractatus de jurisdictione imperiale* (3 vols., Hanover and Frankfort,
1611–14), I, 58-228. (Hereafter this work will be referred to simply as *Monarchia*,
together with the proper volume and page references.) See also, André Lemaire,
*Les lois fondamentales de la monarchie française* (Paris, 1907); he cites heavily from
the French version, *Le songe du vergier*, which I have not used. See p. 47: "Au
roy appartient la souveraineté et le dernier ressort en tout son royaulme, et entant
qu'il ne pourroit mye [*sic*] celle souveraineté donner, transporter ou auetrement
aliener, ne si n'y peut aucunement renoncer, car celle souveraineté et dernier ressort, sont si fort et par telle manière conjoincts et annexés à la couronne, qu'ils ne
peuvent de luy estre séparés;" Jean de Terre Rouge, *Controversia successionis regiae
inter patruum et fratris praemortui filium* in F. Hotman, *Disputatio de controversia
successionis regiae* (Geneva, 1586); Juvenal des Ursins, *Histoire de Charles VI Roy
de France* (ed. Denys Godefroy, Paris, 1653).

[34] For a list of royal revocations see Isambert, *Recueil*, XIV, 185: 1316, 1318, 1321,
1360, 1364, 1388, 1400, 1403, 1413, 1438, 1467, 1468, 1483, 1517, 1519,
1521, 1539, 1540, 1559, and "finally" in 1566.

[35] The works of Ockham used in this study are listed in the bibliography and
are therefore not cited in full here. His views on alienation are briefly noted by
A. Hamman, *La doctrine de l'église et de l'état chez Occam: étude sur le Breviloquium* (Paris, 1942), pp. 152-53; by J. N. Figgis, *The Divine Right of Kings*
(2d ed., London, 1922), pp. 42 and 58; and by A. J. and R. W. Carlyle, *History
of Medieval Political Theory in the West* (6 vols., Edinburgh, 1903-36), VI, 49-50.

An integral element of his position is the idea that the emperor has certain obligations to the people since it is the ultimate source of all his authority. He may not injure the imperial dignity lest his successor receive a diminished *imperium,* and lest future generations of subjects be hurt. He may not alienate rights which he holds in common with the people since these are considered public rights; for any action of possible or potential harm to the public utility he needs universal consent.[36]

In this survey concerning the period and the issues as they relate to the chief nations of Western Europe an attempt has been made to mention the various problems discussed in relation to the concept of inalienability of sovereignty, and to show how vital an issue it was in both political acts and political theories. Stated originally in feudal terms, what later became a theory was at first in reality a *modus operandi* embodied in feudal custom. With the advent of the new Roman law studies and the reciprocal fertilization of the civil and canon law fields, the skilled legists formalized feudal concepts of mutual obligation in terms both of the more abstract ideas of their texts and of the immediate theoretical questions of state and society. As we shall see, three distinct parties made use of the theory of inalienability: the legists in the service of the national states who employed the discussion to free their kingdoms from the supremacy of the emperor; the more traditionally minded Roman lawyers who placed legal obstacles in the path of an emperor who would multilate and ultimately destroy the universal secular *imperium;* and the canonists who were interested in preventing alienation of ecclesiastical property on every level, and especially in preserving intact those countries held in fief from the Holy See. Membership in these groups was not restricted to doctors of the two laws; allied with them in every

---

[36] *Breviloquium,* VI, c. 2; *Consultatio de causa matrimonali* in *Guillelmi de Ockham opera politica* (ed. J. G. Sikes, Vol. I, Manchester, 1940), pp. 283-84; *Octo quaestiones,* cap. IX, in *ibid.,* p. 87; *Dialogus,* 3, 2, 1, 31 in *Monarchia,* II, 902; *ibid.,* II, 3, 2, 1, 29; and 31 in *ibid.,* II, 901-02.

instance was the publicist or apologist who utilized legal arguments, it is true, but who was likely as well to draw heavily upon his theological, historical, and logical training. Not one of these writers, legist or publicist, elaborated what might be termed a well-rounded theory of inalienability of sovereignty. Rather each added elements in a tradition of commentary which in retrospect appears as a theory; and what is more important, those in office tried constantly and consciously to live up to the principles of such a theory. No publicist ever wrote a treatise upon this specific topic, yet almost all utilized its arguments in support of other theses. For despite the absence of a particular treatment, the sum of the legal citations when considered together in all their relationships constituted a very definite political argument which gained in substance through constant use. The repeated appeal to the theory developed from the need of the medieval monarchies and the Empire of a concept which would restrain a ruler in terms of high moral and political significance from participating in his own destruction and, failing this, provide a legal basis for recuperation to a possibly more stalwart ruler.

## II

# *The Concept of Office and Its Responsibilities*

BASIC to the theory of inalienability of sovereignty is its relationship to the medieval concept of office—the central theme of this chapter. Office, conceptualized often in the term *imperium*, was conceived as the sum of governmental powers and functions, exercise of which constituted its essence. Abridgment of office was considered pernicious to the state's welfare since this was linked to the integrity of the *imperium*. No understanding of the medieval concept of office is possible, however, without previous mention of two discussions which, in terms of dramatic effect, served to point up the demands of office upon a ruler: the Donation of Constantine, and the appellation *Augustus* as it appears in the galaxy of Justinian's titles. These were the principal texts upon which canonist and civilian commentators took their general stand upon the legitimacy of imperial and royal alienations. And it was in these discussions, which by their usual method of cross reference the legists related to other pertinent passages and theories in both laws, that they developed legal and conceptual qualifications upon the ruler's freedom of action. As one historian has remarked, the Donation of Constantine was for the canonists " the link between their abstract philosophic reasoning and the realities of life "; [1] while for the civilians, *Augustus* was their perennial exhortation to the living

[1] Walter Ullman, *Medieval Papalism* (London, 1949), p. 108.

emperor, and it served as a natural starting point for consideration of the vexatious Donation.

There was never any question as to canonist acceptance either of the Donation itself or of the emperor's ability to make it. One of the earliest canonists, Paucapalea (fl. 1140–48), treats the Donation as a *fait accompli* about which there can be no question.[2] Following generations widened the implications of the Donation and related it to such problems as the relationship of pope and emperor, pope and king, the origins of temporal power, and the *Translatio Imperii*.[3] Innocent III lauded Constantine and, relying on the emperor's great gift, clearly stated the extreme papal claim to ultimate political supremacy. The archdeacon, Guido de Baysio (d. 1313), whose *Rosarium* became a standard text in the fourteenth century, claimed that Constantine realized that Christ had given the swords of spiritual and temporal power to Peter and so did only what was right by the pope when he made the Donation and removed himself to Byzantium. Moreover, he said, in view of the initial grant of authority to Peter which never had been transferred to the Roman emperors by the saint's papal successors, Constantine had never legitimately ruled the Empire. The *Glossa ordinaria* reduced the discussion to what became a decretalist commonplace, the idea that Constantine's grant merely restored the situation to its original and legitimate state.[4]

---

[2] Paucapalea, *Summa* (ed. F. von Schulte, Giessen, 1890), gloss to *Dist.* XCVII. See Stephan Kuttner, *Repertorium der Kanonistik (1140–1234)* (Vatican City, 1937), p. 3.

[3] See S. Mochi-Onory, *Fonti canonistiche*; Gaines Post, "Some Unpublished Glosses on the *Translatio Imperii* and the Two Swords," *Archiv für katholisches Kirchenrecht*, CXVII (1937), 403 *et seq.*; Ullman, "Medieval Idea of Sovereignty"; Gerhard Laehr, *Die Konstantinische Schenkung in der abendländischen Literatur des Mittelalters* (Berlin, 1926).

[4] Innocent III, *Sermo VII in festo d. Silvestri Pont. Max.* in J. P. Migne, *Monumenta patrologiae latina* (hereafter cited as *M.P.L.*), CCXVII, col. 481: "Urbem pariter et senatum cum hominibus et dignitatibus suis, et omne regnum occidentis ei tradidit et dimisit, secedens et ipse Byzantium, et regnum sibi retinens orientis." Guido de Baysio, *Rosarium decretorum* (Venice, 1481), to *Dist.* X, c. 8: "nullum impera-

The position of almost all the civilians on the Donation question indicates their unwillingness to decide some questions upon purely legal merit, and so, before discussing several opinions on this subject, comment must be made on the civilians' approach to touchy and tendentious questions. For even in the writings of the greatest jurists, Cynus (1270–1336), Bartolus, Baldus, we meet equivocation on crucial issues and an unwillingness to draw logical conclusions from the arguments presented in opposition. Baldus' comparative approach to the Donation has been termed " sceptical " by one authority, but this is an adjective we would hesitate to use. Baldus merely considers carefully the relative legal merits of the issue and then decides on nonlegal grounds. Although he assumes what he wants to prove in his marshalling of the arguments on both sides, on the one hand he appeals to social and political experience as embodied in the written law, while on the other, which is his preference, he recognizes the broad protestations of faith constituted into law by the fervent early Christian emperors. We must note, therefore, the quality of the legal citations upon which he bases his thought. Baldus, when he makes his decision on the Donation, does so on an appeal to the superior nature of the Church, a decision of faith, not of social and political analysis. Like his contemporaries studying natural science, he was trying to " save the phenomena." In the sphere of politics the phenomena were the *de facto* political bodies, other than the Empire, which were leading fully independent lives, exercising the *plena et rotunda potesta*s that once in fact, and in the fourteenth century in theory, was reserved for the Empire.

---

torem onorouiam the gladium, qui illum non accepit a Romana ecclesia, praesertim postquam Christus concessit jura utriusque imperii beato Petro, quod intelligens Constantinus, in resignatione regalium resignavit beato sylvestro gladium, respondens non legitime se usum fuisse gladii potestate nec legitime se habuisse, cum ab ecclesia non recepit." *Glossa ordinaria in decretum,* to *Dist.* LXIII, c. 30, and Johannes Andreae's comment to *Clementines* 2, 9 (Venice, 1497); see also Hostiensis, *Summa aurea* (Venice, 1574), to X. 3, 49.

The legists' minds seem to stop just short of the conclusion which to us would seem imperative. It is as though they were just teasing themselves and amazing their students by a tour de force of extensive exposition. At the end of this " rigged " exhibition they would state a conclusion which they had known before, and which, perhaps, they knew their audience knew they knew before—having not at all been influenced by their own sound arguments to the contrary. In other words, on certain issues, of which the question of the relationship of church and state was one, the opinion of the jurists was formed by more than exclusively legal formulas. Family tradition, employment, city and party allegiance, emotional and religious factors, these are but a few of the elements about which we must speculate but can never be sure.

Azo (d. ca. 1230), while establishing certain positions which became traditional among the lawyers, notably relative to the right of prescription against the emperor and the fisc,[5] avoids the problem of alienation as raised by the Donation. To his pupil, Accursius (1182–1258), however, belonged one of the lone medieval voices raised against its legal validity.[6] It is somewhat strange that his opinions, which otherwise became so authoritative, should have been rejected here. Even Isernia, who was a fierce supporter of the unfettered national state, endorsed the Donation. He suggested that it was a gift not to the pope but to God, and that it had reverted to the Empire after Constantine's death. Besides, he intimated, the Donation was valid since the prince did not diminish the Empire greatly (*enormiter*)![7] Another quibble is attributed to Wilhelmus

[5] Azo, *Summa aurea* (Lyons, 1577), to C. 7, 37, 3, n. 2, and C. 7, 38.

[6] Accursius, *Glossa ordinaria* (Venice, 1591), to the *prooem.* to the Institutes, specifically to *semper Augustus*. Baldus, commenting on the same passage of the Code, notes that Johannes Butrigarius held a similar opinion, but that " postea mutavit opinio et bene quia cum Papa sit superior . . . ." This appears in his commentary upon the *prooem.* of the Code, n. 8.

[7] Isernia, *In feudorum*, tit. I, n. 10; lib. II, tit. 52.

de Cuneo (d. 1335) by Bartolus. Wilhelmus approved of the
Donation because it was not, legally speaking, a gift but rather
Constantine's way of providing for the pope in return for the
latter's success in curing him of leprosy. Bartolus himself
favored this view.[8] Baldus, bothered as he must have been by
his simile of the *imperium* as a sound human body dismemberment of which would produce a monstrosity, and by his general
caution that no feudal alienation be made in prejudice of the
public utility, arrived at a solution sounder than that of his
teacher: Constantine made his grant with the consent of the
Senate and the Roman people; therefore the Donation must be
valid.[9] A similar nod to contemporary political theory is given
by Albericus de Rosate (d. 1354), who approved of the Donation because Constantine acted in his own best interest, inferentially that of the state.[10]

The imperialist theorists, however, familiar as they were with
all the legal arguments, did not quibble. Dante conceived the
*imperium* as a seamless cloak which cannot be rent. The emperor holds his *imperium* from God above and therefore may not
dispose of it. It was inconceivable to Dante that Constantine
could have acted legally against the very concept of his delegated office.[11] Ockham took another step and denied the

---

[8] Bartolus, to col. 1, nov. 6 (*Quomodo oporteat episcopos*) reports Wilhelmus'
opinion: " Quod haec non fuit proprie donatio, sed quedam remuneratio attento quod
Imperator leprosus, sanatus per Papam Sylvestram. Valebat ergo donatio tanquam
remuneratio." Bartolus' own opinion is in his comment on the *Prima Constitutio* in
*Opera omnia* (Basel, 1588–89), I, 4, nn. 13-15. See too Baldus' reporting of
Wilhelmus de Cuneo in his comment on the *prooem.* of the *Digest*, n. 18.

[9] *Super feudis* (Venice, 1516), to *prooem.*; *ibid.*, fol. 3v ad v. *expedita*; also to
*prooem. Digesti* n. 18 (Lyons, 1535).

[10] *Prima et secunda super codice commentarium iuris* (2 vols., Lyons, 1545), to
C. 7, 37, 3, n. 27. For like reasons of royal (public) interest, Philip Augustus
grants the right of immediate election to the cathedral chapter of Langres: " ut
pro utilitate ejusdem et nostra, concedimus eidem ecclesiae . . . " in *Recueil des actes
de P.A. Roi de France* (ed. C. Petit-Dutaillis and J. Morncat, Paris, 1943), II, 772
(1203-4).

[11] Dante Alighieri, *De monarchia* (ed. Gustavo Vinay, Florence, 1950), lib. III,
c. 7 and 10. On Dante and the Donation of Constantine see the article of Bruno

historicity as well as the legality of the Donation . . . first calling the tradition apocryphal on the basis of his study of
chronicles and church history, and then going to the text itself
to show its obvious distortion. Tantalizingly, this approach,
which antedates Lorenzo Valla's by more than a century, breaks
off at the beginning of the textual criticism.[12] But Ockham had
a more familiar argument as well. An emperor must pass on
to his successor the full power of Empire without diminution.
The discussion of the Donation, therefore, served to emphasize
the true obligation of the ruler. Even more significant than
the occasional civilian or imperialist rejection of the Donation's
legality was the common acceptance of it as an unusual action

---

Nardi, " La *Donatio Constantini* e Dante," now in *Nel mondo di Dante* (Rome, 1944),
pp. 107-61. A good part of this article is a summary of previous medieval opinion
on the Donation of Constantine and in this respect is smiilar to Laehr, *Konstantinische
Schenkung*. A fine recent appraisal is A. P. d'Entreves, *Dante as a Political Thinker*
(Oxford, 1952). Vinay rightly criticizes Nardi's oversubtle approach to the *De
monarchia* (pp. 246-47, n. 1), but wrongly, I think, accepts Laehr's judgment that
Dante " hat gleichsam die juristische Schale entfernt und sie zu allgemeiner Bedeu-
tung erhoben." (p. 128). The Sicilian legists, Marinus de Carimanico for example,
were in effect theorizing for *all nations*, and they realized full well the implications
of their doctrine for contemporary politics. See Calasso, *I glossatori*, pp. 127-64.

[12] *Breviloquium de potestate papae* (ed. L. Baudry, Paris, 1937), lib. VI, cap. 4,
pp. 163-65; *Consultatio in causa matrimoniali* (ed. Sikes), pp. 278-79. Yet in
another work, one of his earliest, Ockham accepts the fact of the Donation but
specifies that the Emperor did not return to the pope what was by rights his, but
rather " intendebat sibi illa . . . de novo conferre, concedere, donare, et tribuere.
Ex quo infertur quod Constantinus Papae et clericis, quibus ista temporalia confere-
bat, se superiorem in talibus reputavit. Quare si ista verba eiusdem Constantini
legantur ut videantur innuere quod C. se inferiorem Papa reputavit de inferioritate
in spiritualibus debet intelligi . . ." (*Octo quaestiones*, q. I, c. 12).

Criticism of the historicity of the Donation was made long before the fourteenth century, but the voices in this tradition were few and far between. Otto
III called the Donation a lie, as did Wetzel in his oft-cited letter of 1152 to Barbarossa. However, these critics did not give reasons for their doubt, nor did they
advance the legal arguments which in the thirteenth century became the basis for
attack on the legal validity of the Donation. To my knowledge the only theoretical
argument against the Donation before the controversy of the legists is the statement
of Gerhoh of Reichersberg in his *Opusculum de edificio Dei*, now printed in Vol. II
of the *Monumenta Germaniae historica, Libelli de lite imperatorum et pontificum*
(3 vols., Hanover, 1891-97). Gerhoh says that the emperor may donate freely of
his own property, but must consult with his principal advisors and great men of
the realm before alienating goods of the state (see II, 152).

which demanded special treatment. In other words, the Donation was considered unique, and all were concerned to rationalize or legalize its extraordinary character. By implication, the emperor's normal conduct was indicated to be the preservation of the *imperium,* that is, the original power of his position. Beyond this, in the writers who would deny the legitimacy of the Donation because of its injurious character, there is emphasis upon that view of *imperium* which stresses its abstract and perennial nature.

The emperor, discussing now the implications of the title *Augustus,* must consider as a fundamental duty of the imperial office the aggrandizement of the Empire. This is the essence of all the comments on that title of Justinian as it appears in the *prooemia* to the three main divisions of the *Corpus iuris civilis.* Azo used *Augustus* as an excuse for his opinion on the Donation. He allowed that the emperor is called *Augustus* not because he has always augmented the Empire, but because it is his duty to do so. Accursius employed almost identical phraseology.[13]   Indeed, this passage developed as a favorite place for the idealized statement of the emperor's obligation.   One moment the legists would make an exception for the Donation of Constantine; the next they would hint to the contemporary ruler that this was not the way to act, that in fact he should do just the reverse for the peace and happiness of his subjects.[14]   One canonist went so

---

[13] *Summa aurea* (Lyons, 1557), fol. 268v, to *Inst.* 1, 1: "Sicut et dicitur Imperator Augustus, non quod semper augeat imperium, sed quia eius propositi est, ut augeat." Accursius plagiarizes from his master, and applies this statement to the *prooem.* to *Inst.* ad vv. *semper Augustus,* "Quia huius debet esse propositi quilibet Imperator ut augeat, licet hoc non semper faciat."

[14] See, for example, Petrus de Bellapertica, *In libros institutionem* . . . (Lyons, 1536), fol. 10, n. 9, "Item debet augere Imperium semper, sicut quilibet administrator . . . licet non semper augmentet, tamen in proposito augmentandi debet esse." *Lectura insignis super prima parte codice* (Paris, 1519), fol. 1, col. 2 ad v. *Augustus,* "dicitur ab augendo.   Contra. Constantinus donavit ecclesie quoddam regnum ut dicunt. Responsum. dicitur Augustus ab augendo quo ad propositum . . . dic ergo quod imperator dicitur Augustus quia regulariter semper auget . . . . Queritur ergo utrum donatio quam Constantinus fecit in ecclesiam valeat. Dicitur quod non."

far as to confer the appellation *Augustus* on the emperor's sons
in the hope that this might have some mystical effect upon their
future conduct.  The emperor-to-be would grow up enveloped,
as it were, by the solemnity and sense of office implied by the
title.[15]

Once king or emperor, however, the ruler was by no means
an absolutely free agent, unbound by any legal restraints.. One
intrinsic element of the matured medieval idea of kingship was
the notion that it was an office with functions; and although it
was never denied by theorists in the thirteenth century that the
king had *plenam potestatem et liberam*, it. was also admitted
that he did operate within a certain range of authority the extent of which had been fixed by custom itself tacitly believed
to be sanctioned by a universal *ius gentium*.  As Professor
McIlwain has phrased it, " The sovereign or supreme authority
established and defined by a fundamental law is bound absolutely by that law, though he is free of all other laws." [16]

The concept of inalienability of sovereignty is indeed one of
the circumscriptions placed upon the monarch.  It may seem

---

Isernia, *In feudorum* (Naples, 1571), fol. 247: ". . . sicut Augustus ab augendo
dictus, pro bono statu regni Italiae et Teutoniae, et pro bono statu Imperii pro
quo debet esse solers et sollicitus quia inde resultat commodum pacis et quietudinem
subiectorum . . . ."

[15] Bartholomaeus Brixiensis, *Decretum cum glossis* (Mainz, 1472), to *Dist.* LXIII,
c. 2, ad v. *Augustos*: " nota quod filii imperatorum dicuntur etiam augusti vel ideo
dicebantur augusti quia sperabatur quod essent futuri imperatores et quasi per augur-
ium hic sperabatur vel sicut imperator ·debetur [dicitur] augustus." Frederick II
drew the implications of *Augustus* in an early. donation to the Church in Germany,
*Constitutiones,* II, 64-65 (December, 1214): " Quoniam omnis gloria maiestatis auguste
ad augendam universalis ecclesie . . . tenetur." How far from the violent polemics
against Gregory and Innocent!  The etymology was well-known to chroniclers, too:
Rigord, *Gesta Philippi Augusti,* p. 6, cited by V. Martin, *Les origines du gallicanisme* (2 vols., Paris, 1939), I, 143: "Augustus enim vocare censuerunt scriptores,
Caesares qui rempublicam augmentabant, ab *augeo, auges* dictos."

[16] Charles H. McIlwain, " Whig Sovereignty and Real Sovereignty," *Constitu-
tionalism and the Changing World* (Cambridge, 1939), p. 73.  Also in his *The
Growth of Political Thought in the West* (New York, 1932), pp. 376 *et seq.*  On
the freedom of action of the English kings well into the fourteenth century, see
S. Chrimes, *An Introduction to the Administrative History of Medieval England*
(Oxford, 1952), pp. 1-153, *passim.*

anachronistic to speak of it as an element of the " constitution " of the medieval Empire, or of France or England in the thirteenth century.    Yet, at any and every stage in the historical development of a state there is an operative constitution within which and by which the state is governed.    In a sense it is a rigid framework, the parts of which have hardened over time until they have come to form a basic organizational scheme, about which the substance of new policies and organs of government develops.    One concept vital to the existence of a constitution is the idea that the ruler is under the law, not necessarily private law, but the fundamental law of the state, this constitution which is the essence of a nation's political development.    One of the more specific restrictions placed upon the ruler by medieval law in the historical development of a principle of restraint was its conception of him as *proctor, curator,* public official with a restricted mandate of authority.    Too much emphasis has been placed by modern historians on the Roman law exaltation of the ruler in such phrases as *Princeps legibus solutus est,* and *Quod principi placuit legis habuit vigorem . . .";* not enough has been placed on the medieval restraints.[17]

Even writers who ascribed unique, exalting characteristics to the king limited him by the nature of their qualifications.    It was a civilian commonplace that *merum imperium* inhered in the bones of the prince, and as such was inalienable.    Yet Lucas de Penna for one, in his commentary on the public law of the *Code,* indicated clearly that there were gifts of authority which the ruler might not make, and specified the power to make law, to commission notaries, and to coin money.    These he called *regalia mere.*    (Earlier, Oldradus de Ponte [d. 1335] had spoken of *merum imperium,* but the difference is one of terminology alone.)    Lucas' *regalia* belong to the king not as part of his

---

17 See, for example, the articles of A. Esmein, "Le maxime *Princeps legibus solutus est* dans l'ancien droit public français," *Essays in Legal History* (ed. Sir. P. Vinogradoff, Oxford, 1913), pp. 201-15; and Fritz Schulz, "Bracton on Kingship," *E.H.R.,* LX (1945), 136-76.    For the medieval restraints upon royal absolutism, see Fritz Kern, *Kingship and Law in the Middle Ages* (trans. S. Chrimes, Oxford, 1951).

patrimonial inheritance, but rather from the very logic of kingship.  Hence, if the needs of state demand, they may only be
delegated, not given up.  They would be essential to the king
even were he unwilling.  He cannot deny their intrinsic status
if in truth he is king.  The identification of the ruler and these
essential powers is all the more complete for the reason that he
has been chosen by God and receives his authority directly
from Him.  Lucas' final point is a display of contemporary
logical terminology, the statement that the supreme powers he
assigns the ruler are not " accidental " but rather constitute
the very substance of royal dignity.[18]  Isernia used the same
sort of school language when he spoke of the superiority of a
king over the emperor, and he was again thinking in Aristotelian
terms when he wrote: " realia sunt magis valida quam per-
sonalia."  Why?  Because the office of emperor, being elective,
is a delegation of authority for life.  The king, on the other
hand, is more intimately involved with the powers of his office
since he is given them as an heir in a dynastic succession, designated ultimately by God.[19]  The *Especulo* (1254–55) of
Alfonso X makes the point even more dramatically.  The king
takes the place of God on earth to do justice in the temporal
realm, and should be honored because Christ himself chose the
Castilian royal line.  He is the soul (*alma*) of his people, and
as the body derives its sustenance from the soul, so the people
live through the king.  It is as though the people were to realize
their divine mission through his person.[20]  This is not to state
that the obligations of kingship are fundamentally dissimilar
from those of the imperial office.  Indeed, given the almost

[18] *Lectura* (Lyons, 1538), to C. 12, 29, 1; 12, 59, 8, and C. 12, 35, 14; Oldradus,
*Consilia* (Venice, 1570), cons. 252, n. 6; and Petrus de Ancharano, *Consilia sive iuris
responsa* (Venice, 1585), cons. 339, nn. 1 and 8.

[19] *Andrea de Isernia, Constitutiones regni utriusque Siciliae glossis ordinariis, commentariisque* (Lyons, 1559), to *prooem.*, cols. 14-15.

[20] *Especulo* in *Opusculos legales del rey Alfonso el Sabio* (2 vols., Madrid, 1836),
I: lib. II, tit. 1, ley 5; prol. to lib. II; lib. II, tit. 1, ley 4; see also the *Castigos e
documentos del Rey Don Sancho*, ed. P. de Gayangos in *Bibliotheca autores españoles*,
LI (Madrid, 1860), cap. 10, p. 106.

supernatural character of the king, it is all the more incumbent upon him to fulfill every royal duty.

Exalting as the language was in some passages, it was just as compelling and restrictive in others when it reiterated royal duties. If the ruler were properly to fulfill his office and mission he had to act within the great traditions established as right and just through Christian history. Hence the extensive literature of advice books, and the more prosaic legal and theoretical restrictions in the lawyers.

Cynus put the obligation beautifully when he wrote: " solutus (imperator) legibus de necessitate; tamen de honestate ipse vult ligari legibus qua honor reputatur vinculum sacri iuris et utilitas ipsius." Against this view, he continues, some argue on the grounds that the emperor must always increase (*augere*) his authority and so ought to submit to no one. To these the emperor's answer should be that in acknowledging and observing superior law he is in effect aggrandizing as the office implies.[21] Petrus de Bellapertica (d. 1307) had much the same idea when he asserted: ". . . de auctoritate iuris pendet auctoritas imperii." Although he established a distinction between *Imperator* and *imperium,* he subjected both to higher authority. The emperor is subject to civil law in cases of a minor nature, providing he agrees to be cited. The *imperium,* however, conceiving it as the sum of higher powers, has an obligation to observe higher laws. Its special character stems essentially from the fact that it is a God-given office, while the emperorship is transitory and fortuitous, conferred, as Bellapertica says, by Fortuna. He too gave an imaginary taunt to the emperor because of his submission to law, to which the emperor replies that in truth the ruler gains in honor if he lives in harmony with the law.[22]

---

[21] Cynus, *In codicem* (Frankfurt, 1578), to C. 1, 14, 4 (*Digna vox*).

[22] *Lectura insignis super prima parte codice* (Paris, 1519), to C. 1, 14, 4 (*Digna vox*). See Bracton, *De legibus et consuetudinibus Angliae* (ed. G. E. Woodbine,

Important to the nature of office just described is the idea that title implies commensurate action, and its corollary that its absence loses for the officer the positive significance of his position. Essentially this is again a peripatetic idea concerned with the problem: what is it to be a ruler. Assuming a schedule of obligations which must be exhausted if the definition is to be fulfilled to the satisfaction of contemporary moral and political standards, the ruler is no longer a ruler if he fails to meet his responsibilities. We find this good Aristotelian teleology in both Isernia and Bracton (d. 1268). Isernia's comment is concerned with emphasizing the importance of public as opposed to private welfare. He makes no distinction as to what may or may not be renounced, but speaks protectively of the well-being of the state and the dignity of the *imperium,* referring to the *imperium* as though it were the everlasting embodiment of the state: " bonum rei publicae statum et dignitatem imperii." And then he uses a qualification to which we shall refer again; he says that the prince is to lose his title when he acts with disastrous (*enormiter*) effect against the honor of the Crown.[23] The emphasis upon *enormiter* was both deliberate and necessary, for with this qualification the legist stressed the great danger and singularity of Constantine's Donation, and at the same moment recognized the necessity and function of some forms of alienation, infeudation, for example, in contemporary social and political life.

Bracton is more specific in his chapter concerned with the question, among others, of the king's liberties. Here he states that the keeping of the peace and the administration of justice may not be separated from the Crown since they give the

---

4 vols., New Haven, 1915–42), fol. 5b: " Rex non debet esse sub homine, sed sub Deo et sub lege, quia lex facit regem, attribuit igitur rex legi quod lex attribuit ei, videlicet dominationem et potestatem."

23 *In feudorum,* ad vv. *de prohib. feud. alien.* of Lothar, fol. 232, n. 1: ". . . sciendum quando non auget, sed diminuit, non dicitur princeps. quando diminuit enormiter contra honorem coronae. quando non agit ut Rex non dicitur Rex."

Crown its very essential character: " nec a corona separari
poterunt cum faciant ipsam coronam." [24] There is the suggestion here of something more than " intensification of private
rights," [25] something which would imply a singular nature of
the Crown. For this nature the constitution reserves special
functions, the fulfillment of which is the realization of the inherent potentialities of the office, that which it must do if it is
to be the kingship. Professor McIlwain sees a distinction between a ruler's *gubernaculum* and *iurisdictio* in this passage of
Bracton. The former term refers to royal executive and administrative powers which are " absolute " and beyond discussion; *iurisdictio* covers a much narrower field, essentially treat-
ing of private rights and also their relationship to the king. In
theory he is subject here to the judgments of his own courts,
but it would have been very difficult for one of them, the king
unwilling, to exact a penalty. With respect to his *gubernaculum*, he was in theory unchallenged, for this concerned the very
purpose of kingship: " to exercise justice and judgment and to
maintain the peace." Professor McIlwain notes that in this
view of the *gubernaculum* Bracton was in sympathy with continental political theory of his day.[26] It might also be stated

[24] There is some relationship between the teleology of Bracton's phrase and his
use of such definitions ultimately deriving from Augustine and Isidore of Seville
as " Rex eris si recte facies, si non facies non eris." See Fritz Schulz, " Bracton on
Kingship," p. 151. Schulz rightly remarks that such medieval definitions, which
were already in the eleventh-century dictionary of Papias, became actual " political
and even legal principles." The Bractonian phrase in question in a way is a partic-
ularization of the general definition. It is also linked up with the medieval problem
of tyranny, since Bracton's doctrine is that " the king who violates his duty to maintain justice automatically ceases to be king," and is, rather, a tyrant (Schulz, p. 153).
On Bracton and the *Laws of Edward the Confessor*, and his borrowing of ideas pertaining to the kingship, see II, G. Richardson, " Studies in Bracton," *Traditio*, VI
(1948), 75 *et seq.* Professor McIlwain has discussed this passage in his *Growth of
Political Thought*, p. 381, and also in *Constitutionalism Ancient and Modern* (Ithaca,
1947), pp. 67 *et seq.*

[25] F. Pollock and F. W. Maitland, *The History of English Law Before the Time
of Edward I* (2 vols., 2d ed., Cambridge and Boston, 1905), I, 512.

[26] McIlwain, *Constitutionalism*, pp. 75 *et seq.*

that Bracton's view on the inalienability of the intrinsic aspects of the *gubernaculum* was similarly in line with contemporary continental theory, as was his reasoning.

The history of the term *iurisdictio* in canon law affords an analogy despite the fact that the term eventually was expanded in its conceptual breadth whereas in English law it was contracted.[27] By Gratian the term is used to refer to all levels of administrative authority; the succeeding generation of canonists restricted its scope to the control merely of material possessions; and it was not until the early thirteenth century that it acquired its full force: Innocent IV (d. 1254) used the term to designate the sum of episcopal powers, and it gained even greater significance when Johannes Hispanus (fl. 1235) included legislative power also. As we shall see, the canon law forbade the alienation of *iurisdictio* (*potestas publica regendi societatem*) to the hurt of the Church. This ecclesiastical prohibition was based partly upon the ultimate importance of the public welfare, and partly upon the Romano-canonical maxim *Quod omnes tangit*. Bracton's views on alienation can likewise be referred to these two related principles. It is true that his main reliance upon *Quod omnes tangit* is in private law: those whose interests were affected in any instance were to be summoned to discuss the common problem. Yet it is clear, not only upon the analogy of ecclesiastical public law, but also upon the eventual role of *Quod omnes tangit* in English constitutional history, that Bracton intended the principle to play a like role in public affairs. Indicative of his thinking is the fact that he prohibits alienation of precisely those royal functions which most closely affect the public welfare.[28] Certain rights and duties may be delegated for administrative convenience, it is true, but they

---

27 M. van de Kerckhove, "La notion de jurisdiction dans la doctrine des décrétistes et des premiers décrétalistes de Gratien (1140) à Bernard de Bottoni (1250)," *Etudes franciscaines*, XLIX (1937), 420-55, *passim*.

28 Gaines Post, "A Romano-Canonical Maxim, 'Quod Omnes Tangit' in Bracton," *Traditio*, IV (1946), especially pp. 245 *et seq*.

may never be completely separated from the Crown.[29]   It would
appear then that Bracton is differentiating between the king as
a symbol and protector of rights benefiting the public utility,
and the king as feudal lord who, for reasons of pecuniary advantage, may find it in his interest to allow the use of certain
nonessential privileges.

For analogy to this view of English constitutional development, we may turn briefly to Castile.   The *Especulo* specified
similar and other duties.   Donations of land were deemed necessary for the proper functioning of the state, yet it is clear that
restrictions were placed upon the king's freedom of feudalization.   Upon taking the throne the new ruler is to observe the
debts of his predecessor; but he is also to recall those donations
which may have been made without legal or utilitarian basis.
And this same close surveillance must be made by him of his
own acts.   Also, at the coronation the great nobles of the realm
are to swear to preserve the *señorio* of the kingdom, and should
the new king be a minor, they are to guard lest there be fac-
tional conspiracy against the ruler or a weakening of the territorial extent of the kingdom (*menoscabamiento del regno*).
Conspirators against the *señorio* are to be treated as traitors for
the reason that without the king there cannot be a state . . .
since he is to the state as the head is to its body.   This passage
pertains specifically to the physical possessions of the king, likewise called the *señorio*.[30]   The double significance of *señorio* is
far from clear in these passages.   It may be surmised, however,
that while the term referred to what may be called the royal

[29] Bracton, Vol. II, fol. 14.   For the Thomistic idea of the ruler as *persona publica*
"who incarnates the common good above all individuals," see *Georges de Lagarde,*
*La Naissance de l'esprit laïque au declin du moyen-âge.   Le bilan du XIII* siècle*
(Paris, 1934), p. 108.

[30] *Especulo,* I, lib. II, tit. 16, ley 6; tit. 6, ley 1; tit. 16, ley 5.   See also the
early fourteenth-century chronicle, *Las cronicas de los reyes,* cap. 19, pp. 14-15,
cited by G. Davis, "Incipient Sentiment in Medieval Castile," p. 354, in which the
king is admonished for his renunciation of a tribute due from his grandson, the
king of Portugal.

domain, it referred also to the sum of powers conferred upon the kings of Castile by Divine Grace. Not to the individual king, but to the regal office which would in time be the responsibility of another.[31]

Legists and publicists developed other limitations upon the princely office, but these need not concern us here.[32] This much is clear, that there was a definite tendency as early as the middle of the thirteenth century to conceptualize the kingship as opposed to the individual, to confer exalted powers on the Crown. And, at the same time that the princely office was smothered in honorific titles, it was simultaneously burdened with responsibilities, among which was the duty to maintain undiminished the dignities and rights of the Crown, or office.

Another source for these restrictions which throws light upon the nature of royal office and its responsibilities is the large literature of medieval advice books written for the moral and political instruction of rulers-to-be.[33] Here, however, the emphasis is not on restraint but rather on liberality, and there are few cases throughout the literature of a specific injunction not to alienate the rights of the Crown. Nevertheless, a few writers and views bear mention. Gerald of Wales, in his *De principis*

[31] A century later the prince electors of the Holy Roman Empire were to conceive of themselves as the repository of rights more fundamental than the imperial office itself. See above, note 17, Chapter I, for the relationship of the prince electors and the Emperor Rudolph.

[32] Several examples may be given: Lucas de Penna on C. 12, 46, 1, n. 5: " Dicas omnia iura quae possunt cadere in privatum, in te transtulisse videntur, quae autem non cadunt in alium quam in regem, et quae ipse rex etiam si vellet expresse a se et majori dominio rei publicae, cuius gubernationem accepit, non posset eximere, ut est potestas condendae legis et alia similia non intelligitur concedisse." See also his comment to C. 11, 70, 5 favoring alienation to the Church as part of the princely duty, and Guy de la Pape, *Decisiones Gratianapolitanae* (Venice, 1588), cons. 113: " princeps non debet facere guerram cum praeiudicio subditorum, sed prius debet expendere . . . accipere."

[33] On this entire subject see Wilhelm Berges, *Die Fürstenspiegel des hohen und späten Mittelalters* (Stuttgart, 1952, a reprint of the 1938 edition). This volume is the indispensable survey and bibliography for this literature. Also, L. K. Born, " The Perfect Prince: a Study in Thirteenth and Fourteenth Century Ideals," *Speculum*, III (1928), 470 *et seq.*

*instructione* (ca. 1180), after first approving the virtue of
princely liberality, among the examples of which he mentions
and approves the Donation of Constantine, cautions that there
must be some restraint: the aim of giving should not be the exhaustion of the royal treasury or patrimony.[34]  Aegidius Romanus, in his *De regimine principum* (1277–79), has only a
general admonition for the prince: "jura regni maxime custo-
dire et observare."  This is a usual rule throughout the literary
genus, and common too is his advice that the king always be
generous.   Moreover, since giving should be in relation to
wealth, it is difficult for a king to give enough.   It is worse, he
says, to be called miserly than prodigal, since prodigality is
closer to a virtue, *liberalitas,* than is avarice to this virtue or any
other.[35]   Similar in opinion is the *Castigos e documentos del
Rey Don Sancho* (1292–93), written perhaps by the king himself, and in any event, destined for the instruction of his son,
Ferdinand IV.   The noteworthy statement here is of the duty
of the ruler to give not from vainglory, but for the good of the
public weal (the Church being always included as *res publica*)
and of the king's own person: " por razon de algund bien que
se signe en las cosas de Dios o en la comunidat o en la persona." [36]

Another work which deserves mention is the *Secretum
secretorum,* a pseudo-Aristotelian teatise which appears to have
reached its final pre-Latin form between the seventh and ninth
centuries and which, although based to some extent upon classical Greek ideas, is in the main a product of Syriac and Per-
sian thought.   In the thirteenth century a translation by Philip
of Tripoli made the work available to Europe, and during the

[34] Giraldus Cambrensis, *De principis instructione liber* in *Opera* (London, 1891),
VIII, 28.  Berges, *Die Fürstenspiegel,* gives 1217 as the terminal date of its com-
position.  There are several references to Roman law, one of which, to *C.* 1, 14, 4,
*Digna vox,* illustrates Giraldus' contention that the king should live within the law.
[35] Aegidius Romanus, *De regimine principum* (Rome, 1607), lib. III, pt. 2, cap. 9.
[36] *Los castigos e documentos del Rey Don Sancho* (Madrid, 1891), pp. 181-83.
Berges, *Die Fürstenspiegel,* assigns this work to the years 1292–93.

remaining centuries of the Middle Ages and well into the sixteenth century the work was almost unique in the extent of its
popularity.[37]  For the present study, therefore, the treatise may
be used only to show an analogy between Latin and Islamic
ideals of kingship, which analogy represented an appreciated if
not popular point of view.  For the *Secretum secretorum* after
a preliminary analysis of four types of ruler—the king generous to himself and his subjects, miserly towards himself and his
subjects, miserly towards himself and generous towards his subjects, and generous to himself but miserly to his subjects—proceeds to extol the generous ruler who is beneficent towards his
people yet solicitous for the welfare of his state.  In this connection the treatise mentions that the kings of Chaldea so de-
spoiled their subjects because of a desire for vast wealth that
the people rose up to destroy them.  The conclusion is, therefore, and the similarity here to Western thought is striking,
that " any king who makes gifts beyond the capacity of the
kingdom surely will be destroyed. . . ."[38]

It is not until the 1350's that we find a statement in the advice literature which obviously belongs to the Romano-canonical discussion of inalienability.  This is the treatise *De cura rei
publicae* of Philip of Leyden, a work of practical politics and a
comparison of contemporary actuality and theory.[39]  The most
obvious external characteristic of Philip's work is the frequent
use he makes of legal ideas common to both laws.  We are not
surprised to meet with the accurate reference to *Intellecto*,
therefore, when he approves the habit of royal giving, but opposes alienation " in praeiudicium regni sui," and states: " revocare tenetur [rex] etiam si alienationem iuramento firma-

---

[37] Roger Bacon's edition of the *Secretum secretorum* has been edited by Robert
Steele, *Opera hactenus inedita*, fasc. V (Oxford, 1920).  Professor Lynn Thorndike,
to whom I owe this reference, discusses the work in his *History of Magic and
Experimental Science*, II (New York, 1923), 267-78.

[38] In the Steele edition, pp. 42-45.

[39] Berges, *Die Fürstenspiegel*, pp. 250 *et seq.*

verit; quia iuramentum praecessit et praecedere debet de servando illibita iura regni sui." The nature of prohibited alienation is made clear to us in another passage where he writes: ". . . quod principes aliqua iura habent, quae a se abdicare non possunt, et hoc ut salvetur respublica, cuius salus consistit in potentia principis." [40] In other words, reference is to those rights inextricably bound up with the fundamental, necessary powers of the princely office upon which depends the prosperity of the state.

We do not learn very much from this body of literature. What was common throughout the treatises was a general admonition to maintain the rights of the kingdom as inherited, which, if nothing else, shows an awareness of the idea at the basis of the theory of inalienability, self-preservation. There is no repeated advice specifying the rights never to be alienated, nor is there the developed terminology of the legists and publicists.[41] This absence may be explained by the fact that these treatises were more humanistic and moral in emphasis than political. Their aim was broadly to develop character in accordance with contemporary ethics, rather than present a long list of imperative, practical " don'ts." Hence the universal emphasis on the virtue and seemliness of munificence.

[40] Philippus de Leyden, *De cura reipublicae et sorte principantis* (ed. R. Fruin and P. C. Molhuysen, The Hague, 1915), casus 78, nn. 3-5; casus 1, sec. 7. See also *prooem.*, sec. 3, which is referred to in casus 1: " Visa est per sibi praesidentes respublica infelix et dispersa, et, quod patriae periculosum, principem indigere; cum tuta solum tunc est subditorum opulentia quando non indiget imperator."

[41] Besides the treatises discussed above, I have examined Vincent of Beauvais, *De eruditione filiorum regalium*; Raimund Lull, *Proverbia*; Pierre Desfontaines, *Le conseil que P.D. donna a son ami*; Robert of Blois, *L'enseignement des princes*; Alvarus Pelagius, *Speculum regum*; the Norwegian *Speculum regale*; James I of Aragon, *Libre de saviesa*; Johannes de Viterbo, *Liber de regimine civitatum*; Godofredus de Viterbo, *Speculum regum*; Petrarca, *De republica optime administranda*; *Calila y Dijmna*; William Perrault, *De eruditione principum*; Orfinus of Lodi, *Poema de regimine et sapientia potestatis*; Gilbert of Tournai, *Eruditio regum et principum*; Pedro Belluga, *Speculum principum*. References for these are to be found in Berges, *Die Fürstenspiegel*. At the end of the Renaissance, however, any direct damage to the whole state through abuses of power or neglect of duty was " the equivalent of tyranny." See Otto v. Gierke, *Johannes Althusius* (New York, 1939), pp. 46 *et seq.*, especially p. 52, note 29.

To see how seriously a ruler took his giving one has only to read the stylized, self-conscious donations of Frederick II and other medieval monarchs. In these donation charters two motives are operative: the desire of the king to measure up to the instructional exhortations to give, and the use of giving in the interest of the common good. Since the technical phraseology of the chancery was concerned more with the political than with the moral motivation of the gift, the ultimate benefit to the state was stressed. Frederick II, for example, in an imperial privilege to the Duke of Brunswick, commences his gift: " Nos autem, qui tenemus modis omnibus imperium augmentare, predictum castrum . . . concessimus "; and in another act: " dignum et utile vidimus circa statum et augmentum ipsius imperiali munificientis providere." [42] A half-century later, Pedro III of Aragon is similarly inspired in the great meeting of prelates, nobles, and representatives of the cities and towns at the Cortes of Barcelona in 1283, held to confirm the privileges of individuals and of the various *universitates* of the realm. The king asserts that it is his royal duty to confirm the liberties and privileges conceded by his predecessors since his giving will promote the general welfare. Almost identical inspiration is cited by James II in Barcelona at the Cortes of 1311: ". . . ex debito nostri officii . . . facere bonum et gracias nostris subditis . . . cum redundarent [the donations] et essent ad bonum statum et utilitatem communem tocius chatalonie . . ."

We may note that in the confirmation of 1283 the king uses the term *restituimus* which indicates, possibly, the persistence of the fundamental feudal idea of personal relationship.[43] In

---

[42] *Constitutiones*, II, 263-64 (1235); and Huillard-Bréholles, *Historia*, IV, 485-86 (1234).

[43] *Cortes de Aragon y de Valencia y Cataluña*, I, i, 140 *et seq.* The text of the king's statement in the Cortes of 1283 reads: " Cum ad excellenciam regalem pertineat suis subditis libertates et immunitates concedere et privilegia per antecessores suos eis indulta et consuetudines usus et bonas observancias approbare et inviolabiliter observare . . . ; idcirco nos Rex predictus per nos et omnes nostros restituimus, concedimus et approbamus prelatis . . . baronibus militibus civibus et hominibus

any event, such confirmations are expected in the thirteenth and later centuries on the accessions of kings and emperors. The confirmations of *Magna Carta* by Henry III and Edward I, and of the long series of imperial donations to the Church by Frederick II, are obvious examples. If any new idea is implicit in *restituimus*, it is that the personal participation of the new ruler is needed, or desired, in an act of re-giving, the theory being that all deputations of authority reverted upon the death of the ruler to the everlasting repository which was, so to speak, the royal office, as symbolized by the Crown.

Just as the idea of inalienability was integrated by lawyers, court councilors, and political theorists into the practical constitutions of their states, so too was it arrogated and used by city officials, especially in Italy. The highest municipal magistracy, whatever its local title, was even more of a temporary office than the imperial one. Hence the need for some sort of constitutional provision which would protect the office and its powers through a succession of executive hands.

The earliest municipal constitutions merely indicate the natural desire of the city to preserve its territory and revenues; there is no indication of specific Roman or canon law influence in the terminology of consular oaths or specific statutes. For example, the oath of the official designated by Genoa to govern Tortosa, binds him to preserve the physical extent of the town against any diminution. And from the *societas* empowered to exact the *census* for twenty-nine years the Genoese consuls demanded that it act for the honor and best interests of the city of Genoa.[44] This sort of general provision is to be found straight through the communal period in oaths administered to the *podestà* or the *consul*. But by the end of the thirteenth

villarum et locorum Catalonie, . . . libertates franquitates consuetudines et bonos usus et omnia privilegia et concessiones usitates tempore domini jacobi quondam bone memorie Regis Aragonum patris nostri."

[44] *Liber iurium reipublicae Januensium,* ed. Hercule Ruoffio, in *Monumenta Historiae Patriae* (Turin, 1854), VII, 151 (1150).

century there is no doubt of the influence of legal terminology, and reference to the public utility is commonplace. The official swears to defend and maintain the laws of the city and the privileges of the church.[45]  Just such a general obligation is specified in the specimen oath given by Johannes de Viterbo in his manual of civic rule, *Liber de regimine civitatum* (ca. 1228).[46]

Nevertheless, there were oaths more specifically concerned with observing the rules of action laid down in the municipal constitutions and the commentaries on the civil law.  In 1257 an addition was made to the habitual oath of the Paduan *podestà* which called upon him to act: ". . . ut societas et comunancia populi Paduani manuteneatur, conservetur et augmentetur in suo statu et honore. . . ." The oath of the *podestà*, as given in the early fourteenth-century vernacular statutes of Siena, includes a promise never to make money gifts without the consent of the town council.[47]  In some municipal codes where the oaths contained nothing specific beyond the usual *salvabo et manutenebo*, laws regulating the duties of chief administrative officials did set limitations in terms obviously of legal origin.  An addition of 1275 to the Florentine constitution states that no citizen is permitted ". . . vendere vel permutare, donare vel alienare, obligare vel in alio modo concedere

---

[45] A. Gaudenzi, *Statuti del popolo di Bologna del secolo XIII* (Bologna, 1888), p. 50; G. Fasoli and P. Sella, *Statuti di Bologna dell'anno 1288* (2 vols., Vatican City, 1937–39), I, 8; L. Zdekauer, *Il costituto di Siena dell'anno 1262* (Milan, 1897), p. 25; F. Bonaini, *Statuti inediti della città di Pisa dal XII al XIV secolo* (3 vols., Florence, 1854–70), I, 61; G. Sandri, *Gli statuti veronese del 1276 colle correzioni e le aggiunte fino al 1323* (Venice, 1940), I, 21-22; *Layettes du trésor des chartes*, I, 743, for the regulation of Carcassonne; F. Silopis, *Statuti Niciae*, in *Monumenta Historiae Patriae* (Turin, 1831), II, col. 44.

[46] Ed. G. Salvemini in *Bibl. juridica medii aevi* (Bologna, 1901), III, 229.  The "iuramentum potestatis" demands that the new official ". . . administrare res et negotia huius civitatis . . . et regere, conducere, gubernare, manutenere, et salvare hanc civitatem . . . ."

[47] A. Gloria, *Statuti del commune di Padova dal secolo XII all'anno 1285* (Padua, 1873), p. 41; A. Lisini, *Il costituto del commune di Siena volgarizzato nel MCCCIX–MCCCX* (2 vols., Siena, 1903), I, 167.

aut titulo alienationes transferre aliquas terras . . . vel aliquas
immobiles iura vel actiones . . . sine licentia expressa Consiliae
generalis communis Florentinie " to any citizen or to the commune of Pistoia.  A more general prohibition against alienation to any recipient is in the constitution of Modena of 1306.
Specific mention is made: " quod omnia publica et bona pre-
dicta (bona mobilia et immobilia et omnia alia) non possint
aliquo modo vel ingenio dari, donari, vel concedi aliquo titulo
. . . sed perpetuo, ut dictum est, remaneant in comuni." And
the *statuti* of Bologna issued in 1288 declare that no one may
alienate anything granted to him by the commune for a limited
time.  The Bolognese also forbade the private possession of
public property by the citizenry.[48]

In the twelfth century, at the beginning of the communal
period, at the time when the Roman law itself was in its early
stages of appreciation, such restrictions were self-imposed because of the logic of the situation.  With the importation of a
*podestà* for a limited term of office, it became a matter of wise
policy for a council to hem in the temporary ruler of the city-
state with limitations on his power to hurt his office.  For this
reason, perhaps, the general wording of the oaths which would
make legal action against a lax or traitorous *podestà* all the
easier.  For this reason, surely, the yearly accounting of the
*podestà* to the town council and the frequent stipulation that
he remain in the city after the expiration of his term of office
long enough for an appraisal of his activity, judicial and administrative, to be made.  But beyond such practical explana-
tions for the repetition of limitations on alienation, there was
also, ever more important during the thirteenth century, the
influence of Roman law doctrines.  Legists were important

[48] G. Rondini, "I più antiche frammento del constituto fiorentino," *Publicazioni
del R. instituto de studi superiori di Firenze* (Florence, 1895), p. 38; E. Vicini
(Statuta), *Respublica mutinensis* (Milan, 1929), p. 7; G. Fasoli and P. Sella, *Statuti
di Bologna*, II, 56, and I, 303 *et seq.*

public officials in Italian cities as well as in the national monarchies of the time.[49]   The highly important commercial life of the cities already was regulated by modified Justinianic law.   It is not surprising, therefore, to find discussions in contemporary commentaries which might have offered theoretical inspiration and authority to municipal legislation.

Azo, in his discussion of the legal position of cities other than Rome, gives to the city privileges of restitution similar to those of a minor and the Church.   Moreover, in the case of a loan which is not in the interest of the city, the city shall not be held.[50]   He distinguishes between private and public goods, and specifies which of the latter may be alienated, and when—after first stating exacting requirements for the moral character of the *administrator*.   One general rule of his is that public monies may not be transferred for any use without the consent of the highest authority (*autoritate principali*); and here he cites laws in the *Code* and *Digest* which restrict the actions of public officials and private guardians.[51]   More specifically, with regard to municipal property (*De vendendis rebus civitatis*), he says that movable goods of a city may be lost after proper authorization.   Real property (*immobilia*)—and under this rubric he classifies taxes and revenues—of a royal city may not be alienated save with royal permission; provincial cities may alienate only for evident public utility, and then only with the consent of all or a majority of the citizens.[52]   In other words, aliena-

[49] See, for example, the biographies of Butrigarius, Passagerius, Cynus, Odofredus, and others in Friedrich C. von Savigny, *Geschichte des Römischen Rechts im Mittelalter* (6 vols., 2d ed., Heidelberg, 1834–51), *passim*; M. Sarti, *De claris archgymnasii Bononiensis professoribus a saeculo XI usque ad saeculum XIV* (2 vols., 2d. ed., Bologna, 1888–96), *passim*; and for the French jurists, the *Histoire littéraire de la France,* especially Vol. XXXVI, and the famous article of E. Chénon, "Le droit romain à la Curia Regis de Philippe Auguste à Philippe le Bel," *Mélanges Fitting,* I, 195-212.

[50] *Summa* (Lyons, 1533), to C. 11, 30 (*De iure rei publicae*), fol. 433.

[51] *Idem* to C. 11, 31 (*De administratione rerum publicarum*), fol. 434.

[52] *Idem* to C. 11, 32 (*De vendendis rebus civitatis*), fol. 434v.

tion is forbidden, yet always allowed for reasons of public convenience when made with proper authority. Such is the course taken by later authorities. Baldus forbids alienation of the power to tax because a city which, like a king, has the power of an emperor within its boundaries, may not surrender any part of the *merum imperium*. For convenience, however, a city may rent or sell certain taxes.[53] Albericus de Rosate substantially supports this view. In his estimation, cities may not renounce privileges which have been introduced in their favor, for if they were able to do this, their authority might eventually be whittled away and they would cease to be political entities.[54]

Here, then, is a variation on the idea often expressed in relation to emperor and king—that the city office is the subject of certain rights and privileges which it cannot deny or surrender if it is to survive. What is most interesting about the statement of Albericus is that it is made in relation to C. 1,3,50 (*Si quis in conscribendo*), a passage concerning ecclesiastical privilege which is a major point of departure for civilian discussion of renunciation of personal inalienable rights. In this statement the prefect states as a rule of ancient law that everyone has the right to abjure privileges which have been introduced in his favor. In the late Middle Ages the doctors of both laws developed a complete theory of renunciations which attempted to adapt to contemporary social conditions the privileges given to minors, women, and clerics by late classical law. As we have seen in passing, and as we shall see in detail, the legists cited the private law of renunciations in their discussions of the inalienable rights of heads of state. The criterion for legal renunciation was in one vital respect the same: Inalienable rights were

---

[53] Baldus (Lyons, 1539), to C. 7, 53, 5, n. 21. Bartolus allows alienation of property, real and otherwise, which cannot serve the public weal. See his comment to C. 11, 23, 3, n. 2, cited by G. Post.

[54] *Super codice* (Lyons, 1545), to C. 1, 3, 50, n. 9.

those which touched the public interest. It was at this point that private and public law met, fused, and reinforced each other, giving forth new and stronger theories in both spheres.

The pattern of relationships, then, is apparent although involved. About the Donation and the title *Augustus* the legists and theorists developed theories of simultaneous justification and disapproval which, in the final analysis, condemned the ruler who might gravely damage his aggregate of powers and by so doing run counter to the obligation imposed upon him by his office and title. Perhaps the most important aspect of the notion of office was its service as a conceptual locus for the sovereignty of the state. Kingship as office was not a startling theory to the thirteenth century; what was novel was its integration with a highly developed pattern of public law ideas then in growth. Contemporary were the development of the public utility and welfare as standards by which to judge the propriety of a public act, the abstraction of the Crown as the symbol of the state which bridged generations as the everlasting treasury of public rights, and the teleological concept of office and function which demanded the exercise of inherent or essential authority were the ruler to be, in a full and final sense, a ruler. In law books and theoretical treatises the exact nature of the essential governmental qualities was defined, and the alienation of these requisites was prohibited by a fundamental construction of politics and law. The universal need of the moment for such public law is evidenced by the appearance of the idea— this synthesis of " office " and " inalienability "—in so many different types of political literature and at every level of government.

# III

# The Ecclesiastical Theory
# of Inalienability

DISCUSSION of the canon law aspects of the theory of inalienability properly and necessarily must be made under several major rubrics: the decretal *Intellecto* (*Decr. Greg. IX* 2, 24, 33), by which the pope released the king of Hungary from oaths taken in donation charters which violated his coronation oath, together with its glosses; and the ideas developed in canonist discussion of two distinct although related questions: alienation of church property, and renunciation of ecclesiastical privilege or office. Although *Intellecto* gave rise to opinions of fundamental importance for the theory of inalienability of sovereignty, because of its greater pertinence elsewhere it will be treated more fully later.[1] If it is true that the decretal provided a major locus for canonist discussions of inalienability, it is also true that it is but one of many documents in the elaboration of church theory. What gives it its special significance for our study is the use made of it by the decretalists. They would confirm its principle in a simple *explication de texte*, or in more

---

[1] Yet it might be wise at this point, considering the great importance of the decretal for this study, to give the text of *Intellecto* (X. 2, 24, 33): "Intellecto iamdudum, quod charissimus in Christo filius noster Hungariae rex illustris, alienationes quasdam fecerit in praeiudicium regni sui, et contra regis honorem. Nos eidem regi dirigimus scripta nostra, ut alienationes praedictas, non obstante iuramento, si quod fecit de non revocandis eisdem, studeat revocare. Quia cum teneatur et in sua coronatione iuraverit iura regni sui et honorem coronae illibita servare, illicitum profecto fuit, si praestitit de non revocandis alienationibus huiusmodi iuramentum. Et propterea penitus non servandum."

elaborate commentaries relate the theory of the decretal to other concepts in the domain of other concepts in the domain of ecclesiastical public law: the common utility, provincial representation, capitular consent, and ecclesiastical alienation, to name the most important. Our immediate topic, however, is the influence of church theory as developed in relation to the two other main topics, alienation of property, and renunciation of right, for it was with respect to these that the canonists most successfully integrated their theories of public and private law to produce new concepts of political theory.

Given the basic idea that *res sacrae,* because of their overwhelming importance for the general and individual welfare, could not be separated from an ecclesiastical institution, the general principle of Roman law was to forbid all alienation of church property. The Church concurred, yet as early as Leo the Great (440–61) we have a relaxation of this absolute prohibition in the form of one of the pope's letters which allowed alienation in cases of eventual benefit to the Church. Concomitant with this greater freedom, however, was the institution of new and stricter penalties for violations; and further to avoid abuse, bishops were instructed to confer with all their clergy and to obtain the consent of all before they acted to alienate church property. Leo's legislation and that of Pope Symmachus (498–514) were incorporated into early canonist collections. In these, in the proceedings of the First Lateran Council (1123), in the *Decretum* and the *Decretals,* emphasis rests upon the bishop as the active agent in church affairs. The *Decretum* and the *Decretals* repeat the general injunction against alienation, yet hand in hand with the issuing of new prohibitions went the elaboration of a doctrine of permission linked to principles of representation and consent.[2]

---

[2] Joseph F. Cleary, *Canonical Limitations on the Alienation of Church Property* (Washington, D.C., 1936), pp. 16-17. This is a good discussion of the canonical doctrine, but it does not go into the relationship of the Church doctrine with

The earliest glosses to the *Decretum* for the most part are paraphrases of the canonist texts.[3] One interesting comment of the late twelfth century bears mention, a statement in the Bolognese *Summa Reginensis* which denies the pope the right to alienate church property, and calls upon his successor to revoke any such alienations.[4] In the thirteenth century the decretalists worked the thought of *Intellecto* into the general scheme. For example, Abbas Antiquus (d. 1296) gives an exclusively ecclesiastical interpretation to the decretal, in a sense reversing the usual procedure which was to read the canon law into contemporary political events, thereby extending its influence.[5] The principal desire of canonist theory, we might say then, was for protection. From the time that the Church first began to accumulate property and privileges this had seemed the natural course. In the twelfth century, and even before, exceptions to the generalized prohibition were admitted, providing always

secular public law and theory, and the relationship of this doctrine with others within the canon law itself. I follow Cleary's historical treatment very closely in this discussion of the strict canonist theory.

[3] See the comments upon Ca. XII, q. 2 of Paucapalea, *Summa* (ed. F. v. Schulte, Giessen, 1890); Stephan of Tournai, *Summa* (ed. F. v. Schulte, Giessen, 1891); and Rufinus, *Summa* (ed. F. v. Schulte, Giessen, 1891). Rufinus writes: " sciendum est itaque, quod generaliter res ecclesiae alienari prohibentur," and then, in common with the others, goes on to give the exceptions allowed and the order in which ecclesiastical properties are to be surrendered.

[4] *Summa Reginensis*, Vatican MS Reg. lat. 1061, fol. 18r to Dist. XCVI, which is the text of the Donation of Constantine in the *Decretum*, " Item non licet papa res ecclesiae alienare et si alienate fiunt possunt a successore revocari." For the *Summa Reginensis* see Kuttner, *Repertorium*, pp. 160-66. At the end of the Middle Ages another legist was to declare the pope guilty of mortal sin in cases of nepotistic alienation: Socinus, *Consilia* (Venice, 1579), I, cons. 13, n. 7: ". . . Papam peccare mortaliter si bona ecclesiae alienat in casu non licito, puta dando illa consanguineis."

[5] *Lectura aurea super quinque libris decretalium* (Strasbourg, 1510), to X, 2, 24, 33: " Casus: Quando quis iurat in sui promotione non alienare bona ecclesie: si postea alienet et iuret: alienatio non tenet." Innocent IV's *casus* (Venice, 1491) is typical of the usual treatment: " Intellecto illibita hoc decretale intelligitur quod fecit alienationes propter quas gravitas dignitas regalis. non enim propter hoc interdicitur sibi donare vel aliter alienare." For other opinions on ecclesiastical alienation see Johannes Teutonicus (Venice, 1514), to *Decret.* Ca. X, q. 2; and Bartholomaeus Brixiensis (Venice, 1477).

that ultimately the best interests of the church community were served; this criterion remained the theoretical absolute against which the propriety and legality of actions were measured. And it was in accord with this view that *Intellecto* found its place among those texts upon which the Church relied as it moved more and more into the commercial activity of the day, to say nothing of the political.

Apart from its appearance in the texts of the canon law, the fundamental restrictive theory manifested itself in an important institution of the Church, the oaths taken by bishops and abbots upon their accession to office. These oaths, which were taken before an archbishop, or in cases of immediate relationship before or to the pope, in both terminology and idea provide an analogy to the coronation oaths of contemporary kings. But it was not exactly a contemporary one, for the restrictions on alienation in formal language appear earlier in the ecclesiastical formulas. The canon law collection of Cardinal Deusdedit (1083–87) gives us an early example of such an oath, a simple promise to be faithful to the pope. Slightly earlier (1078) is the oath of an archbishop cited in a letter of Gregory VII: " ea (thesauros . . . et ornamenta et predia ecclesie) non alienabo. . . ." [6] Obviously, this is a step toward the oath required by the Holy See from an archbishop which we find in a late twelfth-century pontifical: ". . . predia, possessiones, ornamenta ecclesiastica, que iuris sunt N. ecclesie, numquam alienabo, nec vendam, nec in pignora ponam, neque alicui sine communi consensu capituli vel potioris partis et sanioris consilii in beneficio vel feudo dabo." [7] Here is precautionary language developed

---

[6] P. Fabre, *Liber censuum de l'église romaine* (Paris, 1889–1910), p. 416; this oath is included in the canonical collection *Deusdedit*.

[7] Michel Andrieu, *Le pontifical romain au moyen-âge* (3 vols., Vatican City, 1938–40), I, 290-91. Emphasis here is upon those aspects of the ecclesiastical oaths which relate to alienation. There is also an approximation of the bishop's oath to that of the feudal vassal to his lord. This feudalization of the episcopal oath during and after the late eleventh century has most recently been stressed by Ernst

by a century of legal thought: the introduction into the oath
of all the variant legal actions leading towards separation, and
the demand for capitular consent. Essentially there is little
difference between these oaths and the somewhat later ones
taken by abbots, bishops, and archbishops to the pope which
are included in the *Liber censuum*. In these, however, there is
no mention of capitular consent; but, as though to compensate,
we find use of the following phrase, straight from the decretals
and commentaries, to denote the category of *inalienabilia* protected by the oath: *ad mensam . . . pertinentes*. This oath was
taken as early as 1234 in England by Henry, abbot of St. Ed-
munds, and by Eadmund, archbishop of Canterbury.[8] And
there is little difference between the form in the *Liber censuum*
and that incorporated by Durandus (1237–96) into his *Ponti-
ficale*.[9] The episcopal oath included by Gregory IX in the
*Decretals* (2, 24, 4) is not as specific as the above examples with
regard to alienation, for as the *casus* indicates, it is only a form
indicating major rubrics. Innocent IV, in his gloss to *damnum*
in the decretal text, stated exactly what his predecessors had in
mind: " id est in diminutionem fidei B. Petri et in derogatione
honoris ecclesiae, vel in lesione personae Papae." [10] And yet another canonist, commenting on *Intellecto*, compared the original oath of the Hungarian king to that taken by a bishop on
his consecration, and because of the justice of the latter, gave

---

Kantorowicz, " Inalienability: A Note on Canonical Practice and the English
Coronation Oath in the Thirteenth Century," *Speculum*, XXIX (1954), 488–502.
Professor Kantorowicz's article appeared after the completion of this study, and so
I have not been able fully to benefit from his conclusions, which, in sum, tend to
substantiate my own.

[8] *Liber censuum*, pp. 285 and 449.

[9] Andrieu, *Pontifical romain*, III, 71; see M. Tangl, *Die päpstlichen Kanzleiordnungen von 1200–1500 (Innsbruck, 1921), nn. 10–11.

[10] *Apparatus* (Venice, 1578), to X. 2, 24, 4. See also the gloss in Bernardus
Bottoni (Rome, 1474), ad v. *alienationis* in X. 3, 13, 8: " largo sumpto vocabulo
sive transferatur dominium sive non." He also states it a duty of every bishop
immediately under the pope to swear: " non alienabit bona ecclesie nec infeudabit
de novo. et idem iuramentum prestant alii episcopi suis metropolitanis."

his full approval to the principle of the decretal.[11] This is to say that contemporary canonists themselves drew the analogy between secular and ecclesiastical oaths and made the connection between the theory of *Intellecto,* the public welfare, and the oath. What is more, besides indicating the relationship of the theory of inalienability to other concepts of ecclesiastical public law, the oaths indicate a possible path for the influence of canonist ideas upon the theory and practice of the national monarchies.

For their part, the civilians repeated the Justinianic prohibitions against church alienation, yet followed the lead of the Church in allowing exceptions. Accursius, for example, lists six cases in which alienation was prohibited—a list he opposes to that of an equal number permitted. Notable among the properties which may never be given up are imperial gifts to the Church. Upon this point there was universal agreement based upon the theory that the emperor gives with an eye to the well-being of his subjects.[12]

Having once admitted the legality of necessitous alienation, canonists and civilians alike elaborated theories which defined the conditions permitting alienation, and established the priority in which forced sales and other alienations were to be made. The basic excuse for alienation was *necessitas,* a requirement obviously open to a great latitude of interpretation. Although many commentators did not bother to define the term and its equivalent *utilitas,* criteria did develop. According to Accursius, the Church might alienate its goods in the following cases: ". . . cum debitum urget; in perpetua emphytusi; cum

11 Bottoni (Rome, 1474), to X. 2, 24, 33: "sic et episcopi iurant in sua consecratione quod iura sui episcopatus non alienabunt . . . . sic ergo patet quod iuramentum istius regis in coronatione sua licitum et honestum fuit . . . ."

12 *Glossa ordinaria* (Venice, 1591), to C. 1, 2, 14 (Hoc ius porrectum); also, Azo (Lyons, 1533), to C. 1, 2, n. 13. See too the statement of the *Siete partidas,* pta. 6, cap. 9, n. 13: "Las cosas sagradas que pertenescen a la Yglesia otrosi las cosas que son señaladamente de los reyes . . . son cosas que non deven ser vendidas, nin enagenados en ninguna manera . . . ."

alia ecclesia permutando; cum principe; ut in redemptione cap-
tivorum ut superflua vasa." [13]   Under such conditions church
property was to be alienated in a specified order. The *Exceptiones Petri* declared that movable goods such as foodstuffs and
livestock should be the first to go, to be followed by real property and the sacred vessels of the Church only in the most extreme circumstances, although the last mentioned category includes this vague phrase in a list which otherwise comprises
grave debts and famine: " vel pro maxima melioratione ecclesiarum." Such is the order generally prescribed from the
late eleventh century onward.[14]

We have seen that both the Roman and canon law were
against alienation of church property save under special circumstances; also, that episcopal oaths which reflected this position in some cases demanded the express consent of the ecclesiastics affected in any instance of alienation. This, of course, is
a use of the maxim *Quod omnes tangit* which found wide application in Roman and canon law, and in the development of
representative procedures and institutions. Glosses from the
late twelfth century give a variety of opinion on the majority
necessary for legal alienation. Huguccio (fl. 1190) simply
paraphrases the text when he says that the consent of the bishop
and of the clerics touched is needed when a cleric wishes to
alienate his prebend or benefice. Without consent a bishop
could not alienate lands under cultivation, even in cases of
necessity, and here Huguccio demands consent where the text
speaks only of *consilium*.[15]   In the thirteenth century, defini-

---

[13] *Glossa ordinaria* (Venice, 1591), to C. 1, 2, 14 (*Hoc ius porrectum*).

[14] *Exceptiones Petri* (ed. H. Fitting, Halle, 1876), lib. I, cap. 65; see also Huguccio, *Summa*, Vatican MS lat. 2280, fol. 190v to *Decret.* Ca. XII, q. 2, c. 41, and fol. 192r to Ca. XII, q. 2, c. 50; Stephen of Tournai, *Summa* (ed. F. v. Schulte, Giessen, 1891), to Ca. XII, q. 2, c. 19; Petrus de Ancharano, *Super clementinis* (Lyons, 1520), to *Clem.* 3, 4, 1, n. 5; Panormitanus, *Commentaria* (Augsburg, 1577), to X. 3, 13, 8, nn. 8-10.

[15] *Summa*, Vatican MS lat. 2280, fol. 190r to Ca. XII, q. 2, c. 37, ad v. *pre-bendam:* " quia possessiones ecclesiastice non possunt alienari sine consensu episcopi

tion of consent became more specific. Besides those glosses cited by Professor Post we may mention in this connection the opinion of Innocent IV, who asked that the *maior pars* of those affected consent to any alienation. Innocent likewise required approval from the *maior pars regni* for the validity of the King of Aragon's devaluation of the national coinage, for the reason: " licitum sit cuiusque renunciare iure suo "—to which concept we shall return.[16] Although consent of the *maior pars* was usually required,[17] there were those who demanded such consent only in cases of great danger, or of possible loss of *magna dignitas* to the Church. Among these were such great doctors of the canon law as Antonius de Butrio (1338–1408) and Johannes Andreae (1270–1348). The latter's comment was made in reference to the possible surrender of a benefice to a layman; and its terminology and qualifying restraint are strongly reminiscent of Innocent IV's words upon *Intellecto* in which he limited the application of the decretal to those diminutions which would hurt the Church gravely.[18]    Andreae's

---

et clericorum nec proprietatem talis prebende possunt clerici sibi acquirere vel in alium transferre."

[16] *Commentaria* (Venice, 1577), to X. 1, 4, 9: " secus tamen in alienationibus rerum ecclesiae, ubi non tenet, quod a paucioribus fit, nisi maior pars ibidem residentium contractum inierit "; and to 2, 24, 18: " et quin negotium Regis negotium universitatis reputatur, et ideo sufficit consensus maioris partis regni." For the maxim *Cum licitum* see below pp. 68 *et seq.* It was in relation to this text that the lawyers developed a good many of their opinions on the fundamental criteria which determined the alienability or inalienability of rights.

[17] For example, Hostiensis, *Summa* (Venice, 1581), p. 159, to X. 3, 2, 1; Bernardus Compostellanus, Jr., in MS Pal. lat. 629 fol. 270v to the decretal *Dudum* of Innocent IV, incorporated into the lib. VI, 3, 9, 1 ad v. *defensore*; Bartholomaeus Brixiensis, *Auree questiones dominicales ac veneriales nec non brocarda* (Venice, 1508), fol. 32v. See also Azo, *Summa*, to C. 1, 2, nn. 12-15.

[18] Johannes Andreae, *In . . . librum decretalium novella commentaria* (Venice, 1581), to X. 1, 9, 8, n. 4: " consensum capituli maioris, vel cathedralis ecclesiae non credimus requirendum, nisi esset magna dignitas, cui renunciatur, vel talis persona, de qua magnus honor, vel periculum immineret ecclesiae. tunc enim quia magnum esset negotium, consensus capituli requirendus." See also Antonius de Butrio, *Pars prima super primo decretalium* (Lyons, 1556), to X. 1, 9, 8, n. 6; Baldus (Lyons, 1539), to C. 6, 61, 7, nn. 1-2, cites the Archdeacon to the effect that when prop-

comment certainly is a step away from the emphasis of *Intellecto* and also of the earlier letter of Innocent III to the guardians of young Frederick Hohenstaufen which was the prototype
of Honorius' decretal. With regard to this letter of 1200, there
is little doubt that Innocent III had the principle of inalienability of sovereignty clearly in mind when he prohibited alienation of the royal demesne save in cases of " the most obvious
and urgent necessity, for example, the mobilization of an army
or navy "; even then action demanded supervision and consent:
" communi omnium voluntate vel ex majori saltem parte consilii sanioris." [19]    The fundamental point was perfectly expressed by Hostiensis (d. 1271) apropos a general injunction
against transfer of property from one church to another without consent of all involved: " authority is not given for destruction or spoliation, but rather for rule, care and defense." [20]

Despite the fact that this ecclesiastical law offered oppor-
tunity for circumvention, its overall emphasis was on the maintenance of church rights and property. Therefore the law on
representation within the Church was in some respects formed
in accordance with this principle. The general mandate given
to ecclesiastical proctors at local or general councils did not allow the representative to act against his principals. The proctor
who intended to ". . . transact, alienate, or to transfer, renew
or change a debt by the *novatio* " until the time of Boniface VIII
had to have special authority in his mandate. After Boniface,
says Professor Post, and perhaps as early as Durandus ". . . *plena
potestas* was the practical equivalent of *libera administratio*,"
which is to say that the proctor might alienate to his principal's

---

erty is " valde pretiosa, ut magna civitas, debet intervenire consensus cardinalium
qui sunt capitulum universale."

    [19] Huillard-Bréholles, *Historia*, I, 57; and for the question of public utility and
consent, Gaines Post, " Plena Potestas and Consent in Medieval Assemblies (1150–
1325)," *Traditio*, I (1943), 355-408.

    [20] *In primum . . . quintum decretalium librum commentaria* (Venice, 1581), to
X. 3, 13, 1, n. 2.

disadvantage but only with proper authority and under conditions which precluded the possibility of fraud, and which were within the realm of legal action. And this was true of diplomatic envoys as well as the representatives of private corporations.[21]

Yet another aspect of ecclesiastical activity with regard to which theories of representation and renunciation were interactive was that of *pariage*. For the essential characteristic of this contractual relationship was the surrender of tangible resources or rights by a monastery or church to a secular authority in return for his protection. And so, the cleric who would make such an agreement needed a special mandate, and in some cases ratification by the congregation. Certain contracts went so far as to provide for automatic nullification in case of papal disapproval.[22] *Pariage,* therefore, presents another limitation upon office. The canon law—Roman law being in complete agreement—was careful to throw obstacles before any delegate potentially harmful to his parent organization.

The restraints placed generally upon proctors and upon church officials negotiating contracts, for example those of *pariage,* indicate the reference of responsibility to be the welfare of the membership of the ecclesiastical institution. Therefore, as we have seen, provision was made for the supervision of churchmen who had to involve themselves in the affairs of the world wherein they were considered incompetent and at an immediate disadvantage.[23] To right the balance canon and Roman law recognized a presumed sacerdotal frailty and

---

[21] G. Post, "Plena Potestas," pp. 360-65.

[22] Léon Gallet, *Les traités de pariage dans la France féodale* (Paris, 1935), pp. 116 *et seq.*

[23] Huguccio, *Summa,* Vatican MS lat. 2280, fol. 188v to Ca. XII, q. 2, c. 23: "episcopo de quo in hoc capitulo habetur mentio dilapidator erat vel suspectus de dilapidatione rerum ecclesiasticarum et ideo remotus fuit ab administratione temporalium. remansit tamen in ordine et officio suo et ita administratione spiritualium ipsa vero cura et administratio temporalium duobus clericis eius ecclesiae sicut archideacono et defensori illius ecclesiae."

granted the Church special rights of redress and restitution. In this connection, Hostiensis, commenting on an ancient law of the Church which brought excommunication upon an alienator of church property, claimed that the original contract could never have been valid, even though confirmed by oath. His supporting citations are significant, for they indicate a view of the church in society which subsequently was carried over into secular theory and applied to the national kings. One is *Intellecto;* the other, the *Senatusconsultum Velleianum* (D. 16, 1, 32) which forbids a woman "to undertake liability for others, either by way of surety . . . or other modes releasing the person primarily liable."[24]  Fundamental to the S.C. *Velleianum* is the idea that female frailty is to be protected legally, and forcibly if necessary, against acts of self-depredation. And *Intellecto* enters the picture here because of its relevance to the legists' theory of the public welfare. In this connection we may note a *consilium* of Oldradus in which he approves the action of an abbot in creating new monks despite an oath he had taken not to do so. This oath, now in conflict with the order of the bishop to whom he had originally sworn obedience, is void for the reason that it was in derogation of his freedom of action and so ultimately prejudicial to the welfare of his congregation: "ecclesiasticae libertatis diminutio. . . . item contra ius publicum, cui pacto renunciare non potest."[25]

The point to be made is this: that the Church was regarded by the civil authorities and law, and regarded itself, as a body to be protected, as an institution highly developed, yet historically incompetent in the world of affairs. The medieval social structure demanded that the Church involve itself in worldly matters; the Church was not unwilling and indeed was

[24] W. W. Buckland, *A Textbook of Roman Law from Augustus to Justinian* (2d ed., Cambridge, 1932), p. 448.

[25] Oldradus da Ponte, *Consilia* (Venice, 1570), cons. 97; see too Cynus, *Super codice et digesto veteri lectura* (Lyons, 1547), to C. 1, 2, 14, n. 4; Hostiensis, *Commentaria* to X. 3, 13, 6.

forced to do so in order that it might fulfill its religious functions. Yet, like the woman who was protected by the S.C. *Velleianum,* and for identical reasons, it was surrounded by special protections which were to insure its existence and service. When legists and theorists wished to enhance the imperial and regal office they did the same thing: they ascribed special natures to the objects they wished to preserve, and based their protections upon the same private law concepts on the basis of which they protected the positions of women, minors, and clerics in a hostile world.[26]

At this point we may document this assertion with reference to the cleric, and show what restrictions were placed upon the individual ecclesiastic in office, what distinction was made between priest and office, and why this discussion is not irrelevant to the history of political theory. The public law of the Church was well known to the legists and political theorists of the late Middle Ages, and they drew inspiration and support as much from one law as from the other.

We have been speaking of restrictions upon the alienation of church property; emphasis now shifts to the renunciation of church privileges. In both cases interpretation of the word is in the broadest sense, for such was the medieval understanding. *Alienatio* meant for the churchmen every act by which possession might immediately or ultimately be lost; *renuntiatio* included every conscious act whereby one's privileges were surrendered.[27]

One crucial ecclesiastical privilege was the right of a cleric to trial in his bishop's court, rather than that of the secular authority: the *privilegium fori*.[28] Canonists were of the unani-

[26] For example, Huguccio, *Summa,* Vatican MS lat. 2280, fol. 122v to Ca. II, q. 7, c. 5.

[27] Hostiensis, *Summa* (1581), fol. 28, " Quid sit renuntiatio "; *Summa* (1574), col. 915, " Quid sit alienatio "; and *Commentaria* (1581), to X. 3, 13, 5, n. 1.

[28] R. Généstal, *Le " privilegium fori " en France du décret de Gratien à la fin du XIV° siècle* (2 vols., Paris, 1925–31).

mous opinion that this privilege could not be renounced, and
it was in relation to the *privilegium* and its significance for the
entire Church that they developed that aspect of the theory of
inalienability which related it to the concept of the supreme
importance of the common good.[29]   The statement of Bernardus Bottoni (d. 1263), whose book of *casus* on the *Decretals*
went through many incunabula editions, and whose apparatus
was accepted as the *Glossa ordinaria,* will serve as sufficient illustration.   Writing in reference to the important decretal of
Innocent III, *Si diligenti* (*Decret. Greg. IX*, 2, 2, 12) in which
the great pope very definitely restrained a Pisan churchman
from fulfilling his promise to appear in a secular court, he
states:

. . . manifeste apparet quod clerici nec inviti nec volentes possint
pacisci ut secularia iudicia subeant, quia hoc non est beneficium per-
sonali cui renunciare possit, sed potius toti collegio ecclesiastico publico
et concessum cui pactum privatum derogare non potest et iuramentum
super hoc prestitum licite servare non potuit. . . . Nota quod ius publicum pacto privatorum non tollitur. . . . Item ius istud publicum est
et ideo nullus ei [*sic*] renunciare potest.[30]

---

[29] T. Eschmann, "A Thomistic Glossary on the Principle of the Preeminence
of a Common Good," *Medieval Studies,* V (1943), 123-66, has brought out the
single case in which private good prevailed over the common: the salvation of the
individual soul.   Here, of course, we are dealing with the institutional aspects of
renunciation, and so the question of individual salvation never appears, save in one
instance.   In the affair concerned with Celestine V's renunciation of the papal office
one argument used by the supporters of the renunciation was Celestine's right to
consider himself.   See H. Denifle, " Die Denkschriften der Colonna gegen Bonifaz
VIII und der Cardinale gegen die Colonna," *Archiv für Literatur und Kirchengeschichte des Mittelalters,* V (1889), 525-26, for the reply of the cardinals supporting Boniface against Jacobus and Petrus Colonna.   On the other hand, the good of
the Church was stressed by both sides.

[30] Bernardus Bottoni, *Casus longi super decretales* (Bologna, 1487), to X. 2, 2, 12.
See also Goffredus de Trani, *Summa super titulos decretalium* (Venice, 1586), to
X. 1, 9 (*De renuntiatione*), n. 5; Innocent IV, *Apparatus* (Venice, 1578), to
X. 2, 24, 28 ad v. *alterius*; Bottoni, *Casus* (Rome, 1474) to X. 3, 31, 23; Vincen-
tius to *Comp. III*, 1, 8, 3 in Vatican MS lat. 1378, fol. 18v ad v. *introducta*; Paulus
Ungarus, Vatican MS Borgh. 261, fol. 84v to *Comp. III*, 2, 2, 4, and fol. 113r to
tit. *De foro competenti.*

The interrelation of the theories of renunciation and public utility are perfectly illustrated here; and the carry-over into the realm of secular politics is shown in the fact that the *Glossa ordinaria* refers to *Si diligenti* as the supporting reference for its approval of *Intellecto*. This is to say that the king could not violate his original oath which obliged him to maintain undiminished the rights of his kingdom, those rights representing by inference the best interests of all his subjects. And Hostiensis, commenting on *Si diligenti* approves the text on the basis of the law *Si quis in conscribendo* (C. 2, 3, 29), perhaps the key passage in the complex civil law theory of private renunciations. This citation is significant because it shows the interdependence of the two laws in the development of a common body of public law dependent upon both the contemporary theory of society and events; and also because it demonstrates through *Si quis in conscribendo* the impact upon each other of private and public law theories of inalienable right.[31]

One other important canonist may be cited to draw the bond of relationships still tighter: Johannes Teutonicus' (fl. 1215–45/6?) gloss on the chapter *Non liceat* (*Decret*. III. q. 6 c. 14) which prohibits what we would call change of venue from one episcopal jurisdiction to another: " patet quod clericus sine consensu sui episcopi non potest consentire in alium iudicem, nam sic posset evacuari iurisdictio episcoporum si omnes consentirent in alium iudicem." What is interesting here is the close parallelism exhibited between this argument relating to the ultimate exhaustion of episcopal authority, and that used by civilian opponents of the Donation of Constantine to the effect that the Empire would ultimately, and inferentially quickly, be destroyed if every emperor were allowed an extravagant freedom of bequest.[32] The exchange of ideas worked

---

[31] *Commentaria* (Venice, 1581), to X. 2, 2, 12.

[32] Johannes Teutonicus, *Decretum cum glossis . . . J. T.* (Venice, 1514), fol. 142v to Ca. III, q. 6, c. 14. This chapter, *Non liceat*, is not, strictly speaking, concerned

in the other direction as well; that is, the civilians, having stated the special position of the clergy, used passages in the canon law dealing with the *privilegium fori* as vehicles for their opinions on renunciations of personal privileges. In other words, it was now the public law (of the Church) lending concepts to private civil law. Accursius' comment to *Si quis in conscribendo,* and that of Wilhelmus de Cuneo on the same passage are indicative of this process.[33]

Yet another aspect of this interrelationship of ideas is evidenced in the canonist treatment of a bishop as *tutor* or *curator* of the goods and privileges entrusted to him. The pope, too, was considered an administrator who did not have ownership (*dominium*) of the perquisites of his office; rather he had, according to Panormitanus (1386–1445/53?) the greatest possible freedom of action (*liberrimam administrationem*). This canonist also defined quite clearly just how an ecclesiastic is to be considered in the nature of *procurator,* a term he set in apposition with *administrator.* The prelate is to have wide powers in the disposition of the properties entrusted to him, but he is bound: ". . . procurare utilitatem ecclesiae. . . ."[34]

---

with renunciation of ecclesiastical privileges. But it is related to several general ideas which enhance that of renunciation itself. In another passage Johannes Teutonicus speaks of renunciation of dignities only into the hands of the original giver: ad v. *laico. Comp. III,* 1, 8, 1 in Vatican MS Chis. E. VII. 207, fol. 154v. And Hostiensis, glossing X. 3, 3, 12 (*Ad nostram*) which calls for restriction to the Church in cases of great harm, speaks of the necessity for stability of Church privileges: "primo propter honorem Dei."

[33] *Glossa ordinaria,* to C. 2, 3, 29; Guilhermus de Cungno, *Lectura super codicem* (Lyons, 1513), to C. 2, 3, 29, n. 1: "Quero nunquid hodie possit clericus renuntiare suo foro? communis opinio est quod non . . . quia non attendimus contractum sed personam clerici . . . quia privilegium quod habent clerici non est introductum mere in favore ipsorum, sed in favorem totius cleri, et ideo non possunt renuntiare. . . . Item quia est introductum in odium laycorum . . . ." He concludes by referring to the S. C. *Macedonianum* which may not be renounced, and the S. C. *Velleianum,* which may be.

[34] *Commentaria* (Venice, 1578), to X. 3, 36, 6, n. 13: "clarius loquitur glossa . . . ubi postea Bernardus dicit Papa non esse dominum rerum ecclesiasticarum nec habere illarum possessionem nomine proprio, sed sunt ipsius ut administratoris principalis. Unde not. concludit post B. Thomas Papam incurrere vitium simoniae si

Failing this use of office, he was to be punished; and Innocent IV indeed urges the cathedral chapter to start proceedings against an erring bishop,[35] Generally speaking, it was the common opinion that properly accredited proctors could bring damage upon the institutions they represented but that the Church was not responsible for the acts of its members. In his statement of this rule Dynus (d. ca. 1300) equates church and ward, and the Renaissance commentator, Nicholaus Boerus, adds the phrase: " civitas et universitas aequiparantur secundum Glossa. . . ." [36] These glosses in relation to the concept of ecclesiastic guardian, and those previously cited relative to the public utility of the Church and the renunciation of the *privilegium fori* lead to the examination of an important incident in papal history.

In 1294 the aged, unwilling Pope Celestine V renounced the papacy and retired to the cloistered life from which he had

---

pro iuribus spiritualibus recipit ab ecclesia aliquid temporale; quod non esset si dominium esset suum . . . . non potest Papa disponere de eis (patrimonialibus ipsorum clericorum) ad libitum, sicut nec princeps secularis de bonis subiectorum." See also his similar comment to X. 1, 3, 19, n. 9; and X. 3, 24, 2; and in the edition of Lyons, 1547, to X. 2, 24, 33 where he compares the duties of the king with those of any ecclesiastical official. This view of ecclesiastical obligations was civilian doctrine as well. See, for example, Guilhermus de Cungno, *Lectura super codicem*, to C. 6, 61, 7: ". . . cum episcopus non sit nisi minister et ideo tanquam peculium sibi venderet." And Lucas de Penna, *Lectura* (Lyons, 1538), to C. 11, 58, 7, n. 4: "Amplius sicut prelatus prohiberetur alienare bona ecclesie . . . ita principes bona fiscalia. Item si alienatio rerum patrimonialium prohibetur . . . fortius bona fiscalia imperii sive regalia inalienabilia sunt . . . . Nam equiparantur quantum ad hoc etiam iuramentum super his prestitum de alienatione facta non revocanda episcopus et rex." See also Albericus, *Super codici* (Lyons, 1545), to C. 7, 37, 3, nn. 26-29.

35 *Apparatus*, to X. 1, 33, 13 ad v. *capitulum*: " et est multum . . . dignum quod capitulum non solum appellavit pro iuribus episcipatus, sed etiam super his causam prosequitur et etiam eius prosequentibus episcopus absolvitur et hoc est ea ratione, quia haec absolutio non personam sed rem tangit, cuius nomine capitulum appellavit, et egit, et quia haec spiritualia et dignitates ecclesiae sunt communia et communiter tenentur ab episcopo."

36 Dynus de Mugello, *Commentaria in regulas iuris pontifici* (Venice, 1572), 159: " Si abbas vel monachus vel alius clericus delinquat iniuriam faciendo, vel damnum dando, vel alicuius possessionem violenter occupando, ecclesia non tenetur, quia delictum personae non debet in damnum ecclesiae redundare, nam qua ratione delictum tutoris non obligat pupillum."

been forced; so doing he moved some of the ablest pens in Christendom to controversy, and brought to the forefront of the polemics the question of the legality of renunciation and its relationships to the public utility. These were not the only problems involved, nor was the primacy of the public utility the single authority appealed to, yet it is notable that every discussion of the renunciation reckons with the reciprocal relationship.[37] Celestine himself pointed up the importance of the intellectual interdependency by basing his renunciation upon the single great exception allowed in canon law to the supremacy of the public good—the salvation of his own soul.[38]

Boniface VIII, in the first recorded document of his pontificate, mentioned canonical precedent for Celestine's renunciation and defended his own election, for the Spiritual Franciscans were already clamoring for the return of their leader.[39] And already in 1295 this question appeared in the *Quodlibeta* of Godefroid de Fontaines at the University of Paris: " Quod liceret praelato renunciare." Godefroid answered succinctly by linking the two bases for the pope's abdication: ". . . et sufficienter casus sit quod non est ad regendum utiliter vel quia ad detrimentum spirituale sui ipsius." In other words, Celestine's renunciation fulfilled both his obligations, to the Church which he had been deputed to protect, and to his soul which,

---

[37] A bibliography of the pertinent literature is to be found in the article of Roger Mols, " Celestine V," in *Dictionnaire d'histoire et de géographie ecclésiastique*, fasc. LXVII (Paris, 1950).

[38] The act of renunciation is given in substance in Baronius-Theiner, *Annales ecclesiastici* (Bar-le-Duc, 1871), XXIII, 145: " Ego Caelestinus V, papa motus ex legitimis causis, id est causa humilitatis, et melioris vitae et conscientiae illaesae, debilitate corporis, defectu scientiae . . . ." Eschmann, " Thomistic Glossary," p. 138, cites the decretal letter of Innocent III (X. 3, 31, 18) which states that a bishop needs a special license (obtainable) from the pope in order to renounce his duties for a stricter spiritual life, while a simple cleric may readily choose the way he prefers for the salvation of his soul; the reasoning is that the bishop is an agent of the public good, and hence may shirk his obligation only on grounds of absolute necessity.

[39] *Les registres de Boniface VIII* (Paris, 1884), fasc. I, col. 1-4.

presumably, now might be saved.[40]   Pierre d'Auvergne (fl. 1275-1304) likewise made the validity of the renunciation dependent on the pope's conscience and judgment, stated conditions similar to those of Godefroid, and emphasized very strongly the pope's obligation to abdicate should he be unable to perform his official duties: ". . . non posset gerere officium ecclesiae." And in answer to the question: to whom shall the pope renounce since he has no superior?—he suggested the college of cardinals or a general council.[41]

This difficulty as to whom the pope might renounce his office, like the appeal to the Church's common good, appeared throughout the contemporary discussions.   It was one of the principal arguments of the Cardinals Jacobus and Petrus Colonna in their two remonstrances of 1297, and as used by them and others it was a step in the elaboration of conciliar theory.[42]   Peter John Olivi, in his letter to Coradus de Offida denying that the pope has no superior to whom he may renounce, notes that St. Francis, with divine inspiration, included in his rule the promise of obedience and reverence not only " to the pope and his successors but also to the Holy Roman

[40] Vatican MS lat. 1032, fol. 197r&v, but P. Glorieux, *La littérature quodlibetique de 1260 à 1330* (2 vols., Le Salchoir-Paris, 1925-35), I, 164, gives from Bibliothèque Nationale MS lat. 14311 the following more explicit incipit: " Utrum posito quod non esset aliquod ius positivum sive statutum quo praelati prohibentur renuntiare statutui et dignitati, ipsi possent libere renuntiare." He gives no other references which indicate similar discussions.

[41] Vatican MS lat. 932, fol. 111r&v, *Quodlibita* I, q. 14 (in the Paris MS cited by Glorieux, *ibid.*, pp. 255 *et seq.*, the question is n. 15).   The date of the discussion is 1296.   In his argument Pierre cites the opinion of Huguccio in reference to *Decret. Dist.* XXI, cap. 7 (*Nunc autem*) with regard to which this decretist says that a monk can refuse to enter a monastery if he feels himself unequal: Vatican MS lat. 2280, fol. 20r.

[42] See too the articles of J. Leclercq, " La renonciation de Célestin V et l'opinion théologique en France du vivant de Boniface VIII," *Revue d'histoire de l'église de France*, XXV (1939), 183-92; V. Martin, " Comment s'est formée la doctrine de la superiorité du concile sur le pape: I. La tradition canonique avant le grand schisme d'occident," *Revue des sciences religieuses*, XVIII (1937), 121-43; H. X. Arquillière, " L'appel au concile sous Philippe le Bel et la genèse des théories conciliares," *Revue des questions historiques*, XLV (1911), 23-55.

Church." This to Olivi meant " the college of cardinals, those to whom the canon law assigns the right to elect the pope." He developed this idea to refute his opponents' argument that the pope is superior to his office. Having inferred the independence of the papal office, and designated the cardinalate as the body in which supreme authority lies during the interregnum, Olivi then distinguished very clearly between the sacerdotal authority of the pope which essentially is that of every bishop, and his jurisdictional power which, although greater than the former, is not coessential with it, being in itself transferable and hence renounceable.[48] The point he makes here is the one Aegidius Romanus later developed into a major feature of his long defense of Boniface's accession; it illustrates quite clearly the Aristotelian element of definition which, in its demand for an essential characteristic of office, provided the basic philosophic environment for the theory of inalienability. For his own polemical purposes, then, Olivi placed his emphasis upon the essentially religious function of the pope. All other characteristics, however important, did not constitute the papacy, and so might be renounced. The theological and canonical justification for such a view is suggested by a comment of Huguccio in which he made it clear that a bishop who might abuse his administrative authority over the possessions of his church nevertheless should be allowed to retain his rank and religious functions since these were, after all, his *raison d'être*.[44]

Citations of the use of the public utility concept in relation

[48] This letter (1297) and his longer treatise (1295–97) are printed by Livarius Oliger, " Petri Johannis Olivi, de renuntiatione papae Coelestini V, quaestio et epistola," *Archivum franciscanum historicum,* XI (1918), 309-73. See especially pp. 347-52, 357-61, and 371-73. Similar arguments are used by John of Paris (*De potestate regali et papali, Monarchia,* II, 143-47), and by the cardinals supporting Boniface VIII in their answer to the two letters of the Colonna cardinals (Denifle, " Die Denkschriften," pp. 525-26).

[44] *De renunciatione papae* in *Bibliotheca maxima pontifica* (ed. J. T. de Roccaberti, Rome, 1695), II, cap. X, XIII. For Huguccio, see above, n. 23, Chapter III.

to Pope Celestine's abdication might be multiplied; sufficient evidence has been presented, however, to show the importance of the relationship between the papal act and its theoretical justification. The idea developed in the polemics of this constitutional struggle was soon incorporated by Boniface in the *Sext* (1, 7, 1), and as an integral text of the canon law was glossed approvingly by succeeding generations of canonists.[45]

Having seen the appeal made to the common welfare in cases of renunciation, we must next examine the thinking behind it, and determine too the interaction here between Roman and canon law. To do this a discussion of the renunciations of personal privileges in the civil law is necessary. Edouard Meynial has examined this subject in great detail, and it is his work that will be summarized now, as it relates to the central problem of inalienability.[46]

[45] Guido de Baysio, *Rosarium seu in decretorum volumen commentaria* (Venice, 1577), to VI. 1, 7, 1 ad v. *resignare*: "hic plane potest, quod potest renunciare oneri et honori . . ."; he then approves the renunciation to the college of cardinals; Johannes Andreae, *Glossa ad librum sextum* (Rome, 1478), to VI. 1, 7, 1: ". . . in dubium an papam possit renuntiare papatui. Celestinus V dum presideret ecclesie romane regimini statuit de concilio et assensu suorum fratrum quod summus pontifex libere possit renuntiare papatui . . ."; Johannes Monachi, *In sextum librum decretalium commentaria* (Venice, 1585), to VI. 1, 7, 1: "Hoc capitulo habetur Papam libere posse resignare ut fecit Celestinus V . . . . Item populus Romanus penes quem erat summa potestas transtulit lege regia lata suam potestatem in Imperatorem . . . . Sic papa, qui habet plenitudinem potestatis. Ista lege data, potuit cedere oneri et honori ut hic."

[46] Edouard Meynial, "Des renonciations au moyen-âge et dans nôtre ancien droit," *Nouvelle revue historique de droit français et étranger*, XXIV (1900), 108-42; XXV (1901), 241-77, 657-97; XXVI (1902), 49-78, 649-710; XXVIII (1904), 699-746. While little can be added to Meynial's exposition of renunciation theory, allowing even his neglect of the canonists, his approach to the subject is open to question. He treats the renunciations as developing from a struggle between two systems of law, the Germanic customary, and the Roman. For him the renunciation, as it appears in the public acts and legal discussions of the twelfth and later centuries, was the weapon of a free folk with a long tradition of individuality against the imposition of the complex Roman legal system which had its origins in a different society. But was not the renunciation an instrument of evasion used by persons forcibly surrounded with legal protections for various reasons of incompetence to shed these restraints and enter into the quickening commercial life of the twelfth century? For a development of this approach, see my article "Roman Law, Renunciations, and

Meynial begins by discussing the renunciations in classical and late classical law; there he finds no theory, only some twenty texts which the medieval jurists later used. The one significant idea inherited from the Romans is that of a hierarchy of rights and protections. Those sanctioned most highly were those most clearly related to the public interest. The renunciation of these was especially difficult and circumscribed by conditions, and it was just this criterion of public interest that the Middle Ages took up, almost unconsciously. It is not, then, until the thirteenth century, in the *Glossa ordinaria*, that we have a significant medieval statement.

Accursius developed his position in relation to *Novella* 94 (to *Senatus-consulto*), C. 2, 3, 29; C. 5, 35, 2, and to the general statement in D. 2, 14, 29: " Unicuique licet contemnare ea quae pro se introducta sunt." Having established the rule that all public rights are inalienable, he divided these into two classes, those deriving their force *auctoritate* and those, *utilitate*. The former class of rights derives from official legislative pronouncements; in other words, the reference is to the source of the law. The other " consists in the peculiar utility of the state which is incarnate in the prince," and is the aspect most pertinent here.[47] Accursius rejected all renunciations in detriment of the public good, as did Cynus, who went beyond him to consider the nature of the rights themselves. The merit of Cynus lies in his estimate of these inalienable rights as being

---

Business in the Twelfth and Thirteenth Centuries," in *Essays in Medieval Life and Thought Presented in Honor of Austin Patterson Evans* (New York, 1955), pp. 207-25.

[47] Meynial, " Des renonciations," XXVI, 660-62. He sites the Gloss to D. 2, 14, 38 ad vv. *jus publicum*: " Sed cum jus publicum aliud sit auctoritate et utilitate ut sunt illa jura quae tractant de iure fisci, vel quod in communi servatur, id est publica auctoritate, aliud utilitate privatum quod et publicum dicitur auctoritate . . . . In secondo autem dicunt quidam idem propter multos casus quos notavimus, in quibus est publicum jus auctoritate sed privatum utilitate, in quo casu renunciare non potest." Note, too, the wide content Accursius gives to *utilitas publica* in the same commentary: " quod in communi servatur, id est publica utilitas."

" natural " and above human conventions.[48] Bartolus took up this approach and developed it in his commentaries on two of the very passages which had served as texts for the Gloss. For him the question is no longer one of authority, but rather of the importance of the causes above and beyond the written law, those causes which reside in the nature of society and the processes of human relations. For Bartolus, too, laws in the best interests of the community may not be renounced.[49]

The importance of this civilian theory for the development of the national monarchies will soon be examined in greater detail. But from the summary of Professor Meynial's researches we can see that the public law aspects of the theory of renunciation were stated initially by Accursius, and that the full elaboration of the idea took place, roughly speaking, in the century 1230–1350. It is highly probable, however, that originality here lies not with the civilians but with the canonists, and that the formulation of the component principles of the idea of inalienability of public rights, if not of the fully developed concept itself, goes back to the late twelfth and early thirteenth centuries.[50] This ecclesiastical priority must be ex-

---

[48] *Ibid.*, 670.

[49] *Ibid.*, 667 *et seq.*; the two passages are *Nov.* 94 and *D.* 2, 14, 38. The same importance was given to the public welfare by Andrea de Isernia of the Sicilian kingdom, *prooem.* to *Constitutiones*, (1559), col. 13-41; and Petrus de Bellapertica, *Lectura* (1519), to *C.* 2, 3, 29. See too Pauli de Castro, *Prima . . . Super digesto veteri* (Venice, 1575), to *D.* 2, 14, 38, .n. 2.

[50] It is foolish dogmatically to ascribe primacy and authorship for any of these principles to an individual man or movement. Ercole gave the legist supporters of Philip IV credit for the Bartolist formula: " Rex imperator est in suo regno," and soon was called to task by Calasso who, in a series of reviews, articles, and books over twenty years has claimed Italian origin for the concept, pushing its authorship back to Azo. Yet, while Ercole has clung to his view with stubborn purpose, Mochi-Onory now is able to show that Calasso too has been wrong all this time, and he claims for the internationally minded decretalists of the late twelfth century the fame of originality. As long as our texts are still in manuscript, as they are still searched through only partially by scholars with special problems in mind, as scholars insist on stretching similarities of phraseology in order to make their points, any statements on priority must be considered speculative and tentative. It is with such limitations in mind that I offer my conclusions.

plained, for it presumes a high level of political sophistication, an appreciation of the needs of the age and of the Church state, and also a desire to apply theory broadly in the service of the Church as a political institution in the world. From the eleventh century the Church had been playing an ever more active role in international affairs, and its leaders were involved on both political and theoretical levels of controversy. Given this participation, and also the scope of its own internal institutional problems, the Church had been highly active in developing legal procedures and theories to satisfy its needs. What we might call a balance of privilege, rights, or justice was one of its *desiderata,* and the Church's efforts to achieve this balance provided the environment for its development and analysis of a hierarchy of rights. The decretists were deeply involved, then, in contemporary problems, and their great book, Gratian's *Decretum,* was recent enough not to provide any formidable difficulties for interpretation. The contemporary glossators were not so fortunate. Their authorities were comparatively unfamiliar and perhaps intrinsically more difficult than those of the Church. The efforts of the glossators, as is well known, were therefore devoted mainly to elucidating the complexities of the *Corpus iuris civilis.* Before the time of Accursius, the civilians were not as alive to current problems as were the canonists, nor were they to any extent in the employ of secular princes, and hence active participants in political controversy. So, therefore, if there is any broad and basic reason for ecclesiastical priority in the development of public law concepts, it might be the concern of the Church with current affairs as opposed to the concern of the civilians with classical texts.

In the *Summa* of Bernardus Papiensis (fl. 1191/92–98) which was " used directly or indirectly by all the others of its type," [51] we find the following statement: " Renuntiare possunt

[51] A. Van Hove, *Prolegomena ad codicem iuris canonici* (Malines, Rome, 1945), p. 447. This is Vol. I of the *Commentarium lovaniense in codicem iuris canonici,*

propria iura; quod vero pro communi utilitate est introductum a me vel alio resignare non potest." [52]  In Huguccio's *Summa,* which was the high point of the Bolognese decretist tradition, we have similar thinking.[53]  With regard to the *privilegium fori,* he says that the cleric may not renounce the jurisdiction of his bishop since it would be to the latter's prejudice, and then repeats the phrase: " quod pro communi utilitate introductum est ab aliquo renuntiare non potest." A marginal gloss in the same hand makes explicit the key word *utilitate*: " favore omnium clericorum." [54]

Commentaries on the *Quinque Compilationes* added little to the development of the canonist theory, and it is not until the time of Hostiensis that we have significant differences in the amplification of this relationship of ideas.[55]  Goffredus de

---

and is usually my source, with Kuttner, for all dating and similar brief biographical information.

[52] E. A. T. Laspeyres, *Bernardi Papiensis summa decretalium* (Ratisbon, 1861), pp. 8-9, ad vv. *De renunciatione.* Vatican MS lat. 2691, fol. 21v, has: " Renunciare posset propria iura quod non pro communi utilitate est introductum."

[53] Kuttner, *Repertorium,* pp. 157-58, ascribes the work to the period not earlier than 1188, and not later than the *Compilatio prima* (1198). Van Hove, *Prolegomena,* p. 436, says only that it is not certain whether it was written before 1188 and cites the literature.

[54] Summa, Vatican MS lat. 2280, fol. 134r, to Ca. III, q. 6, c. 14: ". . . et nota quod clericus huic privilegio, scilicet ut non conveniatur sub alieno iudice sine consensu episcopi sui, non potest abrenuntiare cum quia inde fietur preiudicium et iniuriam episcopo, cum quod pro comuni utilitate introductum est ab aliquo renuntiare non potest." See also fol. 188r to Ca. XII, q. 2, c. 20, ad vv. *alienare,* and *pro aliqua necessitate*; also fol. 192r to Ca. XII, q. 2, c. 52, ad vv. *ut meliora prospiciat.*

[55] I have examined the following manuscripts in the Vatican Library: to *Comp. I,* lat. 1377 (Tancredus); Pal. lat. 652 and 696 (Richardus); *Comp. II,* lat. 1377 (Tancredus); *Comp. III,* lat. 1377 (Tancredus); lat. 1378 (Vincentius); Chis. E. VII. 207 and Ottob. 1099 (Johannes Teutonicus); V, in microfilm Brit. Mus. Royal 11.C.VII (Jacobus de Albenga). For example, Vincentius commenting on *Comp. III,* 1, 8, 3 (*Causam*) ad vv. *his que pro se*: " hec ratio non videtur hic locum habere quia abbatia sibi collata fuit ob communem utilitatem immo non licuit ei renuntiare ut infra. de foro competenti, Si diligenti." in Vatican MS lat. 1377, fol. 169v. This comment is included in the gloss of Tancredus to the same passage.

Nor is the *Glossa ordinaria* (Venice, 1586), much of an advance, the comment, for example, to X. 2, 2, 12 (*Si diligenti*) ad vv. *pacto privatorum* being by this time common: " Sed si aliquid ius introductum est in favorem quorundam pro publica utilitate ipsorum et odio aliorum, nullus potest tali iuri renuntiare." See

Trani (d. 1245), who wrote his *Summa* in the 1240's, and Innocent IV will serve as examples of the state of the discussion before Hostiensis. Like his predecessors Goffredus made the distinction between protections granted by the law to persons, and those which pertain to the public utility, forbidding the renunciation of the latter. Also, again in the common tradition, he differentiated between rights *in odio* and *in favorem*; and showed his reliance upon contemporary civilian discussion by relating his opinion to the benefits protecting minors and women, the S.C. *Velleianum* and S.C. *Macedonianum*.[56] Innocent IV similarly referred to contemporary discussion of the *senatusconsulta*, and very explicitly rejects renunciations of those Church privileges which had been introduced *in odio* because of the presumed corruption of the world. And, in sympathy with Accursius, or perhaps influenced by him, he adopts the distinction *auctoritate et utilitate*. Innocent is clear that *auctoritate* refers to the source of law; yet it is only when a right or privilege has been introduced *utilitate* that it may not be renounced.[57] In this his classification is somewhat more in-

---

also the *casus* to the decretal of Honorius III, *Intellecto* (X. 2, 24, 33), which is identical in thought.

[56] Goffredus de Trani, *Summa* (Venice, 1586), ad vv. *De renunciationibus*, fol. 16, n. 1. This *Summa* was written c. 1241-43, at the time of the first redaction of the *Glossa ordinaria* to the *Decretals* of Bernardus Bottoni. See S. Kuttner and B. Smalley, "The 'Glossa ordinaria' to the Gregorian Decretals," *E.H.R.*, LX (1945), 97-105.

[57] Innocent IV, *Apparatus* (Venice, 1578), to X. 2, 2, 12 (*Si diligenti*), ad v. *renunciare*: "Solutio iuri privato quod tantum in alicuius favorem introductum est, renunciari potest, secus in iure publico, quod est introductum in favorem ordinis, et odium, quale est hic, quod in favorem clericorum et odium laicorum est introductum, sunt enim laici clericis oppido infesti . . . vel potest dici, quod iuri publico auctoritate et utilitate non potest renunciare publico autem tamen auctoritate potest: D. de pac. pacisci, et ideo iuri publico quod consistit in sacris sacerdotibus et magistris, renunciare non licet." See too his comment to X. 2, 26, 16 (*Cum ex officii*) n. 1, where he gives an example of the unrenounceable Church laws, the *ius visitandi* ". . . quia illud non posset, cum sit ius publicum visitare et corrigere." The fact that Innocent's use of "auctoritate et utilitate" comes sometime after the publication of the *Glossa ordinaria* to the civil law does not, I think, completely vitiate my thesis. As I have tried to show, the public utility was appealed to constantly by a century of canonists. Besides, as Savigny says, although the gloss to the Institutes may be dated to 1234, and that on the *Code* to 1227, Accursius worked on his commentary to the

clusive than Accursius' in that the latter established a category *auctoritate tantum* which arises from the limited authority of a specific privilege. If a privilege of this category had been granted in favor of the renouncer, it might be surrendered; if, however, in favor of both the renouncer and the common good, it might not.[58]

Since the distinction *in odio* and *in favorem* is so integral a part of the discussion, a word upon it is necessary. Meynial admits great difficulty in finding a precise definition, pointing out that it was often the equity of the case and the inclination of the jurist which determined the final evaluation. For as the distinction touches the problem of renunciation, the basic questions were: for whose benefit did the law grant protection, and why? Protections were granted by the Roman law to minors, clerics and women; yet the same Roman law provided that all persons, including clerics, were allowed to reject these protections. Therefore, some further criterion had to be added to the legal theory if the protections were not to be nullified by the existence of the contradictory evasion. As it developed— and the distinction is to be found in the twelfth century commentaries upon both laws—emphasis was placed on the historical and social reasons for the institution of the protection. The

---

*Digest* until his death in 1260 (*Geschichte des Römischen Rechts* . . . , V, 262 *et seq.*). For the date of Innocent's *Apparatus* see Stephan Kuttner, " Die Novellen Papst Innozenz' IV," in *Zeitschrift der Savigny-Stiftung*, Kan. Abt. XXVI (1937), pp. 462-63. Kuttner puts its completion between 1246 and 1251. Hostiensis' *Summa* is dated 1250-61, and his *Lectura* was worked on until his death in 1271 (Johann F. von Schulte, *Geschichte der Quellen und Literatur des Canonischen Rechts* [3 vols., Stuttgart, 1875-80], II, 125-27).

58 *Glossa ordinaria* to *Nov.* 94 ad v. *senatusconsulto*: " sed nunquid semper, et cuilibet iuri renunciari potest? Plene dicas: quia aut est publicum auctoritate et utilitate: ut quia ius fisci, vel alias publica utilitas ibi vertitur et tunc renunciari non potest . . . Aut auctoritate tantum non tamen utilitate, nam et hoc dicitur publicum . . . et tunc aut est statutum tantum utilitate renunciantis: aut renunciantis et communis. Primo casu potest renunciari sive sit privilegium, sive ius ex aliquo contractu vel pacto . . . his accipe casus illos quos not. secundum Ioan . . . . Si vero communi utilitate, id est publica, et renunciantis, tunc non licet." Accursius was perhaps inspired by Azo, *Summa aurea* (Lyons, 1512), to *Inst.* 2, 1, nn. 8-9: " Publica autem nedum non conceduntur occupanti sed etiam interdicte proponuntur contra eum qui aliquid fecit in eis laesionem publicam."

*S.C. Velleianum* was universally held renounceable since it was introduced in favor of the woman; because of her limited incapacity she might or might not take advantage of it. The presumption of frailty in the case of minors was greater; therefore they might never renounce the *S.C. Macedonianum* whose protections had been instituted as much *against* the Macedonian money lenders (whence the title) as *for* the minor. Likewise in the case of the privileges of the clergy: the world of affairs was presumed hostile and more cunning in matters of property, so the *privilegium fori* was meant to act not only for the clergy but against certain secular scheming.[59]

Hostiensis adopted these criteria, and more closely than had ever been done before linked them up with the social theory of the common good. Like Accursius and Innocent IV he categorized rights with regard to alienability, but his classifications are much more ramified than theirs. He starts from a broad definition of public law—that given its force by virtue of the promulgating authority be it prince or municipal council—and follows the classic definition of the *Digest* in setting the limits of the public law jurisdiction of his discussion: " specialiter et proprie consistit in sacris et sacerdotibus." [60]

[59] Meynial, "Des renonciations," XXVI, 667, has discussed this hazy point. Johannes Teutonicus gives us a typical discussion: " sed si aliquod ius introductum est in favorem quorundam et in hodium aliorum, illi non potest renunciare, tale est hoc ius de quo hic agitur quod non tam in favorem clericorum quam et in hodium laycorum est introductum . . . ." He then cites *Decret.* Ca. II, q. 7, c. 14 (*Laici*) which states that " Laici in accusatione episcoporum audiendi non sunt, quia oppido eis quidem infesti sunt "; he continues, stating the usual opinions on the *S. C. Velleianum, Macedonianum,* etc. (gloss to *huius pacto tenere* in c. *Si diligenti, Comp. III,* 2, 2, 4, Vatican MS lat. 1377, fol. 189r; also Vatican MS Chis. E. VII. 207, fol. 171v ad v. *privatorum*). See also Cino da Pistoia, *Super codici et digesto veteri lectura* (Lyons, 1547), to C. 2, 3, 29, n. 4; Abbas Antiquus, *Lectura aurea super quinque libris decretalium* (Venice, 1587), to X. 2, 2, 12, n. 5. The latter's discussion of the hard days of the Roman Empire, the jeopardy in which the young were in those days because of the death of their parents—" et plures cives Romani interfecti sunt hac occasione quare in odium illius [the usurer's] constitutum fuit . . ."—is an example of this socio-historical approach.

[60] Hostiensis, *Summa aurea* (Lyons, 1568), to X. 1, 9 (*De renunciatione*), n. 2. The reference in the *Digest* is 1, 1, 1.

Ecclesiastical public privilege breaks down into several types. The first of these, *reale sive temporale,* is granted to churches lest they alienate their property, and this privilege may never be renounced.[61] Its purpose is to maintain the status of the Church. The *ius . . . publicum divinum et spirituale* consists in the practices of the cult itself, and in manifestations of divine teaching such as religious feasts; these may not be renounced, says Hostiensis, specifying that custom has no force. Next he discussed privileges classified under the heading *publicum divinum collegiatur aliud commune* which refers to those introduced in favor of the entire ecclesiastical community. The *privilegium fori* is to be included here, as his reference to the appropriate chapter of the Decretals indicates. Such rights are not to be renounced *expressim* which indicates some latitude. Related closely is the group embracing certain privileges —still under the general rubric *ius publicum divinum*—conceded to an individual church or corporation, and these may be renounced under certain conditions. Privileges granted for reasons of personal honor or dignity may be renounced only insofar as the renouncer alone is affected. And then, with added degrees of approbation, those enjoying privilege because of their position, or because of rights intended for them personally are allowed to renounce. Finally, still under the same heading, is the category pertaining to the proper administration of the Church, *publicum statum respiciens,* and these may not be renounced.[62]

He then established a new general rubric, this one clearly

---

61 On the question of oaths accompanying and fortifying renunciations, see A. Esmein, " Le serment promissoire dans le droit canonique," *Nouv. rev. hist. de droit fran. et étranger,* XII (1888), 248-77, 311-52.

62 Hostiensis, *Summa aurea (De renunciatione),* n. 3. An identical scheme is developed in his comment to X. 2, 2, 12 (*Si diligenti*), n. 12 in his *In primum . . . quintum decretalium librum commentaria* (Venice, 1581). The above passages are concerned with general principles. His comment on the inalienability of the *privilegium fori* may be read in the *Summa* (Lyons, 1568), *De foro competenti,* n. 13; the similar opinion on Church fairs, *De feriis,* n. 6 in *Summa* (Venice, 1574).

having its inspiration in Accursius and Innocent: *Ius vero humanum publicum, aliud publicum auctoritate et utilitate.* Example is given of the *ius fiscale* and this is inalienable. Thereupon his treatment is the familiar one: protection of privileges granted by the public authority in its own interest, and permission to renounce in cases of private privilege in which the protection was established *in favorem* and not *in odio*. In regard to this distinction his words on the *S.C. Macedonianum* point up its relation to the common welfare by showing that *D.* 27, 1, 8 says that the minor, because he cannot renounce the *S.C. Macedonianum*, will not be a charge of the state, not that he is not a public charge.[63] That is to say, the minor is a state charge in the general sense that he and his property are to be protected and preserved so that he never becomes a liability to the state in the other sense of public ward.

Although this classification and position of Hostiensis was that adopted by the canonists, discussion never ceased. Abbas Antiquus termed it *solutionem generalem,* as had Damasus (fl. 1210–15) in his *Burchardica.* Durandus emphasized the reasons in history for the *S.C. Macedonianum.* Johannes Andreae remarked that the public utility is involved when the interests of all are touched, that priests are not to be deprived of their functions, and then went ahead to join these statements in an exposition of the theory of *auctoritate et utilitate.* In sum, his statement is an almost word for word repetition of Hostiensis'.[64]

---

[63] *Summa* (Venice, 1574), *idem.* The phrase is: " lex alleg. [*D.* 27, 1, 8, *Athletae* in ed. 1591] non dicit quin sit munus publicum, imo quod non est munus reipublicae et hoc quod non possit renuntiari fragilitas aetatis . . . ."

[64] Abbas Antiquus, *Lectura,* to X. 2, 2, 12; Damasus, *Veteris iuris ecclesiastici . . . Burchardica sive regulae canonicae* (Cologne, 1564), *regulae* 22 and 138; Guilelmus Durandus, *Speculum iuris* (Venice, 1585), lib. II, pt. 2 (*De renun. et concl.*), nn. 8 and 9; Johannes Andreae, *In libros decretalium novella commentaria* (Venice, 1581), to X. 2, 2, 12, n. 19.

The opinion of Parnomitanus is differently organized but in result essentially the same. This last of the great medieval canonists, profiting from several centuries of speculation, based himself upon the natural law theories of Bartolus: "who is known to speak clearer than anyone else." His major division is *ius naturale aut positivum;* the former category is inalienable. Within the second group the criterion of alienability is always the public utility, and Panormitanus runs through a list of cases, on the one hand emphasizing the right of the individual to renounce personal benefits, and on the other, restricting renunciation of these and other privileges so that the common good is left unharmed.[65]

Then, following Bartolus, Panormitanus adds a reason to the theory *auctoritate et utilitate* which heretofore had been sufficient to justify opposition to a renunciation. This is the important Bartolist idea, ultimately stemming from Cynus as Professor Meynial has shown, that rights and privileges are to be considered in themselves. The determinant no longer is the nature of the authority behind the right, or the public welfare in whose ultimate benefit protection has been afforded; rather the criterion develops from the nature of the person protected, his essential status which presents one or more aspects to be safeguarded. Meynial criticized Accursius because he never investigated the nature of the rights, but instead discussed the problem on the basis of the laws found in Justinian's texts. And he condemns the canonists for merely adopting the Gloss's criteria as their own, and confusing them at that.

But is this criticism justified, and are not the theories which Meynial sees behind the merit of Cynus and Bartolus identical with the rationale of the original distinction in favor of the public utility, that held by Accursius, Hostiensis, and most of

[65] Meynial, "Des renonciations," XXVI, 662-80. In these pages Meynial gives the texts and his analysis to which my words are a comment.

the later commentators on both laws? Meynial notes that there
is little or no recognition of Bartolus' general theory by his
contemporaries or successors; and this may be because they
found little novel in it.

For what Bartolus did was to erect new categories, just as
formal and exegetic as those of Accursius and Hostiensis; and
he based his division upon principles clearly in the minds of
both these predecessors and of those earlier canonists who constantly appealed to the common welfare in their opinions on
immediate church problems. It is necessary to go but one step
back of the term " natural " to perceive this. What Bartolus
saw was the necessity to preserve the condition of the minor,
to protect the woman against her own indiscretion, her hus-
band's or society's machinations. In the sense that all societies
have regarded such frailties in the same light, these rights are
natural. It is against the best interest of every state, every society to allow the despoiling of its propertied classes, of its
women—assuming always a natural inclination towards self-
preservation on the part of the state—if for no other reason
than to save itself the expenses of public maintenance. Was it
not this that Hostiensis had in mind when he played upon the
words *munus publicum* and *munus reipublicae*? The protection of the minor was an obligation of the state, one of its very
defining functions, and were this obligation to be left unful-
filled, the state would have a different type of obligation on its
hands: the physical support of the defrauded and now indigent.
That beggars in the Middle Ages were in fact legion, and that
states commonly failed in this responsibility is beside the point
—which is that the theorists of state and society with whom
we are dealing were after all considering ideas and ideals and
were relying upon fundamental Christian principles of *caritas*.
The reduction of such tensions in the state likewise was their
object, and of the importance of this goal to the common good
there can be no doubt. The reasons which were " natural " in

the considerations of Cynus and Bartolus were fundamentally the same as those of their predecessors and, according to Professor Meynial, the majority of writers.

What may be considered new in Cynus and Bartolus is the shift in emphasis, for in his discussion of rights and privileges, the former practically ignores the Accursian distinction between rights deriving their force *auctoritate* and *utilitate*. From this fact we may draw several conclusions relative to our thesis. To the time of Cynus the emphasis among both canonists and romanists was upon the source of authority of a privilege and the evident, consciously expressed reference to the common good as final criterion. Thereafter the basic appeal remains the same, but consideration shifts to the nature of these rights in regard to the essential character of the person protected. Stoic natural law concepts have been taken up by a jurisprudence greatly influenced by Aristotle which is now concerned with defining the essence of a person in his peculiar or changing relationship to society. The prince, to the time of Cynus, benefited from arguments which conceived him as the active agent of the state, fountain of law and justice, and inspirer of administration, and which therefore circumscribed him with protections intended for the general welfare of the nation. With the shift we have been discussing these protections remained, but the stress now was on his peculiar nature as king which inhered and which never could be renounced. And, in sympathetic parallel development with the new emphasis marched the doctrine of the public good. For essentially it was unconcerned with the ideological source of the king's new position, and so without difficulty it offered its support to the revised concept of the kingship. The direction of such thought is towards a concept of divine right. For the difference, say, between kings Henry III and James I of England is that the latter is no longer considered a natural person. Inalienability of prerogative does not necessarily rest upon theo-

ries of divine right; rather the other way around. For it is
only when the ruler is surrounded with an aura of intrinsic
power that he may be removed from the plane of mortal action.
And it was in just this surrounding and protecting, that legal
theories, developed originally in relation to clerical and individual (private law) privileges, were put to use by the theorists of
the new monarchies. It might almost be said that the authority which rulers lost during this period of growing secularization, the late Middle Ages, by the separation of kingship and
priesthood, was regained by them from a new source, the protection afforded by a synthesis of the public and private law
doctrines of the two great universal laws of Christendom.

Finally to be noted relative to this shift that comes with
Cynus is that formerly, and first in the medieval discussion, inalienable rights were so considered because of their politico-
social implications. It was the ecclesiastical community or the
secular state that categorized a right alienable or inalienable.
At this turning point, although the public utility remains the
ultimate reference, the force of emphasis is on the individual's
rights. The force of authority too, for whereas previously
sanction had come from the importance of the rights for the
state, it now came from a new recognition of the individual . . .
in himself and in his relationship to the community; and rights
and privileges took their brand, alienable or inalienable, from
their relationship to the essential nature of the person.

## IV

# The Lay Theory of Inalienability:
# The Crown

MORE IMPORTANT than the theory of inalienability itself is the
pattern of its integration with other contemporary political
concepts and its significance in political events. Hence we
must turn to an examination of two issues, one theoretical, the
other eminently political, which will indicate the theory's role.
One major development of the thirteenth century was the
growth of national monarchies—in Italy, city states—which
governed themselves without regard for the theoretical supremacy of the Empire. Insecure in the possession and exercise of
their authority, the young political bodies felt the need for intellectual justification of their independence. The first subject
of this chapter, therefore, will be the development of the
theory of national independence, itself an example of the process whereby the monarchies arrogated to themselves protections
once enjoyed exclusively by the Empire. This question merits
discussion because in large measure it was treated in relation to
the Donation of Constantine and other passages in the two laws
which served as points of departure for civilian and canonist
theories of state powers and responsibilities. Also, it brought
up the problem of precisely which powers could be stripped
from, or alienated by, the emperor—a question fundamentally
important for the legal status of the national kingdoms, and
important, too, because once it was answered, the criteria were
immediately applied to the kingdoms. Coeval with the emer-

gence of the kingdoms vis-à-vis the Empire was the development within their borders of characteristic institutions. The study of one of these, the Crown, will be our second topic.

Although the canonists' principal concern was to define the limits and powers of Church and Empire—with the balance of favor never in doubt—they did touch upon relationships within the secular sphere. Indeed, the extent of canonist support for the theoretical pretensions of the national monarchies has only recently been explored. The formula *Rex in suo regno imperator est* which is found in Bartolus and the legist advisors of Philip the Fair, which even recently was thought to have been the creation of Azo, must now be ascribed to the canonists of the late twelfth century.[1] Nationalistic bias and indeed opportunism on the part of these canonists who came from every country of Europe was common, and did not wait for modern scholarship for its critics.[2] This, however, cannot be represented as their principal motivation. It may be true that they were biased, that they were instruments of papal policy as Professor Mochi-Onory suggests; yet at the same time they were concerned with interpreting contemporary reality. To a certain extent, as their very names of origin indicate, national entities did exist, and of this fact these sophisticated canonists were surely aware. By integrating political reality into their discussions, by supporting their theories with references ranging from scriptual precedent to chronicled history, they acted to make political reality explicit. The support their theories gave to papal claims of supremacy at the expense of

---

[1] Mochi-Onory, *Fonti canonistiche,* especially pp. 96-103.

[2] The great French legist of the sixteenth century, Charles Dumoulin, in his *De iuribus et privilegiis regni Franciae* in *Opera* (Paris, 1681), II, 539, criticized Johannes Teutonicus' gloss to *Venerabilem* (X. 1, 6, 34): "licet Glossa dicat quod de facto et non de iure, Rex ipse superiorem recognoscat, tamen illi non est credendum; nam ut iniquit Alex. illa glossa est Ioannis, qui fuit theutonicus, et Imperatori subjectus; et sic tanquam suspectus spernendus est." Earlier, Cynus had criticized his contemporaries for their intellectual prostitution and opportunism: cited by Walter Jones, "Cino da Pistoia," in *Essays in Honor of Roscoe Pound* (New York, 1947), p. 386.

the universal Empire is important, as is too the use which theorists of the national states eventually made of these canonist opinions. Here is a perfect example of the historical process whereby incipient fact forms theory which in turn acts back upon original reality to strengthen it, and in a continuous process is nurtured again by the events which have occurred during the previous cycle.

The origin of the formula of independence, *Rex in suo regno,* lies not with Azo nor even Marinus de Carimanico (fl. 1290), the great chancellor of the Sicilian state; rather, with Huguccio, Stephen of Tournai (1128–1203), Johannes Galensis (fl. ca. 1210), Vincentius (d. 1248), Petrus (fl. 1180–1220), and Laurentius (fl. 1210–15), the last three surnamed Hispanus, and others who, as their names often indicate, represented the great states. Commenting upon the chapter *In apibus* (*Decret.* VII q. 1, c. 41), which declares that in the world as among the bees there must be a single ruler, and which served, therefore, as proper locus for political commentary, Huguccio made his declaration of royal independence in reference to the words *imperator unus:*

Quid ergo de greculo? abusive et sola usurpatione dicitur imperator, solus enim romanus dicitur iure imperator, sub quo omnes reges debent esse, quicquid sit. *Iudex provintie unus:* sed nonne debent X iudices sive presides in una provintia ubi sunt X civitates? sic, set nomine iudicis ego intelligo regem, quia in qualibet provintia debet esse unus rex, et in qualibet civitate unus iudex sive potestas ut VI q. III *Scitote* [c. 2] alibi videtur quod alius sit iudex provintie et alius rex . . . set rex ibi dicitur imperator vel potest dici quod in qualibet provintia debet esse unus iudex principalis et maior coram quo tractentur negotia provintialia.[3]

If one object of canonist politics was to posit general independence of the Empire for the national kingdoms, *de jure,* an-

[3] *Summa, Vatican* MS lat. 2280, fol. 154r.

other was the desire of each canonist to fortify the general principle with theories pertaining to his own country.[4] For example, in a gloss on the *Compilatio tertia* otherwise attributed to Johannes Teutonicus, Professor Post has noted that the words *excepto regimine hyspanie* have been interpolated into the glossator's description of the papal transfer of the Empire to the Germans.[5] And long before Innocent III's decretal *Per venerabilem* (*Decret. Greg.* IX 4, 17, 13) which furnished a text on French independence to the decretalists, Stephan of Tournai has already attributed to the king many of the most important imperial powers.[6]

*Per venerabilem* was seized upon by canonists as the ideal passage upon which to discuss the relationship of the kingdoms to the Empire. In this letter addressed to the count of Montpellier in 1202, Innocent rejected the request of the count for the legitimization of his bastards, and stressed the exalted position of the king of France to whom he had recently allowed such dispensation, in these words which became the key text: " Insuper quam rex ipse superiorem in temporalibus minime recognoscat. . . ." Once stated and incorporated in the *Compilatio tertia* (4, 12, 2) which was devoted to Innocent's decretals, the import of the words was generalized by the canon-

---

[4] The exception is England.

[5] Gaines Post, " Some unpublished glosses," pp. 407-9. However, Professor Post does not estimate when this interpolation was made. Johannes Teutonicus was of no like mind. In his gloss to *germanos* in the same decretal *Venerabilem*, *Comp. III*, 1, 6, 19 in Vatican MS Chis. E. VII. 207, fol. 153r, he writes: ". . . est tamen imperator super omnes reges . . . et omnes nationes sub eo sunt . . . et omnes provinciae sub eo sunt . . . nec aliquid regnum possit probare exceptionem cum non habet in hoc loco praescriptio . . . nec aliquid regnum possit (potuit) exivi ab imperio quia illud esset acephalum . . . et esset monstrum sine capite . . . ." See also the gloss of Bartholomaeus Brixiensis to the *Decretum* (Mainz, 1472) to *Dist.* LXIII, c. 22 (*Hadrianus*). The reason given for the independence of Spain refers not to papal privilege (as in the case of France) but to the historical fact that Spain had been won back from the Moslems, and therefore never had been under the emperor.

[6] *Summa*, to *Decret.* Dist. II, c. 4 ad v. *rex, cited by* Mochi-Onory, *Fonti canonistiche*, p. 97: " rex, in regno suo. Vel eundem vocat regem et imperatorem."

ists and integrated into their great anti-imperial scheme.[7] Laurentius Hispanus claimed that French independence, and Spanish, were *de facto;* yet he recognized that, like the emperor, the kings received the *gladium materialem* directly and *de jure* from God, and were limited in their use of temporal power only by the superior *imperium spirituale* of the Church. But whereas Laurentius particularly stressed the fact that every king derived his supreme position *de jure* from God, Johannes Galensis' concern was to exalt the pope. Johannes Teutonicus, supporter of the Empire that he was, did no more in his gloss than assert the *de jure* subjection to the Empire of the kingdoms, and at the same time admit that the *de facto* situation was beyond defense. And as we have noted, he may have weakened his stand even more by accepting the freedom of Spain which had been won back from the Moslems.[8] Vincentius Hispanus took the next step. Disagreeing in part with Laurentius and Johannes Galensis, he declared that France was indeed independent of the Empire *de jure.* That secular authority came directly from God—and here he based himself on Laurentius—had more than political significance and was more than chance history; rather it was a necessary development of the law and history of Christian society. The final, or rather typical, word in this pre-Gregorian discussion was written by Tancred of Bologna (d. 1234–36?) who attempted a compromise of the two positions. Being unable to deny the existence of the free kingdoms, yet remaining faithful to the traditional concept of universal Empire, he reconciled this difficulty which existed between the two distinct realms of reality and ideal

---

[7] For what follows, see Mochi-Onory, *Fonti canonistiche,* pp. 271-86. The pertinent texts given by him need not be cited again. I shall give only those texts relevant to the present discussion.

[8] It would appear that the insertion described by Professor Post is indeed the thought of Johannes Teutonicus. For in *Glossa ordinaria* to *Decretum* Dist. LXII, c. 22 ad vv. *per singulas,* he repeats the exception. See Mochi-Onory, *Fonti canonistiche,* p. 280.

with a view which allowed the perpetuation of this contradic-
tion, and which in itself was no real difficulty for a medieval
intelligence which could hypostatize hieratic levels of reality:
" De facto . . . De iure tamen sub est romano imperio." [9]

Canonists of succeeding generations maintained this distinction, or took one of the extreme positions.   So Innocent IV
used his commentary on *Per venerabilem* as a statement of
papal absolutism.   Following Johannes Galensis—although he
never mentions him—he asserts that kingdoms are *de jure* independent of the Empire but subject to the pope.[10]   Hostiensis
similarly; although more moderate in his views on the free interference of papal jurisdiction, he nevertheless was one with
other canonists in holding that the emperor's person was always subject to papal authority and that the emperor's obligation was to revere the pope as would a son his father.   And
Durandus, too, although he was most interested in the independence of France, allows Spain and England the full privileges of empire.   These kings are assumed to have *supremum
et merum imperium* since it is only rulers with such power who
may commission notaries, with respect to which he had raised
the question of the monarchies' status.[11]   Durandus' equation
of *Imperator* and *Rex* touched another aspect of monarchy, one
of those which made the king greater in his realm than the emperor was in his.   For, he says, only the great barons, palatine
counts, dukes, and kings recognize the emperor as their liege

[9] Important for the legal impregnability of the Empire (at this moment) was
Tancred's belief that prescription was invalid in this case against the Empire.   The
independence of the monarchies was absolute and original, and had to be, for " nec
aliquis regum potuit prescribere exemptionem, cum non habeat in hoc prescriptio."
Mochi-Onory, *Fonti canonistiche*, p. 285, cites F. Gillman, " Tankreds oder Laurentius Hispanus . . . ," *Archiv. für katholisches Kirchenrecht*, CXX (1940), 206.

[10] *Apparatus* (Venice, 1578), to X. 4, 27, 13 ad v. *recognoscat*: " De facto, nam
de iure subest Imperatori Romano, ut quidam dicunt.   Nos contra, imo Papae."

[11] Durandus, *Speculum iuris* (Venice, 1585), lib. II, partic. 2, n. 8 (*De instrum.
edit.*), nn. 22-24; and to tit. *De appel.*, § *Nunc tractemus* (ed. 1547), fol. 188.

lord; the king of France is unique in that he does not recognize the emperor, and also in that all men of his realm admit a direct relationship to him.[12] Here, in relation to a feudal problem, basing himself upon a traditional canonist-papalist theory of monarchical independence, the great French canonist had again stated, but for his time, ready more than ever for such pronouncements, the individual destinies of the states he saw about him. Succeeding generations were to do no more, only extend the authority of the lesser political entities, as fact in the fourteenth century demanded, at the expense of the Empire.[13] They also became more conscious of the direction in which their ideas were heading. So Panormitanus accepted the *de jure–de facto* compromise of Tancred; and then in his comment on *Intellecto,* in the section entitled *Reges fiunt per successionem non per electionem,* writes: " bona regni non sunt propria ipsius Regis sed dignitatis regalis." [14] *Dignitas* here approximates the idea of the Crown in meaning and purpose: it is a broad abstraction standing for the authority, territory and history of the monarchy. Perhaps, by the time of Panormitanus, the mid-fifteenth century, we need not hesitate to speak of " nations."

That it was the canonists who first developed the theory of national independence is a fact of major importance, because the canon law, international as it was, carried their doctrines across all frontiers. And although the full use and extreme statement of many of these principles was not made for per-

---

12 *Ibid., De feudis,* § *quoniam*: " omnes homines qui sunt in Regno Franciae sunt sub potestate et principatu Regis Franciae et in eis habet imperium generalis iurisdictionis et potestatis." This thought is developed in his discussion of the familiar school problem discussed among others by Azo, " Queritur utrum homo hominis mei sit meus homo."

13 In this sense, Panormitanus, *Lectura in quinque decretalium libros* (Lyons, 1547), to X. 4, 17, 13, n. 26.

14 *Ibid.,* to X. 2, 24, 33.

haps a half century, the texts were available in monastic and
episcopal libraries throughout Europe.[15]  If, therefore, the
Angevin legists, Andrea de Isernia and Marinus de Carimanico,
are to be praised because they stated their theories in univer-
salized terms and so made them applicable to every monarchy,
similar praise for similar reasons may be granted the earlier canonists.[16]  Yet priority is not everything, and it must be admitted that the glosses, at least those before Gregory IX, did
not have too great an influence, if one is to judge by the in-
frequent use made of them by later civilians, and, indeed, by
succeeding canonists as well.  Citations of Hostiensis and Innocent IV abound, but, generally speaking, there is less immediate
reliance upon the *Summae* of the late twelfth century and the
glosses upon the *Quinque compilationes*.  Exceptions must be
made, however, for Johannes Teutonicus, Huguccio, and
Alanus (fl. 1200–15), with whose names we do meet frequently.  We do find, however, references to the pre-Gregorian
writers in the works of the early commentators upon the *Decretals* who provided, therefore, a more immediate source for
succeeding generations.  When, from about 1250, a sustained
legal-political statement of *Rex in suo regno* appears, we find
it in the writings of civilians, and specifically among those who
would defend the position of their king against the traditional
claims of imperial supremacy.  The anti-imperial sentiments of
the Sicilian Angevins; the difficult relations at the end of the
century between France and England on the one hand, and the

[15] An idea of the distribution of canon law manuscripts will be given by the
very arrangement of Kuttner's *Repertorium*.  See also Ullman, *Medieval Papalism*;
Eduardo de Hinojosa, "La reception du droit romain en Catalogne," in *Mélanges
Fitting*, II, 391-409; G. Post, "A Romano-Canonical Maxim," p. 217, note 104;
and, more recent, S. Kuttner and S. Rathbone, "Anglo-Norman Canonists of the
Twelfth Century," *Traditio*, VII (1949–51), especially pp. 321 *et seq.*

[16] Calasso, *I glossatori*, p. 158, makes much of Isernia's statement " quilibet in
regno suo Monarcha est; quod ergo in uno regno dicitur, idem in alio dicimus,
quando est rationabile " in *Super usibus feudorum*, II, 56 (*Quae sunt regalia*), n. 2.
And Marinus was almost certainly a student at Bologna, the great international
law school.

Papacy on the other—these situations produced a literature both legal and political which so fractured traditional relationships that they never were fully repaired.[17]

Marinus gave complete authority (*plena potestas*) to his Sicilian king, including that to make law. Isernia repeated the formula, and rated the king's power greater than the emperor's because of its hereditary, as opposed to elective, quality. Moreover, he developed the idea of the forced, hence illegal, origin of the Empire, and allowed defections for this reason. And what is also significant, he sanctioned the operation of prescription against the Empire as a means of obtaining independence. Lucas de Penna, last of this great line, here did no more than repeat *Rex in suo regno*, and like Isernia he used the hereditary nature of the kingship as justification for royal superiority.[18]

What these jurists meant by this emphasis on the greater intrinsic importance of hereditary succession must be understood in Aristotelian terms. For besides the idea that God had tapped a certain royal house to furnish His vicars on earth for Spain or France or England, the implication was that continuity intensified the essential authoritative power of regality. Therefore, a king, although but a temporary official, exercised rights and powers sanctioned by repeated anointings in his ancestral line. The emperor, however, although his office was greater in scope than the king's, could not obtain for himself the same degree of authority which the king achieved because of a better,

[17] On the Angevin monarchy see Calasso, *I glossatori*, and Gennaro Monti, " La dottrina anti-imperiale degli Angioni di Napoli . . . , i loro vicariati imperiali e Bartolomeo da Capua," in *Studi in onore di A. Solmi* (Milan, 1941), II, 13 *et seq.*; " Intorno a Marino de Caramanico e alla formula *Rex est imperator in suo regno*," *Annali del Seminario giuridico della Università di Bari* (1933); " L'influenza francese sul diritto publico del regno angioino di Napoli," *Riv. stor. di dir. ital.*, XI (1938), 556 *et seq.* Still fundamental for the period of Boniface VIII is J. Rivière, *Le problème de l'église et de l'état au temps de Philippe le Bel* (Louvain and Paris, 1926). .

[18] Marinus, *prooem.* of *Liber constitutionum*, now in an appendix to F. Calasso, *I glossatori*, especially pp. 181 *et seq.*, Isernia, *Praeludia* of *Feudorum* (1571) fol. 5r, n. 36; and Lucas de Penna (1538), fol. 209, ro C. 11, 76, 71, and C. 11, 51, 1.

higher approach to office: heredity. This view of kingship
which emphasizes the mode of accession to office is not necessarily at variance, logically, with the other concept we now
must study: the office and Crown as opposed to the person of
the king, and the superiority of the former. For it does not
emphasize the personality of the king at the expense of the office, but rather does just the opposite; it implies that the
heightened office of the king was due to the unique continuous
relationship of the anointed kings. In other words, this added
superior quality of the royal Crown derived from nonlegal
theories or sanctions, for in the legal sphere royal and imperial
powers were equated and it was conceded that the area of the
emperor's jurisdiction was greater than that of the individual
king. The Crown, however, the ultimate symbol of royal authority, always remained within the royal family and this continuity itself was regarded as both divine approbation and as a
sign of superior quality.[19]

Among the Italian legists the *de facto* independence of the
national kings was admitted by others outside the southern tradition. Oldradus, for example, devotes an extremely important *consilium* to the question: " Imperatori omnes reges et
principes non debent de iure sub esse de iure positivo." [20] And
as is well known, the question of the relationship between the

[19] Marsilius of Padua reached the opposite conclusion. For a long discussion of
the arguments advanced for the relative superiority of king and emperor, see the
*Defensor pacis*, I, xvi, *passim* (ed. R. Scholz, Hanover, 1932).

[20] *Consilia seu responsa et quaestiones aureae* (Venice, 1570), cons. 69. This is,
more or less, the unique *consilium* cited by modern writers on political theory.
Actually there is much to be learned in the *consilia* of Baldus, Petrus de Ancharano,
Alexander da Imola, and others. In another paper I plan to survey this literature
with regard to its relevance to medieval political theory. Besides Oldradus we may
note Guilelmus de Cuneo as reported from a Turin MS by B. Brandi, *Notizie intorno
a Guillelmo de Cuneo. Le sue opere e il suo insegnamento a Tolosa* (Rome, 1892),
p. 126; Cynus, *In codicem et aliquot titulos . . . digesti veteris . . . commentaria*
(Frankfurt a.M., 1578), to C. 1, 1, nn. 1-2; Baldus, *Consiliorum sive responsorum*
(Venice, 1575), I, cons. 327, n. 13. The position of Bartolus forms a major part
of the book of C. S. Woolf, *Bartolus de Sassoferrato. His Position in the History
of Medieval Political Thought* (Cambridge, 1913).

old order and the new political entities, kingdoms, and city states, was one of the most vital issues to the post-glossators.

The French jurists, too, wrote particularist apologies for king and country.[21] At the time of the Renaissance glorification of the monarchy, Charles de Grassaille recalled Pierre Jaime (fl. ca. 1300) and his statement of French independence. According to the earlier jurist, Roman law has force in France only by courtesy of the king who neither *de facto* nor *de jure* is under the emperor. The tension in the mind of Jaime between the traditional conception of the emperor as the pope's counterpart in the secular sphere with all the social and moral responsibility that went with the office, and the undeniable independence of the kingdom which he desired to support—this tension is evidenced by his continued belief in the theoretical moral primacy of the emperor.[22] Another example of the hesitancy and conservatism of the jurists is to be found in the work of Johannes Faber (d. ca. 1340) who admitted that prescription could not operate against the emperor, and even repeated the injunction against the emperor alienating to the eventual hurt of his successor. It was only with some difficulty that he affirmed the

[21] For a fine presentation of the problem of inalienability of royal landed property in France see A. Esmein, " L'inalienabilité du domaine de la couronne devant les Etats Généraux du XVIe siècle," in *Festschrift für O. v. Gierke* (Weimar, 1911), pp. 361-82. Mention of the problem is found in the standard histories of French law. Yet, despite the works of Ercole and Calasso, F. Olivier-Martin, *Histoire du droit française . . .* (ed. 1951), p. 302, dates the origin of the formula " Rex in suo regno . . ." to the early fourteenth century, and ascribes it to Spanish origin since it appears in the *Siete partidas*. Also questionable is his remark that this concept was formulated by the jurists and never made an integral plank of royal policy.

[22] *Regalium Franciae* (Paris, 1538), p. 316. Cited by Emile Chénon, " Le droit romain à la *curia regis* de Philippe Auguste à Philippe le Bel," in *Mélanges Fitting*, I, 211; De Grassaille also compares emperor and king in his denial to the king of the power of alienation: " quod sicut Imperator dicitur Augustus ab augendo, ita quod bona Imperii alienare non potest, sic Rex Franciae bona coronae alienare non potest, et ita iurat in eius coronatione," in *Regalium Franciae* (Paris, 1545), p. 104. Note the use of " coronae," which indicates the direction and final significance of the theories of nonalienation. See also Guy de la Pape, *Decisiones Gratianopolitanae* (Venice, 1588), decis. 239.

*de jure* independence of his own country. Primarily, he writes,
because the custom could eventually bring freedom; [23] and in
another passage he claims that that *Francia* held to be part of
the Empire is in reality Franconia which is in Germany
(" quadam Francia quae est in Alemania ").[24] Yet a third of
his arguments involves the violent origin of the Roman Empire,
and the complementary idea that the people, through whom
God acts to create worldly authority, may withdraw its support and call to itself new princes. He assumes that any such
action would have to be accomplished with God's permission,
and in this thought effects a classic synthesis of Roman law
representation and divine intervention . . . in favor of the king
of France and not of the Holy Roman Emperor.[25] This legal
discussion was not lost upon the publicists of Philip the Fair
who time and again utilized the twin arguments of national independence and the equality of royal and imperial authority.[26]
The king himself discounted any imperial pretensions to supremacy over France when he wrote the Emperor Henry VII
to express annoyance with the universalist assertions made at
the recent imperial coronation.[27]

The rulers of Spain had an even clearer title to independence,

[23] *In codicem . . . priores libros IX annotationes* (Lyons, 1594), p. 2, ad vv.
*Cunctos populos, C.* 1, 1, 1.

[24] *Super institutionum in quattuor libros* (Lyons, 1557), ad v. *Franciscus* in
*prooem.*

[25] *In codicem, idem,* nn. 6-8: " Nam licitum est cuilibet recuperare ius suum
authoritate propria, quando per superiorem non potest. Unde quamvis imperium
fuit a Deo institutum permissive: populus tamen fuit author et depositor."

[26] See Pierre Dubois, *De recuperatione terrae sanctae* (ed. C. Langlois, Paris, 1891),
p. 8, sec. 5. Langlois notes that a similar equation occurs in the *De abbreviatione,*
fol. 23v: ". . . dominus Rex Francorum, quantum ad suum feodum et dominium
temporale nullum cognoscit superiorem in terris; " see also the anonymous *Rex pacificus* in P. Dupuy, *Histoire du differand d'entre Pape Boniface VIII et Philippe le
Bel, Roy de France* (Paris, 1640), p. 675; also the *Disputatio super potestate
ecclesiae . . . inter clericum et militum* in *Monarchia,* I, 17. It and the other treatises
of this period are analyzed by Rivière, *Le problème.* And, towards the end of the
century, the treatise, perhaps by Raoul de Presles, *Quaestio in utramque partem . . . ,*
in *Monarchia,* II, 98.

[27] *Constitutiones,* IV, ii, 813.

and the Spanish canonists stated why at the time of Innocent III, when they pointed out that Spain never had been included in any transfer of the Empire from the Greeks to the Germans but had been won back from the infidels. The next step was to grant to the king imperial powers, and at mid-century in the *Especulo* we have the following statement: " Ninguno non puede fazer leyes sinon enperador o rey o otro por su mandamiento dellos." [28] Contemporaneously the same assertion was made in the *Siete partidas* in terms more closely related to the usual expression: " vicarios de Dios son los Reyes, cada uno en su Reyno . . . bien assi como el Enperador en su Impero." [29] And here, too, we find one of the earliest statements of the superiority of the king on the basis of heredity. Even in the use of *señorio* in this passage which defines the relationship of sovereign and emperor, we see the implication of an overall authority which rises above the feudal structure and is transmitted as an entity from ruler to ruler:

Ca ellos (reyes) non tan solamente son señores de sus tierras mientra biven mas aun a sus finamientos las pueden dexas a sus heredores proque han el Señorio por heredad, la que non pueden fazer los Enperadores, que lo ganan por eleccion.[30]

Against such pretensions imperial supporters, legists, and publicists could do no more than repeat the old arguments.

---

[28] *Especulo*, tit. 1, ley 3: " Quien puede fazer leyes."

[29] *Siete partidas*, 2, 1, 5.

[30] *Ibid.*, 2, 1, 8. It must be noted that this passage which ranks the powers of the king above those of the emperor goes on to give as illustration the royal ability " dar Villa o Castillo de su Reyno por heredamiento a quien quisiere, lo que non puede fazer el Emperador porque es tenudo de acrescentar su Imperio, e de nunca mengiarlo . . . ." This may be reconciled with the texts of the *Partidas* already cited in that such donations of towns or castles were feudal arrangements necessary for the administration of the country and not theoretically harmful to the monarchy. Also there is a parallelism here in the sense that the hereditary king may enfeoff with hereditary privilege, while the elective emperor may grant only for life. In both cases, I believe, the theoretical restraints in favor of the preservation of the monarchy were understood to stand.

For example, Ockham, partisan of Ludwig of Bavaria, reiterated throughout his political works the theme of the indestructability of the Empire and the *de jure* subjugation of France to it. He pointed out that the *Per venerabilem* said only that Philip Augustus recognized no superior, not that he had no superior. And, although he admitted that the emperor might delegate many powers to the king, he limited the extent of such delegations by the standard *reductio ad absurdam* . . . which was that the Empire would soon be reduced to nothingness, a state which, by his previous proof, could not be.[31]

By the time of Ockham, therefore, the emperor was very much on the defensive in both theory and fact, and the fictions of courtesy which still were observed towards him by political entities within the Empire should not blind us to this fact. The legists and state theorists had found it necessary legally to justify the actual independence of both the national monarchies and the city states, and by so doing they had hollowed out the substance of imperial authority. One theory that developed from a discussion of the emperor in relation to the Donation of Constantine was a view of him as a temporary official who theoretically could not injure the substance of his authority, the *imperium*.

Our discussion to this point has brought out the canonist contribution to the theoretical justification of national independence. This was accomplished at the expense of the Empire by churchmen who quite consciously meant to undermine its uniqueness. Soon afterwards the civilians and publicists of the monarchies relied upon this canonist precedent for their own separatism. Herein lies the significance of the canonists'

---

[31] *Dialogus,* pars. III, tr. II, lib. II, cap. 7 in *Monarchia,* II, 908, cited by John Figgis, *The Divine Right of Kings* (2d ed., London, 1922), p. 42: "Licet imperator possit multas libertates concedere regi Franciae et aliis; tamen nullo modo potest regnum Franciae vel aliud totaliter ab Imperio separare, ut nullo modo subsit Imperio. Quia hoc esset destruere Imperium, quod non potest Imperator." See also *Octo quaestiones,* q. 4, cap. 3, in *Monarchia,* II, 358-59, and *Breviloquium de potestate papae* (ed. L. Baudry, Paris, 1937), pp. 114 *et seq.*

work. Moreover, the formula *Rex in suo regno* has been seen to have represented first an aggressive claim, and later, a statement of fact . . . in the sense that it sums up in a phrase the process whereby imperial power was made royal. Now we must turn again to the concept of office, and examine its relevance to the concept of the Crown. Although the idea of office has already occupied us at some length, further emphasis upon certain of its aspects will not be in irrelevant at this juncture.

The idea of the *imperium* or kingship as office was not new to the twelfth or thirteenth centuries.[32] Manegold of Lautenbach in the late eleventh century had developed a theory of the ruler's responsibility to the people (i.e., the king's electors) which ultimately derived from his equation of bishop and king.[33] John of Salisbury too, although this is not his principal approach to the kingship, refers in several places to the king as officer of the *universitas*.[34] And in the thirteenth century the new Aristotle, with its great concern for substance, and the Thomistic canalization of this idea into a theory of the superiority of a single ruler into whose hands the public office is given for the betterment of all, provided the background elements for the more technical legal theories.[35]

[32] Gerhart Ladner, "Aspects of Medieval Thought on Church and State," *Review of Politics*, IX (1947), 403 *et seq.* See also, for an indication of the general problem of office vs. person throughout the Middle Ages, Otto v. Gierke, *Political Theories of the Middle Age* (Cambridge, 1938), notes 123, 212-20. Ladner develops the Augustinian concept of states themselves as offices or functions fulfilled by persons.

[33] Augustin Fliche, "Les théories germaniques de la souveraineté," *Revue historique*, CXXV (1917), 44-51. On the equation of lord and bishop, see, for example, Bernardus Compostellanus, Jr.: "quod apparet quod rex iste negligens erat et remissus circa regnum et subditos eius . . . unde debuit privari regno quia propter negligentiam removeretur prelatus . . ." in *casus* of VI, 1, 8, 2 (*Grandi*), in Vatican MS Pal. lat. 629, fol. 263r.

[34] John Dickinson, "The Medieval Concept of Kingship and Some of Its Limitations as Developed in the *Policraticus* of John of Salisbury," *Speculum*, I (1926), 312-13.

[35] On the Thomistic aspect, see Georges de Lagarde, *La naissance de l'ésprit laïque*, pp. 171-72. See also Dante, *De monarchia*, III, 7 and 10.

The lawyers, as we have seen, emphasized the theory of representation, and the views of Hugolinus (fl. ca. 1160), Placentinus (d. 1192), and, a century later, Petrus de Bellapertica may be mentioned.[36]   Petrus, in his comment upon *Semper augustus*, declares that the exhortation to augment the Empire is addressed to the *Princeps* conceived as perpetual office.[37] And after Petrus, perhaps the most vivid legal introduction to a discussion of the Crown is a statement of Baldus which appears in a *consilium* upon the question " Contractus factus per Regem an obliget regem? " under this rubric: " Respublica regni nunquam moritur, et ideo non habet heredem." Baldus begins by calling the emperor *procurator maximus*, and proceeds to describe the twofold nature of the kingship which results from the eternity of the state.   The state cannot act save through the majesty concentrated in the person of the king in whom, he says, two aspects of character are united, his person and his *significatio*.   Whereas the former is merely a physical instrument receptive to authority, the *significatio* has a more important, albeit intangible quality which vitalizes the material person of the king and makes of him the active agent of the

---

[36] Hugolinus in *Dissensiones dominorum* (ed. Gustave Haenel, Leipzig, 1834), *Dist.* CXLVIII, p. 585: " . . . sed constituit eum (Imperator) quasi procuratorem ad hoc." Also Placentinus, *In summa institutionum* (Lyons, 1536), I, p. 2 (*De iure nat. gent. et civ.*): " id est vicem, nam cum imperator proprie sit vicarius . . . ."

[37] Petrus de Bellapertica, *In libros institutionum* (Lyons, 1536), *prooem.*, nn. 10, 11.   See also *Lectura insignis super prima parte codice* (Paris, 1519), ad vv. *De emendatione Just. Cod.* fol. 1, col. 2 ad vv *semper augustus*: " sed certe quod dicitur princeps generaliter: hoc est improprie, quia in rebus est generalitas ut forma est generalis. sed in hominibus non est generalitas . . . . unde possumus dicere quod princeps est perpetuus quod verum est inquantum princeps.   non inquantum Titius vel Robertus . . . et sic officium durat." Earlier the French feudist Johannes Blanosc applied these ideas of office to the fief, which is not at all surprising.   See his *Tractatus super feudis et homagiis*, ed. Archer, *Nouv. rev. hist. de droit fran.*, XXX (1906), 157; and *Epitome feudorum* in *Tractatus universi juris*, X, i, 269v. The idea of emperor as *administrator* is also found in Johannes Faber, *In codicem* (Lyons, 1594), to C. 1, 1, 1; and in the contemporary publicist who relies very heavily upon the legists for his arguments, John of Paris, *Tractatus de regia potestate et papali*, in *Monarchia*, II, 140.   By the fifteenth century it had become a secure part of the French constitution.   See André Lemaire, *Lois fondamentales*, p. 62.

state.[38] It is clear, then, how important for Baldus too is this legal tradition, the whole force of which is to distinguish between an abstraction of sovereignty and its momentary possessor, and which, at the same time that it exalted the ruler by identifying him with all the cumulative authority of his office, yet circumscribed him in his eminence with restrictions upon the full use of his majesty. For this, in effect, is what these writers did. The comments of Faber, Bellapertica, Baldus, Cynus, Dante and the others were made in relation to the question of imperial or royal alienation, principally to the Donation, and to *Augustus* which always implied the Donation. The significance of the relationship of the two ideas was reciprocal. Those who would deny the Donation or restrict the medieval emperor's powers of alienation, or apply imperial attributes to their kings, leaned on the traditional concept of office for support. And at the same moment, those who were creating, slowly, new ideas of disassociated, symbolic sovereignty based on the distinction between man and office found in the Donation an arch example of the grant of territory and authority which was anathema to their theory.[39]

[38] *Consilia*, I, cons. 327, n. 7; III, cons. 159, n. 5: "nam verum est dicere quod respublica nihil per se agit, tamen qui regit rem publicam agit in virtute reipublice et dignitatis sibi collate ab ipsa republica. Porro duo concurrunt in rege: persona et significatio, Et ipsa significatio, quae est quoddam intellectuale, semper est perseverans enigmatice, licet non corporaliter: nam licet Rex deficiat quid ad rumbum, nempe loco divinarum personarum Rex fungitur et persona regis est organum et instrumentum illius personae intellectualis, et publicae et illa persona intellectualis, et publica est illa, quae principaliter fundat actus: quia magis attenditur actus, seu virtus principalis quam virtus organica." See also Cynus, *Super codice* (Lyons, 1547), fol. 307, col. 1 to C. 7, 37, 3. Baldus, ad vv. *nos imperator* in *Extravagantes ad Lib. feud.* (Venice, 1591), p. 126, speaking of the Peace of Constance, says that it is final for all time "quia Imperator facit hanc pacem nomine sedis, non nomine proprio . . . et Imperium non moritur . . . ." But, on the other hand, the lesser entities, the cities, may be destroyed by imperial order.

[39] Other expressions of the idea of delegated office may be found in Ockham's *Breviloquium*, pp. 156-60; Hermanus de Schildiz, *Contra hereticos negantes emunitatem et iurisdictionem sancte ecclesie* in Richard Scholz, *Unbekannte kirchenpolitische Streitschriften aus der Zeit Ludwigs von Bayern* (2 vols., Rome, 1911-14), II, 137; Antonius de Rosellis, *Monarchia sive de potestate imperatoris et papae,*

It is by this path that the question of the Crown enters our discussion, for the theory of inalienability served, as it aided in clarifying the idea of office, to contribute to the concept of the Crown as well. And in this contribution to political thought it entered directly into the constitutional and institutional development of the monarchies. It goes without saying, therefore, that our whole approach to medieval politics is based upon the belief that men of action in the Middle Ages were not all the sword-swinging knights of *Ivanhoe*. Those who would deny that theoretical sophistications entered into the plans and actions of, say, the English barons of the late thirteenth and fourteenth centuries must explain away the more than empirical approach evidenced in the growth of the judicial and administrative systems, to say nothing of the appeals to principle made by both parties during the constitutional crises of the same period. Moreover, if the Papacy and the Empire had been aware of the political implications of their every statement for at least a century, it would be strange that French, English, and Spanish clerics and diplomats would not have brought something of the same approach to their high advisory and administrative positions in the service of their kings. Also, given the high degree of self-consciousness in contemporary theology, law, and science, we might expect that at least a tolerant ear was turned by the leaders of state to their political consultants.

The use of *corona* as a symbol above and beyond the king, indicating the residuum of rights and privileges that he temporarily enjoyed, may be traced in England to the middle of the twelfth century.[40] In English constitutional history the theory

---

in Goldast, *Monarchia*, I, 290. Also two important French writers of the sixteenth century might be mentioned, for the monarchist writers of the Renaissance used the idea to exalt the monarchy itself: Charles Loyseau, *Des seigneuries* (6th ed., Paris, 1600), lib. II, cap. II, n. 42; and René Choppin, *De domanio Franciae* (4th ed., Frankfurt, 1701), lib. II, tit. 1.

[40] Fritz Hartung, "Die Krone als Symbol der monarchischen Herrschaft im ausgehenden Mittelalter," in *Abhandlungen der Preussische Akademie (1940–41), Phil.-hist. Klasse*, XIII, 6. The Crown has not yet received the systematic discussion

of inalienability aided in the development of the Crown
through its relationship to the ancient demesne and the prerogative; and, as the doctrine, fortified by continental examples and theory, so acted, it was in turn strengthened by its
contact with the Crown which itself had been the beneficiary,
so to speak, of a sum of influences and theories. The points to
be emphasized are these, that *corona*, like *dignitas* and *majestas*,
was from the beginning a very imprecise concept whose very
vagueness lent it strength and capacity for growth, and that
the inalienable aspects of the Crown included not only landed
property and feudal rights over the royal demesne, but also a
freedom of action and prerogative which pertained to the ruler
as king and which were qualitatively different from those of
the feudal lord.

Essentially it was in regard to this second aspect, the non-
feudal superior prerogative, that the general theory of inalienability of sovereignty developed, for the first was well
regulated by feudal custom, and by their more obvious and de-
finable nature was more amenable to control by traditional
means. Yet, as the researches of Professor Hoyt have shown,
from the time of Henry II the monarchy consciously based its
growing authority upon an intensive exploitation of the royal
demesne, and although alienation was both frequent and necessary, such dismemberment was calculated in terms of new feudal revenues which were more substantial than what had been
forthcoming before. Moreover, the royal demesne served as
proving ground for the judicial and administrative techniques
which later were applied to the rest of the kingdom.[41]

---

it deserves, and Hartung's study, although it compares the development in France,
England, and Eastern Europe, does not touch upon all the related problems. On the
development of other nationalistic ideas see, for example, Joseph Strayer, "Defense
of the Realm and Royal Power in France," in *Studi in onore di Gino Luzzatto*
(4 vols., Milan, 1950), I, 289-96, and Ernst Kantorowicz, "Pro Patria Mori in
Medieval Political Thought," *A.H.R.*, LVI (1951), 472-92.

41 Robert S. Hoyt, *The Royal Demesne in English Constitutional History: 1066–
1272* (Ithaca, 1950), *passim*, but especially the passages listed in the index under
"crown," and pp. 106-7.

Although revocations of lands granted from the royal demesne had been made by Henry II, action had not been taken
with a theory in mind, but rather with a view toward resum-
ing those titles which were based upon bad charters. Very
probably this was a prime objective of these inquisitions, not
only until the oath of 1257 mentioned by Professor Hoyt, but
even later in the general survey of his demesnes and rights
made by Edward I in 1274.[42]   This sort of general stocktak-
ing, which became common in the late Middle Ages in both
England and France, was as much the result of the ruler's desire to ascertain the exact state of his resources as of a royal
theory which eventually would demand resumption on the basis
of the information obtained.   On the other hand, given the
stated identity of purpose of both the theory and the efforts at
resumption, the influence of theory upon political practice is
more than likely.   Moreover, the theory, stated in explicit
terms and evident by analogy, had been available to the English for several generations.

At the time of John, if not earlier, a new element entered
the history of the Crown, a general theory of inalienability
composed of Roman and canonical elements.   As has been suggested, the canon law was the probable path of influence.   In
the last decade of the twelfth century an interpolation was
made in the *Laws of Edward the Confessor* which called upon
the king to maintain unimpaired his lands, and in addition,
" omnes . . . honores, omnes dignitates et iura et libertates
corone regni in integrum. . . ."[43]   A few years later, Pope Innocent III, in his capacity as John's feudal suzerain, declared
*Magna Carta* to be illegal, claiming that the concessions to the

---

[42] *Ibid.*, pp. 95-96. See also Helen Cam, " The Quo Warranto Proceedings Under
Edward I," *History*, XI (1927), 143-48. The survey ordered by Edward I in
1274 was to touch three kinds of royal rights: military, judicial, and territorial.
See *Foedera*, II, ii, 517.

[43] A most recent discussion of the coronation oath may be read in B. Wilkinson,
*Constitutional History of Medieval England* (London, 1952), II, 85-111.

barons were in his, the Pope's, prejudice.[44]  Henry III received
several bulls from Gregory IX referring to the oath he had
taken: "ut moris est, iura, libertates et dignitates conservare
regales." Twenty years afterwards his royal brother St. Louis
asserted that the participation of the council of barons in the
affairs of state was in derogation of the royal position: "iuri
et honori . . . quod dictus rex plenam potestatem et liberum
regimen habeat in regno suo et ejus pertinentiis." Moreover,
in so judging, he disclaimed for himself and his decision all intention of changing the existing monarchical constitution of
England.[45]  And two years later, in 1266, Henry restated his

---

[44] Charles Bémont, *Chartes des libertés anglaises* (*1100–1305*) (Paris, 1892), pp.
41-44. This incident is noted, among others, by McIlwain, *Growth of Political
Thought*, p. 376, and by J. N. Figgis, *Studies of Political Thought from Gerson
to Grotius* (*1414–1625*) (Cambridge, 1931). The latter's treatment is indicative
of the summary treatment usually accorded to our subject. He writes, " Innocent III
denied the right of a king to diminish his regality, even though he had sworn to
the concessions. This was erected by Bartolus into a general principle of the inalienability of sovereignty." The bull itself reads in part: ". . . tandem rex illis
proposuit quod . . . ipse nec poterat nec debebat absque nostro spetiali mandato
quicquam de illo in nostrum prejuditium immutare, unde rursus ad nostram audientiam appellavit. . . . Unde, compulsus est per vim et metum, qui cadere poterat in
virum etiam constantissimum, compontionem inhere cum ipsis non solum vilem et
turpem, verum etiam illicitam et iniquam, in nimiam diminutionem et derogationem
sui juris pariter et honoris." Note that John had used the idea of the inviolability
of his crown rights when he wrote to Innocent to complain about the Great Charter
forced by the barons: " Et cum post motam inter eos discordiam rex et barones de
pace tractuari multotiens convenissent, idem rex publice protestatus coram eis,
regnum Angliae ratione dominii ad Romanam ecclesiam specialiter pertinere, unde
nec potuit nec debuit praeter conscientiam domini Papae de novo aliquid statuere
vel quicquam in ejus praeiudicium in regno immutare," in Matthew Paris, *Chronica
majora* (ed. H. R. Luard, 7 vols., London, 1872–93), II, 615. Interesting in connection with inalienability at this period is the statement of V. H. Galbraith, *Studies
in the Public Records* (London, 1948), p. 127, to the effect that "Already from
Richard I's reign the most solemn Charters, or *perpetuities*, which for ever alienated
royal prerogatives or demesne, were fully dated and closed with a special formula
taken from Papal Bulls . . . ." And recently Professor Kantorowicz has noted that
from the late eleventh century certain bishops were required to swear defense of
the papacy as well as its material and intangible rights (*papatus Romanus* and
*regalia sancti Petri*). See his article, " Inalienability," *Speculum*, XXIX (1954),
491-93.

[45] The *Mise of Amiens*, printed in W. Stubbs, *Select Charters* (9th ed., Oxford,
1913), pp. 395-97. Sir Maurice Powicke has described this quarrel between the

conception of the Crown's authority in the Dictum of Kenil-worth. The king was to enjoy and freely exercise his *dominium* without interference, nor might the dignities of the Crown be diminished.[46]

Edward I made similar reference to his Crown rights and in one case claimed his inability to alienate without the consent of the *prelates et proceres* of the realm.[47] No doubt, in his effort to range the nation behind him, he remembered public dissatisfaction over his father's treaty with St. Louis by which Henry surrendered England's claim to Normandy.[48] In any event, the determination is there to safeguard the privileges of the monarchy against both the church and the barons. With reference to Edward's reign we might mention again those passages in *Britton* and *Fleta* which restated in standard terminology the general principles of inalienability. *Fleta*, especially, shows Roman influence in its application to the English king of the principles established at the supposed conference of Montpellier: prescription is invalid against prerogative deriving from either the *ius gentium* or *ius naturale*; and, as was

king and the vassals as a "moral issue" which raised big questions such as "The nature, rights, and obligations of Kingship, the standing of the magnates, the sanctity and limitations to attach to sworn agreements," in *King Henry III and the Lord Edward* (2 vols., Oxford, 1947), II, 422. The document is now translated in B. Wilkinson, *Constitutional History* (Toronto, 1948), I, 175-76.

46 Stubbs, *Select Charters*, pp. 407-11. Section 6 reads: "Omnia loca, jura res et alia ad coronam regiam pertinentia, ipsi coronae et domino regi restituantur . . . nisi ostendant (the possessors) se illa per rationabilem warantiam ab ipso domino rege vel a suis antecessoribus possidere."

47 *Calendar of Close Rolls*, 3 Edward I, pp. 397-98. Also, Pollock and Maitland, *History*, I, 524, cite the case from the *Placita quo warranto* which concerns a donation by Edward I before his accession to the throne. Once king, Edward demanded the return of the vil of Stamford from the Earl of Warenne, and his counsel declared that the king was bound to resume all rights unlawfully detached from the Crown even though he, not yet king, was the guilty one who had alienated the land. Important is the description of the king: "est alterius conditionis quam prius fuit et quasi altera persona."

48 *Chronicon domini Walteri de Heminghburgh* (ed. H. C. Hamilton, 2 vols., London, 1848-49), I, 303, and the *Annales Nicholai Triveti* (ed. T. Hog, London, 1845), p. 247.

also specified in the civilian discussions, protracted violation of
the king's rights must not be considered a positive claim which
acknowledgment of prescription would one day validate, but
rather as an aggravation of the crime.[49]

Throughout both reigns, then, covering the greater part of
the century there was a protracted effort by the monarchy to
recover alienated lands and what it considered the rights of the
Crown; also an effort to retain unimpaired its rightful freedom
to govern. The constant reiterations of these royal claims in
fact stimulated a consciousness of the Crown. That the kings
did not in every instance gain what they wanted through reliance upon the Crown's symbolic authority is not all-important.
They were making good propaganda which, although it had
only limited effect in their own time, eventually had great consequences for English constitutional development.

By the time of Edward II the distinction between king and
Crown was sufficiently established for the barons to declare
their allegiance due the symbol rather than the person.[50] And
in their opposition to Piers Gaveston they based their position
on a concern first for the *status ecclesiae* and then for the *status
coronae* which, coming as it does before the final *pax terrae*
would indicate their equation of Crown and realm.[51] Finally,

[49] *Fleta* (2d ed., London, 1685), lib. III, cap. 6, sec. 3: "Res quidam coronae
sunt antiqua munera, regis homagia, libertates et hujusmodi, quae cum alienentur,
tenetur Rex secundum provisionem, omnium regum Christianorum apud Montem
Pessaloniam et si de escartis suis proinde satisfacere debent ad valentiam, nec valebit
deforciantibus longi temporis praescriptio . . ." (Britton [ed. and trans. M. Nichols,
2 vols., Oxford, 1865], I, 221).

[50] In the famous *Declaratio* following on the coronation of Edward II. The text
may be read in *Statutes of the Realm*, I, 182, and in translation with commentary
in B. Wilkinson, *Constitutional History*, I, 111. Not only was this idea expressed
by the barons in 1308; it was repeated in more or less similar circumstances in 1321.
See T. F. Tout, *The Place of the Reign of Edward II in English History* (2d ed.,
Manchester, 1936), p. 136. See also George Haskins, "The Doncaster Petition,"
*E.H.R.*, LIII (1938), 481, where he notes the strong statement of the king in
rejecting the petition of the nobles against the Despensers.

[51] *Chronicles of the reigns of Edward I and Edward II* (ed. W. Stubbs, 2 vols.,
London, 1882), II, 270.

the concern of the barons for the royal demesne is indicated by Article 23 of the Ordinances of 1311 which condemned Lady de Vescy for beguiling the king into making gifts harmful to the Crown.[52] This particular criticism, combined in the same document with the complaints against usurpation and misuse of wider powers of justice and administration indicates the point of tangency of the two aspects of the monarchy in relation to which the idea of inalienability had developed and been applied. What proved significant for the kingship was the broad language of the many statements of the king's position which gave the Crown protection across a wide front. Not only did the principle as stated in the coronation oath give the monarch an excuse to fend off foreign demands and resume titles and privileges lost to baronial pressure; it also—and perhaps this is its ultimate significance—was accepted by the barons to the point that they were willing to defend it, as part of the constitution, or, if that seemed anticipatory, as the legitimate legal position of the Crown.[53]

By the time of Edward II, therefore, the problem of the identity of the original and principal supporter of the theory of inalienability, the monarchy or the baronage, is anachronistic. But, looking backwards a century from the *tractatus* at York, the question is a real one. Most probably, assuming canonist and Roman inspiration, the concept entered the armory of the royal household first. It was in the royal interest to foster a principle which sought to preserve intact its authority and material foundation. Moreover, the king was perhaps in a

[52] *Statutes of the Realm*, I, 157. No attempt has been made to be "final" in this cursory examination of English constitutional practice. Rather incidents have been selected to show the use of the doctrine of the Crown through this critical period of English history.

[53] Hartung, "Die Krone," p. 44, points out that the gradual increase in the power of the Crown is accompanied by a decrease in the personal power of the king. This does not necessarily follow, for a strong king was always able to use the powers of the Crown to his own advantage; this is what happened in France during the Renaissance.

better position to command intellectual talent which would be awake to the possibilities of such an idea.[54] Over the thirteenth century, however, the barons' historical consciousness developed, and they began to conceive of themselves as in some way protectors of the realm and of the Crown. The francophile policy of Henry III no doubt accelerated the growth of this incipient national feeling. It might be estimated, therefore, that during the second half of the thirteenth century the principles of inalienability were viewed favorably by both the baronial and royal parties—and here is another argument against the view which dichotomizes too cleanly the interests and goals of the two factions. From the royal point of view, the principle of inalienability was useful when the lands or governing power of the monarchy, its *plena potestas* or *gubernaculum*, were threatened. And to the barons the principle acted as an exhortation to preserve for posterity the lands and governing powers of the kingdom which still for several centuries, all men would regard as properly in the hands of the king.

France presents an analogous development; as in England, already in the twelfth century reference was made to the Crown as being something above the personality of the individual ruler.[55] And, as in England, the idea of inalienability touched both the royal demesne, which may be considered the

---

54 Much has been written since the time of Maitland upon the influence of Roman law upon the English legal development in the thirteenth century. Recent studies which have emphasized the relationship include those of Post, Richardson, Schulz, and Ullman, and will be found in the bibliography.

55 Hartung, "Die Krone," p. 20, where he refers to a letter of Suger (1155) wherein the abbot uses the phrase "ex iure fidelitatis, quam regno et coronae debent." I have noted several more examples: the donation by Louis VII of an episcopacy together with all its regalia, "cum regalibus ad nostrum coronam pertinentibus" (1168), in *Layettes du trésor des chartes*, I, n. 168; and the call to arms of Philip II (1197): "videlicet quod idem comes (Flandriae) terram nostram in multitudine gentium violenter intravit in damnum corone . . ," in *Recueil des actes de P.A.*, II, n. 566. See the article of J. Strayer, "Defense of the Realm."

antique feudal and physical foundation of the state, and the newer powers which pertained to the king in the name of the nation. The general principle of inalienability was known and used in France early in the thirteenth century, for the dauphin Louis of France claimed in 1216 that John had sworn in his coronation oath to preserve the rights of the realm (*regni Anglie*) and never alienate them without the barons' consent. Although, as Mr. Richardson has noted, the assertions of Louis are without foundation, " still, it is evidence that men might be led to believe that such an oath had been taken and that it was customary to do so." [56]

Even before this, however, in a long series of charters issued to bishops, new towns, and feudal nobles, Louis VII and Philip II had sworn never to alienate the territories taken under their protection.[57] The aim of the king in all these agreements was, of course, the aggrandizement of the royal demesne; the motives of bishops and nobles were equally selfish in desiring the protection that agreements of *pariage* or liege homage would bring. Yet the element of perpetual inalienability is there, and the importance with which the relationship to the Crown was regarded is evidenced in one instance by the great dissatisfaction of the nobles of Aquitaine with the provisions of the treaty of 1259.[58] In the mid-fourteenth century this type of

[56] Richardson, "English Coronation Oath," p. 54, where he also prints the text. See also the *Chronicles of the Reigns of Edward I and Edward II*, I, p. 18, for another chronicle account of the incident.

[57] The earliest is cited by Professor Strayer, "Defense of the Realm," but he either overlooked or preferred not to refer to many similar documents: *Layettes du trésor des chartes*, I, n. 143 (1156), also n. 181 (1163); A. Luchaire, *Etudes sur les actes de Louis VII* (Paris, 1885), n. 611 (1171–72); and more frequent in the following reign, *Recueil des actes de P.A.*, I, 22 (1181), 71 (1183), 117 (1184), 188, 189 (1186), 205 (1187), 253 (1189), 330 (1190), 332 (1190); II, 479 (1194), 527 (1196), 531 (1196), 799 (1204); and in L. Delisle, *Catalogue des actes de P.A.* (Paris, 1856), n. 1409 (1212). It should be noted, however, that not all the documents of *pariage* and protection indicate this everlasting attachment to the Crown. See, for example, *Recueil*, I, 218 (1188), and *Layettes*, I, n. 713 (1204).

[58] See below, pp. 133 *et seq.*

royal protectionism continued to be practiced, and a petition of a town in the vicinity of Toulouse of 1341 indicates both the continuing desire for protection, and the operation of a general principle of inalienability. In return for 100 *livres Tournois* the town is to remain forever under royal jurisdiction immediately subject to the king.[59]

Despite the fact that there was reasoned desire on the part of many to remain in the royal demesne, the French kings, especially during the fourteenth century, were constantly forced to make donations from it. As one historian puts it, " la munificence est un vertu royale "; and, as we have already seen, the emphasis on moral education was always upon the largess rather than the niggardliness of kings.[60] This generosity was not always voluntary, however, and it was common practice for the new ruler to resume what had been granted away and to base his actions upon his obligation to the realm.[61]

The earliest of these revocations dates to 1318 and was an element of Philip V's general policy of repairing the damage done to the realm by his ancestors.[62] His order is very explicit, stating the duties of the king and the purpose of the ordinance which is the " review of gifts made from the royal demesne since St. Louis," and listing the abuses which have occurred " to the great dismay and harm of ourselves and our kingdom." [63] Charles IV, in 1321, found it necessary to repeat this complaint and to order his bailiffs to recover all illegal donations for the Crown in the interest of the public welfare. And this type of revocation occurred again in 1349 and 1351.[64]

---

[59] Bib. Nat. MS Nouv. Acq. Fr. 7420, fols. 10r-13v: " remaneat in futurum sub Domanio et iurisdictione immediata Domini nostri Franciae Regis. Et quod non possint, nec debeant per Dominum nostrum Franciae Regem, nec per ejus successores de Domanio et Jurisdictione Regia abstrahi, nec in alium transferri . . . ."

[60] Olivier-Martin, *Histoire du droit français*, p. 320.

[61] A. Esmein, " L'inalienabilité du domaine de la couronne," p. 366.

[62] *Cambridge Medieval History* VII, 334-37.

[63] Isambert, *Recueil général*, III, 179, and 294.

[64] *Ibid.*, p. 295; and *Ordonnances des rois de France*, II, 315, and 455.

Throughout the century there is a growing abstraction in the
language used, and in 1364, in the middle of his financial difficulties with Edward III, King John I deplored the excessive
gifts the Crown had been forced to make, and made full pro-
testation of his desire for the growth of the nation and the
Crown. In the next year these sentiments were expressed at his
coronation by the new king, Charles V, in an oath which indicates quite clearly the application of the theory of inalienability as a fundamental law of the state: ". . . et superioritatem
jura et nobilitates coronae Franciae irrevocabiliter custodiam et
ille nec alienabo." [65]

Through this entire series of protest, revocation, and oaths,
there runs a theme of consciousness mixed with hopeless ex-
asperation. The royal house knew its rights and theories but
could do little to maintain them: the necessities of families,
court, and the nobles could be met in no way other than sub-
sidization from the royal demesne. Yet, on the other hand,
the theory was always available to a strong ruler for him to
grasp at the proper moment, and it was recognized as having a
legitimate tradition. The very frequency with which it was
appealed to is an indication of the force rulers would have liked
it to have had.

Inalienability of sovereignty was involved with more than
the physical aspect of the royal demesne, the preservation of
which this series of orders was primarily concerned to effect.
Although known to French legists for perhaps a century, the
theory first appeared in political controversy with relation to
the higher rights of the monarchy in connection with the quarrel between Boniface VIII and Philip IV. Since acceptance of
the Donation of Constantine would have implied the admission,
first, of France's quondam subordination to the Papacy, the

[65] Isambert, *Recueil*, V, 240. This phrase is almost identical with the episcopal
and municipal forms which have already been discussed.

French publicists were at pains to deny the legal validity of the Donation.[66] John of Paris, whose *De potestate regia et papali* may be dated 1302, will serve as an example of the publicist approach.[67] Although, by and large, his views are only moderately partial to the French with respect to questions of Church and Empire, he is very decided with regard to the Donation. First he declares that France was never included in it, and then to make sure he produces four proofs of the invalidity of Constantine's great act. Most striking is his reliance upon authorities of the two laws for his choice of proofs and for his supporting references as well.

He first mentions the responsibilities of *Augustus,* and correctly observes that the emperor as an individual may donate as much as he will to the Church, but not so of the property of the fisc which, having been established for the use and benefit of the state, may never perish. This dovetails well with his final point which was the usual argument from logic, tradition, and law proving that the Empire soon would cease to be were it left to the discretion of every emperor to make extravagant donations. His other two arguments were equally familiar to the legists: the emperor is only *administrator* of the *imperium* and therefore must not alienate his trust; and the law prohibits officials of equal rank from coercing each other, therefore making it impossible for Constantine legally to have prejudiced his successor.[68] The major point is this: here we have a philosopher-publicist, probably in the employ of and certainly sym-

---

[66] See Jean Rivière, *Le problème, passim,* for this period. I have used the anonymous *Disputatio super potestate ecclesiae . . . inter clericum et militum,* in *Monarchia,* I, 13-18; Pierre Dubois, *Deliberatio,* in Dupuy, *Histoire du differand; Rex Pacificus,* in Dupuy, *Histoire,* and recently examined by W. Ullman, "A Medieval Document of Papal Theories of Government. Rex Pacificus," *E.H.R.,* LXI (1946), 180-210; and besides the work of John of Paris discussed below, the *Quaestio in utramque partem,* in *Monarchia,* II, 96 *et seq.*

[67] *Monarchia,* II, 1094. He is known also as John Quidort.

[68] The reference is to *D.* 4, 8, 4.

pathetic to the monarchy, using the full schedule of imperialist arguments against the Donation, but against the emperor as well, and in support of the king of France.

A generation later the argument from inalienability was again used by the Crown, this time at the Council of Vincennes called in 1329 to discuss the relative jurisdictions of ecclesiastical and civil courts. Widespread encroachment upon the king's justice was the immediate reason for the council; the basic issue remained the growing secularization of society. Here the king's spokesman was Pierre de Cuignières, professor of law at the University of Paris from 1311, and until his death in 1345 a trusted diplomatic and legal plenipotentiary of the royal house.[69]

It is important to place Pierre's royalist arguments in their proper setting: to show that in denying the king ability to alienate rights essential to the Crown he was neither unique nor original. Indeed, his arguments were merely a French variation on a universal theme. Beyond this general pronouncement, Pierre denied the application of prescription and custom against the king in his official capacity, and against the fisc. He emphasized the temporary nature of the kingship, and also that of trusteeship which is its complement. And, in a statement which creates for historians a mystery about the phraseology of the French coronation formula akin to that which surrounds the English oath, he mentions that the king has sworn at his coronation to maintain the status of the Crown, not to alienate its powers, and to revoke all alienations his predecessors may have made.[70] In sum, this is his major argu-

[69] Standard is F. Olivier-Martin, *L'assemblée de Vincennes de 1329 et ses conséquences* (Rennes, 1909); pp. 117 *et seq.* relate to Pierre's discussion of inalienability of royal rights.

[70] The problems surrounding the English oath are discussed by Richardson in "English Coronation Oath." As far as I know there is no comparable treatment of the French oath—probably for the reason that the known sources allow merely the statement of certain questions relative to its date and use.

ment against the relaxation of additional royal jurisdiction to the Church.[71]

Nor was Pierre's use of the argument its last service to the French Crown, for some fifty years later Philip de Mézières emphasized this defense of jurisdictional powers in his *Somnium viridarii*. This treatise, known also in a French version as the *Songe du vergier*, takes the form of a debate between a cleric and a knight over the relative powers of pope and king. In the passage bearing on our problem Philip denied that *regalia* are prescriptible and forbade the prince to dispose freely of them; but, should a king have alienated them, and this is especially true of jurisdictional powers, he may revoke his grant. Should he plan to transfer his subjects to an alien regime, their objections must be heard—in accord with the principle *Quod omnes tangit*. With regard to the church, he denies the king ability to give up his rights to the clergy, for by so doing he would merit the title *Angustus* rather than *Augustus*. In other words, here is the teleological approach to office which is familiar in these discussions. Familiar, too, are his reasons for restricting the king: the temporary nature of royal authority, prejudice of successor, and equality of office as a bar to coercion. Appropriate references to the two laws are frequent and accurate, and it should be noted that although he mentions the Donation of Constantine rarely in his discussion, the author always returns to it as though it were the understood focal point of his whole argument.[72] Early in the next century these views were reiterated by Jean de Terre Rouge, and, towards 1450, by Juvenal des Ursins.[73] In fact, discussion was con-

---

[71] *L'assemblée*, p. 122. Olivier-Martin is unable to verify Pierre's statement on the coronation oath. See A. Esmein, *Cours élémentaire* (9th ed., Paris, 1908), p. 329, where he gives the text of the 1365 oath of Charles V, which is also printed in Isambert, *Recueil*, V, 240.

[72] The Latin text is printed in *Monarchia*, I, 58-228. André Lemaire, *Lois fondamentales*, cites heavily from the French version.

[73] Lemaire, *Lois fondamentales*, pp. 56, and 62.

tinued throughout the sixteenth and seventeenth centuries, and closely linked with the rise of monarchial absolutism was the ever more important doctrine of the Crown.

This chapter illustrates the most dramatic and immediate influence of the doctrine of inalienability; that on the Crown whose development in theory and fact it aided. Yet sight should not be lost of the way by which its influence was ultimately felt. The entire problem of the *Rex in suo regno* enters our discussion because of its relevance to the theoretical debilitation of the Empire; and also because the scholars of both laws used the issue to theorize on the singular nature of the kingship. To this idea they linked civilian and ecclesiastical concepts of office, and ultimately joined the two in developing an abstraction, the Crown. If it is true that the idea of inalienability of sovereignty was most influential in its effect upon the Crown, it is also true that for contemporaries it was but one more political argument common to the publicist armory of every ruler. And as we shall see in further detail, it entered into a mutual relationship with other constitutional ideas which were growing up side by side with that of the kingship.

# V

# *The Decretal* INTELLECTO *and the*
# *Coronation Oath*

OF PRIMARY SIGNIFICANCE for the theory of inalienability was
the decretal *Intellecto,* perhaps the most explicit statement of
the theory medieval legists had.  As such it served them as a
text with respect to which they could expound the idea's universal application.  However, although *Intellecto* had this importance, it was not by any means the sole component of the
medieval theory; an attempt has been made to emphasize this
fact.  Doctors of both laws brought other concepts to their
interpretation of *Intellecto,* and simultaneously utilized the idea
behind this decretal in support of other principles.  Hence, despite the relationship which approaches identity between *Intellecto* and the theory of inalienability itself, we must continue to emphasize that it is a pattern of integration which
gives the theory stature.  From this viewpoint *Intellecto* takes
its proper position in the discussion of statements of nonalienation in certain coronation oaths, and it is with these oaths
that we are here concerned.

The decretal itself is both brief and clear.  The text is that
of a letter sent by Pope Honorius III in 1220 to the Archbishop
of Kalocsa in reference to an oath taken by King Andrew II
of Hungary.  The king had sworn in his coronation oath:
" iura regni sui et honorem coronae illibita servare," but non-
theless had been forced to make " alienationes in praeiudicium

regni sui et contra regis honorem." [1]   To repair the situation
Honorius freed the king from observing the oaths he might
have taken in donation charters contrary to the one sworn at
his coronation.   The pope's letter was incorporated originally
in the *Compilatio quinta* (1226), and later in the *Decretales*
(1234).

Comparable use of papal powers was not without precedent,
as we have seen.   In fact, this was the third such action of the
Papacy in regard to major powers within twenty years.   In
1200 Innocent III had written to the guardians of his ward,
Frederick Hohenstaufen, enjoining them not to alienate the
royal demesne except in cases of " extreme and evident emer-
gencies."   And in 1215 the same pope quashed the legality of
*Magna Carta* because of the damage it did to John's regality
and to his, the pope's, rights.   It is important that in both these
cases, and in that of Andrew of Hungary, the Papacy was as
much concerned to preserve its own feudal position as to protect or exalt the local ruler.   For all three rulers were, at the
moment in question, vassals of the Holy See.[2]   The doctrine of
inalienability had its natural origins in feudal society, and the
strength it developed was due in part to its harmonious relationship with existing feudal ideas.   In the early thirteenth
century the idea of royal sovereignty was by no means what it
was four hundred years later, yet more than a germ of the later
idea is evidenced in the reference to " iura regni sui et honorem
coronae " in Gregory's collection, and the earlier writings of
Innocent III.

Taken together with the traditional view on episcopal oaths
which, as we have seen, regarded the bishop as an officer responsible to his community for the public welfare, these two

[1] This is the purport of the oath as given in the decretal letter, X. 2, 24, 33.
Kuttner, *Repertorium,* p. 382 is my source for the date of the *Comp. quinta.*

[2] This is implied in the words of Bernardus Bottoni in his *Casus longi* (Strasbourg,
1493), to X. 2, 24, 33: " Rex ungarie fecit quasdam alienationes in preiudicium
regni sui et contra honorem regis . . . . Significatum fuit hoc domino pape."

letters of Innocent may be termed the immediate constitutional or political background of *Intellecto*. The opinions of the early canonists provide the moral and canonical factor. Their general conclusion was that forced oaths need not be honored. Although, as Johannes Teutonicus severely put it, there is an element of necessity in every oath-taking, and absolution may be granted only in extreme cases,[3] other commentators upon this same passage—which concerned an oath forced by the king of Navarre upon his nobles after an invasion by the kings of Aragon and Castile—were more lenient.[4] Tancred, especially, took issue with Johannes Teutonicus and, as we learn from one of his glosses, with Laurentius as well. Commenting upon a letter of Gregory III to the bishop of Laon in which the pope absolved the prelate from an oath which he had been forced to swear sanctifying the renunciation of his right of redress, Tancred agreed that the bishop was not bound.[5] Another decretal which drew his attention concerns the bishop of Clairvaux who complained to Clement III that he had had to swear to an agreement: ". . . in dampnum episcopalis iuris et dignitatis canonicis Claramontanae ecclesiae." The pope replied that the bishop's oath need give him no cause (*impedimentum*) for worry, which absolution Tancred explained by restricting the force of the decretal to *iuramenta temeraria*.[6] In general, therefore, these writers recognized that the immediate fact of extortion was more important than the broad injunction to observe all oaths.

From this brief discussion of analogous cases, it should be

---

[3] Johannes Teutonicus to *Comp. III*, 2, 15, 3 (*Ad audientiam nostram*), in Vatican MS Chis. E. VII, 207, fol. 182v, ad vv. *quod iuramentum*.

[4] Vincentius, *idem*, ad vv. *ab his*, in Vatican MS lat. 1378, fol. 45v; Tancred, *idem*, ad v. *coactus*, in Vatican MS lat. 1377, fol. 205r&v, and in Vatican MS lat. 1378, fol. 196v ad v. *iuramentum*. Also Paulus Ungarus, *idem*, in Vatican MS Borgh. 261, fol. 86r.

[5] Tancred, Vatican MS lat. 1377, fol. 29 to *Comp. I*, 2, 17, 10, ad v. *posse*. This letter was incorporated into his collection by Gregory IX (*X*. 2, 24, 2).

[6] Tancred, Vatican MS lat. 1377, fol. 102v to *Comp. II*. 1, 3, 4, ad v. *impedimentum*.

clear that *Intellecto* presented no new canonical doctrine. Most likely, had political developments not given good reason for its great service to canon and civil lawyers, it would have remained just one more title in the law of oaths. What happened because of the developments in national histories during the thirteenth century was that it became an important authority for the new royalist doctrines of state which then were being formulated.

It is not until the middle of the century that we have significant commentaries on the text of *Intellecto*. Jacobus de Albenga (fl. 1210–74), whose apparatus to the *Compilatio quinta* is the only one extant, gave no more than an *explication du texte*.[7] But in the following great period of legal scholarship, while not all the canonists were interested in the public law aspects of the decretal,[8] there were many who related its implications to the body of theories which constituted in sum the current working constitution of the Church.

Innocent IV is important here as in so many other phases of canonical development. Although his comment is extremely succinct, he introduced, perhaps for the first time, a certain qualification into the discussion. He does not forbid all alienations but only those because of which the royal dignity is impaired or burdened (*gravitur*).[9] Soon afterwards Hostiensis changed *gravitur* to *graviter* and formalized the emphasis on moderation which was implicit in Innocent.[10] This sensible

---

[7] I have examined a microfilm of the British Museum MS Royal 11, C. VII, fols. 246r–271v. See Kuttner, *Repertorium*, pp. 382–83.

[8] For example, Goffredus de Trani, *Summa* (Cologne, 1487?), to X. 2, 24 (*De iureiurando*) where he merely refers to *Intellecto* as an example of the kind of "iuramenta . . . illicita et temeraria" which are not to be observed. And Abbas Antiquus, *Lectura aurea* to X. 2, 24, 33, gives a purely ecclesiastical interpretation to the decretal "Quando quis iurat in sui promotione non alienare bona ecclesie: si postea alienet et iuret alienatio non tenet."

[9] *Apparatus* (Venice, 1481), to X. 2, 24, 33, *casus*.

[10] *Commentaria* to X. 2, 24, 33: "Haec decret. intelligatur quando fecit alienationes per quas graviter laeditur regalis dignitas. Non intelligas quod propter hoc interdicatur ei quod nihil possit donare vel alienare . . . ."

approach no doubt strengthened the doctrine, for as these great canonists realized, had an absolute prohibition on alienation been imposed, the decretal would have lost all its practical effect, and would have been ignored completely by society . . . the structure of which, although changing, was still essentially feudal. Any idea, therefore, if it was to have a chance of acceptance, could not ruthlessly attempt to alter the basis of society; rather it had to integrate itself into the old pattern, in interaction with which it might eventually produce change. Since this is what happened in the case of *Intellecto*, we find these opinions of Innocent and Hostiensis cited repeatedly, not only by canonists, but also by civilians. Even the most extreme of the latter group recognized the importance of alienation for the maintenance of the social and political structure. So, for example, Isernia, who explained the necessity of feudal donations in the sense that they were signs of office and nobility which ultimately benefited the state.[11] The later canonists maintained this viewpoint. As Johannes Andreae wrote, apropos his agreement with Innocent and Hostiensis, it would be very difficult for a legist to make a strict and contrary interpretation.[12]

It is not strange, however, that none of the legists ever arrived at a clear definition of *graviter, enormiter* or of another term frequent to the commentaries, *magna laesio*. One looks in vain and perhaps foolishly for quantitative precision despite the constant and significant use of such expressions. Certainly rules of thumb were worked out for common cases. In unusual ones, and in controversies which concerned public officials

---

[11] *In feudorum*, lib. I, tit. 1, n. 10. See also his comment to the constitution of Lothar, lib. II, tit. 52: ". . . non dicitur princeps quando diminuit enormiter contra honorem coronae . . . ." And n. 3 of his comment on the title *Quae sunt regalia* (lib. II, tit. 55 [56]), where he specifically refers to *Intellecto*.

[12] *Commentaria* (Venice, 1581), to X. 2, 24, 33, ad v. *praeiudicium*. See also Panormitanus, to *Intellecto* (ed. Lyons, 1547), n. 7, where he says that the decretal "non debet intelligi de modica donatione."

and properties, each case must have been decided on its own merits and within its own sphere of influences. As Cynus said, referring to the question: " quid sit magna leasio: dico arbitrio iudicis relinquendum. . . ." [13]

At this point the relation between the oath and the public welfare might be brought again into the discussion. That bishops, as representatives of their ecclesiastical communities, took an oath to preserve the goods entrusted to them has already been mentioned; likewise the fact that the canonists almost invariably equated bishop and king in regard to the concept of office and the obligations of the lay or ecclesiastical official towards it and his community.[14] The *Glossa ordinaria* established opinion in this respect for the thirteenth century, and Panormitanus summed up medieval thought in his gloss on *Intellecto* at the beginning of the fifteenth.[15] And linked to this notion of office which treated bishop and king alike was the idea that oaths in derogation of the public welfare were not to be honored. This view was expressed by Bernardus Bottoni and Hostiensis, among others, in relation to *Intellecto*. Noteworthy is the fact that their supporting reference is to the decretal *Si diligenti* which, as we have seen, is a prime support of the theory of the renunciation of the *privilegium fori* and other rights introduced in favor of a community.[16] We have here, then, a wonderful example of the integration and mutual support of principles of moral, social, and public law. Moral in

---

[13] *Ad codicem* (Lyons, 1527), fol. 8, n. 1, to C. 1, 3.

[14] The comparison was a familiar one long before. See the Retold coronation *ordo* of the late tenth century, cited by P. L. Ward, "An Early Version of the Anglo-Saxon Coronation Ceremony," *E.H.R.*, LVII (1942), 351: "Et defensionem quantum potuero adiuvante domino exibebo. sicut rex in suo regno unicuique episcopo et ecclesiae [sic] sibi commissae per rectum exibere debet."

[15] *Casus longi* (Rome, 1474), to X. 2, 24, 33, and the *Glossa ordinaria*, and Panormitanus, *Lectura* (Lyons, 1547), to this passage.

[16] Hostiensis, *Summa* (Venice, 1574), to X. 2, 24 (*De iureiurando*), n. 6; Bottoni and Panormitanus, *idem*, to X. 2, 24, 33. See also Panormitanus' comment on X. 2, 2, 12 (*Si diligenti*), n. 4, where the same thought is expressed.

the sense that the admitted illegality of the forced oath permitted the pope to declare in *Intellecto* that King Andrew's sworn charters of alienation were null and void. Social in the sense that the reference to *Si diligenti* implied sympathy for the view of woman in society as someone special, to be protected because of her presumed weakness and intrinsic importance. And public in that the canonists related to the decretal on the Hungarian incident, itself a political manifestation of a moral principle, their ideas upon the special nature of the bishop (whom they equated with king), upon the individual's subordination to the obligations and dignity of his office, and upon the primacy of the public good.[17]

Something has been suggested in an earlier chapter about the role of *Intellecto,* of the concept of inalienability in general, in the development of the national states, and of their symbol, the Crown. Theoretical rejection of the Empire's inviolability by jurists in the employ of the young monarchies was tantamount to acceptance of *Rex in suo regno.* And once the realm had been established in theory, its supporters recognized the strength the Crown, its symbol of permanence, could receive from a doctrine which posited the existence of rights which were inalienable because they truly defined the office of the king. Moreover, as we have just seen, the idea was current that an oath taken by a ruler in derogation of his Crown and regal dignity was invalid. Lately much has been written about the significance of the coronation oath in relation to the growth of the monarchy and the Crown—especially in England and France—about which it is necessary to say something in the light of comparative research.

The problem of the English oath waits upon the discovery of new manuscript sources for its further elucidation or final solution. It is known that at his coronation Edward II took

---

[17] The exception to this rule was the salvation of the individual soul, as has been mentioned.

an oath which included a provision, based upon the theory of
*Intellecto,* to safeguard the rights of the Crown.    It is also
known that both Henry III and Edward I referred to such a
provision in their coronation oaths; yet, no office or other document has survived from their reigns which includes such a
promise.    Recently Mr. Richardson and Professor Wilkinson
have examined the sources in great detail; the former has observed the relationship between *Intellecto* and the coronation
oath of Edward II, and has stated at some length the reasons
for believing that both Henry III and Edward I took such a
special although unrecorded promise.[18]    Mr. Richardson gives
nine statements of Edward I which refer to his obligations under such an oath.[19]    We may add another, and say something
too about the evidence forthcoming from the reign of his father.    Our purpose is to emphasize the influence of the *Intellecto* tradition upon English constitutional history.    The theory
of inalienability was available to English thinkers early in the
thirteenth century, and its appearance in the coronation oaths
shows one path of its eventual significance.

Besides the bulls of 1233 and 1235 in which Gregory IX released Henry III from the oaths forced upon him by the

[18] An outline of the problem is given by Professor Wilkinson in the second
volume of his *Constitutional History of Medieval England* (London, 1952), pp.
85-112.    Mr. Richardson's summation of some twenty years interest in the oath
is his article "The English Coronation Oath," pp. 44-75, in which will be found
references to his earlier studies made in collaboration with Professor Sayles.    Unfortunately I came upon Mr. Richardson's article after the greater part of my
researches into the English aspects of *Intellecto* were completed.    For this reason,
and for the sake of clarity, I shall take the liberty of repeating something of what
has been well covered by him.    Since constant reference will be made to Mr.
Richardson's article and the sources cited therein, I shall not bother in every case
to repeat his references or to give the page to which my argument is directed.

[19] In connection with the nine appeals to the oath made by Edward I, mention
should be made of the "Statute of Fines Levied," in *Statutes of the Realm,* I, 126
(27 Ed. I).    Edward I confirms the Charter of Liberties and the Charter of the
Forest ". . . salvis tamen juramento nostro, jure corone nostre, et racionibus ac
eciam aliorum."

nobles,[20] another series of papal letters later in the reign indicates the possible influence of *Intellecto*. This group runs through three pontificates, and consists of three bulls all to the same effect. In the words of the foremost historian of the period, these popes, Alexander IV, Urban IV, and Clement IV, " opposed the pretext of reforming the state of the realm to the depression of royal liberty." [21] What is most noticeable from our point of view is the similarity of certain phrases in all these documents, and the similarity of these phrases to the text of *Intellecto* and the glosses upon it written before the promulgation of the first of these bulls in 1261.

The decretal itself speaks of " alienationes . . . in praeiudicium regni sui et contra regis honorem," and of the royal oath sworn " iura regni sui et honorem coronae illibita servare." Hostiensis wrote of the " alienationes per quas graviter laeditur regalis dignitas "; Bernardus Bottoni of the " alienationes in praeiudicium regni sui et contra honorem regis," and again in the *Glossa ordinaria* of the royal oaths, " in damnum suae dignitatis "; Innocent IV wrote of the " alienationes propter quas gravitur dignitas regalis." [22] Alexander IV used the words: " in diminutionem potestatis tuae, ac depressionem regiae libertatis "; Urban IV used the same phrase with a minor variation; and Clement IV spoke of Henry and Edward as " detentos

---

[20] Besides the two letters discussed by Mr. Richardson on pp. 51-52, we may note the bull of Gregory IX of March, 1238, in *Foedera*, I, i, 234. Here the pope permits the king to revoke donations made in " enormem laesionem ejusdem regni " and " in grave praeiudicium ecclesiae Romanae ad quam regnum Angliae pertinere dignoscitur . . . " despite the oaths he may have taken to observe the alienations. This is clearly the doctrine of *Intellecto* with which Gregory for one would certainly have been well aware.

[21] Maurice Powicke, *King Henry III*, II, 423. Although he refers here to the first of these bulls, that of Alexander IV, the same might be said of those of Urban IV and Clement IV.

[22] Hostiensis, *Commentaria* (Venice, 1581), to X. 2, 24, 33; Bottoni, *Casus longi* (Strasbourg, 1493), *Glossa ordinaria*; Innocent IV, *Apparatus* (Venice, 1481); all to the same decretal.

taliter in suae libertatis, dignitatis, honoris, status vel iurium suorum aut dicti regni praeiudicium. . . ." [23] Given the natural limitations of the language's vocabulary, the similarities here in idea and terminology are too great to be passed off. Noteworthy too is the fact that the canonical justification for papal action was the legal theory expressed in *Intellecto*. These three papal letters cannot be considered of the same value as evidence for the existence of a restrictive clause in Henry III's coronation oath as the two bulls mentioned by Mr. Richardson. Yet, although they do not make a specific appeal to the oath, they are important in showing a reference to the *Intellecto* theory which is independent of the oath. By so doing they imply the existence of a clause in the oath, the violation of which would have been sufficient provocation for papal interference.

Another addition might be made to Mr. Richardson's presentation of the subject. He states that " the draftsman of the king's petition of 1232, which led to the pope's letter of 10 January 1233, had another document before him . . . Innocent III's bull of 24 August 1215, annulling John's great charter." Although he mentions the similar passage in the *Laws of Edward the Confessor* as a " closer parallel," the assertion nevertheless is made that the evidence " practically excludes the possibility that he [Henry's draftsman] had in mind the decretal which he could have found in the *Compilatio quinta*." [24]    It

---

[23] *Foedera*, I, i, 405-6 (1261); 416 (1262); 459 (1265). See also the terminology of King Henry's letter to Urban IV, *Foedera*, I, i, 414; and his proclamation the same year, 1262 (p. 419) based on the pope's absolution, to the effect he is no longer bound by his oaths to the barons ". . . in praeiudicium et derogationem iuris regii et turbationem pacis nostrae . . . ."

[24] Richardson, " English Coronation Oath," *Speculum*, XXIV (1949), p. 52. On p. 62 Richardson gives the texts of the passage in the *Laws of Edward the Confessor* and of a writ to the sheriffs of 1312 mentioning the royal duty " regiam dignitatem ac pacem et tranquilitatem ecclesie sancte et tocius populi nostro regimini commissi integra et illesa manutenere . . . ." He too has caught the familiar ring of certain phrases. The canon law texts offer similarities, for example the statement from the *Apparatus ius naturale* (1210-15) to *Decretum* Ca. XII, q. 2, c. 69 *Ecclesiarum*, ad v. *proposcit*: " Poscere debet ecclesia regem ut ecclesie iura servet illesa ut xcvii.

seems useless to attempt to pinpoint a specific inspiration for the idea as it appears in the letters of Pope Gregory to King Henry. Even if the specific document before Henry's drafts-man was Innocent's letter to John, that very letter was by no means original or unique. The same pope had written similarly fifteen years earlier to the tutors of Frederick Hohenstaufen, and identical language had been used by canonists in regard to ecclesiastical affairs in analogous circumstances.

Several points, then, must be noted. First, that Henry's chancery relied in its appeal upon familiar ideas which already by the time of Innocent III, if not before, had gained general acceptance. If nothing else, the little phrase in Gregory's letter of 1235 shows this. He writes that an oath to preserve the rights of the Crown was customary: " ut moris est." Second, the language describing the objects of preservation is broad and unconcerned with specific feudal rights. Rather both royal and papal chanceries used such elastic terms as *dignitas* and *majestas*. The extent to which such terms were stretched varied from ruler to ruler and moment to moment; and in a sense English constitutional history for two centuries can be viewed as an expansion and contraction of royal authority rela-tive to baronial and later parliamentary views of the exact limitations of royal dignity.[25]

---

Di. ecclesie." I owe this reference to Professor G. Post, who noted the phrase in Bibliothèque Nationale MS 3909. We might also note the phrase used by John in 1212: ". . . ut libertatem et dignitatem qua corona Anglie hucusque gravisa est integram conservet et illesam " (cited by Richardson, p. 53, n. 54).

[25] I have not ventured at this point to enter the lists on the *Statute of York*. My purpose in these pages is to substantiate Richardson's thesis on *Intellecto*, and to show the broader continental aspects of the problem of inalienability as it applied to the oath. Many documents might be cited for the fourteenth century to show the acceptance in the English constitution of this principle. Incidentally, it might be pointed out that Richardson answers his own question and surprise about the presence of *legistae Francigeni* at the side of Edward at the Parliament of York. In his next note he remarks that both men were trained lawyers at the Parlement of Paris. Given the importance of Roman law doctrines of royal supremacy which were well known by the French kings, it would not have been unusual for Edward

Although the available documents do not permit a discussion of the French oath in such detail, enough do exist to show that at one time an oath was taken to preserve and never alienate the rights of the Crown. And, although the earliest text of such a provision comes from the coronation oath of Charles V in 1365, references to such an oath are to be found in earlier documents.[26] The idea that there were certain Crown rights which could not be alienated was expressed by the dauphin Louis in 1216, as we have noted with respect to the Crown. In his remonstrance against the surrender of England to the Papacy by King John, Louis wrote, emphasizing the commonplace nature of such an oath as Pope Gregory was to do later in 1235: " Ad hec, cum prefatus Iohannes in coronatione sua solempniter, prout moris est, iurasset se iura et consuetudines ecclesie et regni Anglie conservaturum. . . ."[27] The concept never appeared, however, in any French oath during the thirteenth century. The closest approximation to the standard terminology was the promise of Louis VIII: ". . . ea quae Imperatoribus, et Regibus Ecclesia commissis collata et reddita sunt inviolabiter conservare."[28] But such a promise to main-

---

to have obtained for himself advice from a different legal camp. For their arguments see the *Annales Londonienses* in *Chronicles of the Reigns of Edward I and Edward II*, I, 211-15.

[26] As far as I know, no systematic study has ever been made of the French coronation oath, and the works of Professor P. Schramm unfortunately do not help us here. The question brought up by references previous to the oath of 1365 to such a clause in the coronation oath has been raised frequently by historians, but never solved, and never related to the broader problem. See, for example, Olivier-Martin, *L'assemblée*, pp. 117 *et seq.*; Jean de Pange, *Le roi très chrétien* (Paris, 1949), p. 413; Esmein, *Cours élémentaire*, 3d ed., pp. 328-29; Lemaire, *Lois fondamentales*, p. 47. The text of Charles V's oath is given in Theodore Godefroy, *Le cérémonial français* (2 vols., Paris, 1649), I, 31 *et seq.*; and in Isambert, *Recueil*, V, 240: ". . . promitto . . . et superioritatem, iura, et nobilitates Coronae Franciae inviolabiliter custodiam, et illa non transportabo nec alienabo."

[27] Cited by Richardson, in " English Coronation Oath," p. 54. It is also discussed by Charles Petit-Dutaillis, *Etude sur le vie et le regne de Louis VIII* (Paris, 1894), pp. 75-87.

[28] Godefroy, *Cérémonial*, I, 223.

tain the lands and rights of the Church was the most traditional part of every coronation oath.

The most important reference to such an oath before 1365
was made by Pierre de Cuignières at the Council of Vincennes
in 1329. Referring to the king's inability to recognize jurisdictional authority which the Church now claimed, Pierre
argued:

nec Rex etiam posset tale jus a se abdicare sicut probabat per multa
capitula. . . . Quare cum Rex in sua coronatione juravisset jura Regni
non alienare, et alienata ad se revocare, si per Ecclesiam aut quemcum-
que alium erant aliqua usurpata Rex tenebatur per juramentum ad se
illa revocare.

It is almost certain that Pierre knew well the discussion which
embraced *Intellecto* and the Donation of Constantine, for the
arguments he throws against ecclesiastical pretensions are based
upon familiar themes: the fisc may not be the subject of prescription; the king is a temporary official who may not diminish his powers, especially that of secular judgment; the king
must pass on his powers undiminished to his successor whom he
would injure were he to do otherwise.[29] By the time Pierre
used them, all these arguments were standard repertory, and
had been employed to the same effect for at least fifty years.

Perhaps the only other early reference to the elusive oath is
the *Ordonnance* of 1357 which ordered the royal bailiffs in
Auvergne and Montaignes to reunite to the demesne all land
wrongly alienated since the time of Philip the Fair. The king
declared his perennial obligation:

accroistre le prouffit, les Hautesses et Noblesses de ladite Coronne de
France et ycelles garder, maintenir et deffendre de tout nostre povoir,
ayens promis en bonne foy aus dictes Genz desdiz Troix Estaz. . . .[30]

---

[29] Cited by Olivier-Martin, *L'assemblée de Vincennes*, pp. 156-57 from the *Libellus
Petri Bertrandi*, which is our only source for Pierre's arguments.

[30] *Ordonnances*, III, 162 *et seq.*

Even this may or may not refer to a specific clause in the coronation oath, but in any event the sense is that expressed eight years later in the oath of Charles V.[31]    And having once appeared, the principle of inalienability remained in the *ordo* until late in the sixteenth century.    It dropped out only when the monarchy no longer needed to use such an oath in defense of its status, that is, at the moment that inalienability of the royal demesne became in practice as well as theory one of the fundamental laws of the French state.[32]

In France as well as in England, then, the principle of inalienability as manifested in the coronation oath became an incipient principle of state.    In England where the development of the nation was more rapid, the clause was eliminated from the oath after 1308 because the barons and the commons as well as the king recognized the wisdom of such an idea.    All were alive to the fact that England was a kingdom whose destiny was, so to speak, immortal and independent of that of the

---

[31] The recent work of M. David, " Le serment du sacre du IX⁰ au XV⁰ siècle," *Revue du moyen-âge latin*, VI (1950), 256 *et seq.*, adds nothing to the discussion other than the nationalist statement that French events alone would be enough to explain the presence of such a clause in the oath of 1365 (p. 259).

[32] On this point see Olivier-Martin, *Histoire du droit français*, p. 320. For the several references to such an oath after 1365 see Philippe de Mézières, *Somnium viridarii* (ca. 1366/67), in *Monarchia*, I, pt. II, cap. 293; Alfred Coville, *L'ordonnance cabochienne* (Paris, 1891), pp. 35-36; French Renaissance legal opinion is indicated in the comment of F. Hotman on *Intellecto* in his *Quaestionium illustrium liber* (Paris, 1573), p. 53, quaest. 1: " Rex qui fidem publicam subiectis datam et iureiurando confirmatem violat, iam non Rex . . . ."    At one time or another, according to Godefroy, *Cérémonial*, I, 76, the German emperor and the kings of Hungary, Bohemia, England, Denmark, Sweden, and Poland took oaths to preserve and never alienate the rights of their kingdoms.    He expresses surprise that there should have been no such oath in the French *ordo* until 1365, but imagines that perhaps it had been regarded as " superflu et inutile " to request that the kings not alienate their rights in view of the fact that they did swear to protect their subjects and to maintain the peace.    This, incidentally, is the essence of Mr. Richardson's conclusion with regard to the oath of Edward II (" English Coronation Oath," p. 75).    He believes that the first promise " required of the king the observance of the whole body of law granted by ' ancient kings ' . . ." and " it especially singled out the laws of St. Edward . . . a reference to a particular edition of the laws attributed to the Confessor which embodied a tract on the duties of the king. A separate promise to maintain the rights of the Crown was consequently unnecessary."

king. This was so despite the existence of centrifugal feudal forces which were to divide the state for another two centuries. Development as a nation against feudal opposition was made easier for England because of her insularity. There was no such positive geographic factor to aid the French monarchy, and what in retrospect seems the most " natural " boundary for France had to be created slowly. Feudalism was still the basis for society and government throughout most of northern Europe in the fourteenth and fifteenth centuries, and the French kings were forced to use and manipulate feudal relationships in their prolonged effort to erect a centralized state.[33] Hence the slowness with which all parties admitted the principle of inalienability; hence, also, the constant reiteration of the idea in the oath long after it had ceased to be necessary in England. The fact that such a promise was demanded of the emperor into the sixteenth century would substantiate these conclusions. Like France, the Empire was far from being a centralized state, and, as in France, the ruling authority was eager to have the dramatic coronation ceremony as setting for the assertion of its inviolability.

If such assertions were not made by the monarchs themselves, they were made by their legal advisors who drew from a tradition by this time the common property of all who wrote political theory. And so we find that the theory of a restrictive clause in the coronation oath passed over into the armory of the speculative thinkers. It is referred to, for example, by Alvarus Pelagius in his *Speculum regum* (1341–44) under the rubric: *De malis regibus et principibus et in quibus peccant.* One of the evils on his list is the alienation " of the properties

---

[33] For a substantial exposition of the view that France was essentially a feudal as opposed to a centralized kingdom long after the end of the Middle Ages, see Samuel Chevallier, *Le pouvoir royal français à la fin du XIII⁰ siècle: Les droits régaliens* (Laval, 1930); and Gustave Dupont-Ferrier, " Où en était la formation de l'unité française aux XV⁰ et XVI⁰ siècles? " *Journal des savants* (1941), 10-24, 54-64, 106-19.

of the kingdom in violation of the coronation oath." Alvarus refers immediately to *Intellecto,* and what strikes one is the familiar way he mentions such a promise: as though the author could assume that his readers, whatever their nationality might be, would be conversant with such an idea, and almost as though *Intellecto* had established a pattern for all nations to follow.[34] The unity of the various themes composing the *Intellecto* tradition is further brought out by Alvarus, for he rests his belief that the king would do evil by alienating in violation of his oath upon the familiar view of kings as mere " defensores et administratores et augmentatores," and not as proprietors of their realms in the strict legal sense of *dominium.*[35]

But long before this theoretical presentation of the middle fourteenth century, the theory of *Intellecto* had begun to play its constitutional role in the histories of England and France. We cannot point with certainty to the document or documents through which its influence passed from the public law of the church into that of the monarchies. Only the function of the canon law as transmitter may be stressed. This, and the fact of integration that is evidenced by the mutual reliance of the concepts of office, Crown, inalienability, and what has received particular emphasis in this chapter, the coronation oath.

[34] Long sections from the *Speculum regum* are printed by Richard Scholz in *Unbekannte kirchenpolitische Streitschriften* (Rome, 1914), pp. 514-29.

[35] Scholz stops his excerpt after *administratores.* For the complete text I have consulted Vatican MS lat. 1477, fol. 16r. Reference is also made to C. 7, 37, 3, which was the locus for much civilian commentary on the question of alienation.

# VI

## *The Theory of* INTELLECTO *and Contractual Agreements*

WE SHALL TURN NOW to examine several incidents and issues which reveal medieval attitudes as to the proper conduct of royal diplomacy, and in so doing we shall treat another of the political problems in terms of which the theory of inalienability was discussed and further developed: the question of the ruler's responsibility with respect to certain basis contractual agreements. Treatises of princely instruction and the more philosophical concept of the king as active agent of the state imposed moral restraints upon his freedom of action; the coronation oath added constitutional responsibilities besides. As the representative of the state in foreign affairs as well as its guardian, the king theoretically was in a position to do as much evil as good. Hence, to supplement broad exhortations to good rule, pressures were exerted upon him for the ultimate protection of the state. These pressures were made manifest in legal discussions over the validity of agreements, and, perhaps more important in indicating an atmosphere of nationality, in popular reaction to unpopular treaties. The examples chosen are English and French.

From the twelfth century the French kings consciously used treaties of *pariage* to enlarge the area of royal jurisdiction, a technique which indeed was exploited by Philip II.[1] Very

---

[1] Achille Luchaire, *Louis VII, Philippe-Auguste, Louis VIII (1137–1226)* (Paris, 1902), p. 205.

often a town, noble, or religious community was forced by weakness and fear to petition the king for such a charter, and, as the system worked in practice, the king who was always the more powerful party tended to increase his influence.[2] We have already taken note of some of these contracts in relation to the early development of the Crown; these documents are valuable in showing that *pariage* was an element of the general theory of inalienability in the sense that certain legal obligations or limitations were placed upon the king. Although the language of these agreements becomes more and more formalized during the reign of Philip II, throughout all the documents run two themes: the royal promise to retain the area under his immediate jurisdiction, and the royal assurance that the contract will be observed by his successors. Such agreements covered the entire gamut of the feudal hierarchy: from the act of 1189 which brought the village of d'Escurolles directly under the royal wing, to that of 1212 in which Philip received the homage of the count of Perigord and promised never to detach the county from the Crown.[3] As we shall see, the violation of this last had interesting consequences. But before turning to the treaty of 1259, the implications of which will lead to further aspects of the theory of inalienability, we must examine another diplomatic incident, the sale of Avignon to the Papacy in 1348.

The story of Queen Joanna's sale of Avignon to Clement VI is really quite amusing if pieced together from the conflicting versions of the seventeenth-century Frenchman, Pierre Dupuy, and the Roman, Gaetano Tanursi, who in 1792 published a violent but defensive apology for the papal claims on Avignon.[4] Dupuy, who wrote a century and a half earlier and was a better

[2] Léon Gallet, *Les traités de pariage*, pp. 63 *et seq.*, 140 *et seq.*

[3] *Recueil des actes de P.A. Roi de France*, II, 253; L. Delisle, *Catalogue*, p. 320.

[4] *Allegazione istorico-critico-diplomatico-legale . . . concernante i diritti incontrastibili del Papa sulla città, e stato di Avignono . . .* (Rome, 1792), especially pp. 13-30, 72 *et seq.*

historian, will serve as our guide. In truth, his version of the story is evidence for the subsequent tradition of the doctrine of inalienability as well as for the actual events of the fourteenth century, for his three reasons why the queen should not have alienated the city present the view of inalienability held by the monarchy of Louis XIII.

First, he mentions that Avignon belonged to the Crown from 1270 to 1290; therefore Philip IV could not legally have surrendered his rights to the city to Charles of Anjou. Second, the queen was but twenty-three, by contemporary definition a minor, at the time of the sale and was under the specific injunction of her grandfather, who had designated her his heir, that she alienate nothing before she was twenty-five. Moreover, she had not received the advice of her magnates. Finally, he writes, her action would have violated the treaty of 1125 by which the counts of Toulouse and Barcelona divided Provence between themselves. One stipulation of this agreement prohibited alienation of Provençal territory to persons outside the two comital families. Following the alienation, according to Dupuy, the princes of Naples and the magnates of Provence, on the legal grounds of bad management and because of the queen's violation of the edict of Frederick II which forbade the alienation of Provence, declared that her sale could be revoked.[5]

Two aspects of this history must be noted. First, the fact that contemporary opposition was based upon certain specific legal documents. The treaty of 1125 did forbid alienations to persons outside the families of the two counts.[6] Frederick II issued a constitution in March, 1232, which forbade alienation of Provence, as Dupuy says.[7] And, in his testament, Joanna's

---

[5] Dupuy, *Histoire*, pp. 397 *et seq.*

[6] C. Devic and J. Vaissete, *Histoire générale de Languedoc* (15 vols., Paris, 1872–93), V, 935-39.

[7] *Constitutiones* II, 198-99. See also VIII, 679-81, for the renunciation by Charles IV of the rights of the Empire over Avignon, preparatory to the sale by Joanna.

grandfather, Roger, did forbid alienation while she was still a minor and, providing for her future even as an adult, required eventual consent of the great nobles.[8]  Second, the nobles' opposition to the queen is important, for it implies the validity of the restraints which Joanna ignored and also consciousness of the fact that she had alienated what never was hers to give. Given the date of the incident, 1348, and the location of Avignon in the area of civil law usage, it may be assumed that the complex of ideas developed around *Intellecto* was known to those who protested the queen's action.  Interestingly enough, Tanursi goes through special gyrations to prove that the elaborate renunciations of her privileges made by the young queen were valid, that the public welfare in fact benefited from the sale, and that it was not until the sixteenth century that there was any public law of the Empire which would have barred the queen's alienation.[9]  In other words, the arguments he feels he must destroy are just those medieval ideas which would have made logical and necessary the act of the queen in 1365 in which she admitted her ill-considered action and reunited her lost territories to the realm.[10]

The Treaty of Paris of 1259 meant for Henry III the renunciation of all English claims to Normandy, Maine, Anjou, Poitou, and Touraine, and his homage to St. Louis for a reduced duchy of Aquitaine and Gascony.  Upon the French it had little practical effect, since their counterconcessions were mainly of future rights and ultimately were blocked by the skilled duplicity of their lawyers.[11]  This treaty enters our discussion on two accounts.  First, because English reaction to the harmful provisions indicated patriotic resentment that per-

---

[8] Johann C. Lunig, *Codex Italiae diplomaticus* (4 vols., Frankfurt and Leipzig, 1725–35), II, col. 1125.

[9] *Allegazione*, 14–23.

[10] Dupuy, *Histoire*, p. 404. I have not, however, been able to find this act of the queen.

[11] See Michel Gavrilovitch, *Etude sur le Traité de Paris de 1259* (Paris, 1899), and Powicke, *King Henry III*, I, 252 *et seq.*

tinent rights of the Crown had been surrendered to the prejudice of future generations. In the words of one chronicler, the
treaty was a *pudenda concordia* which the king contracted in
order to keep something of Aquitaine; [12] another emphasized
the great dissatisfaction of Prince Edward, who had been per-
suaded to renounce his rights that the treaty might be con-
cluded.[13]

The second and greater significance of the treaty is that it
illustrates, and brings under discussion, a topic which demonstrates another area of contact between the theory of inalienability and the political issues of the day: the idea that the king
was bound to honor and preserve the allegiance of his subjects
and never alienate them without their consent. The feudal
dissatisfaction with the violation in the treaty of solemn contracts calling for perpetual relationship to the Crown was at
the heart of the controversy. Many of the nobles and towns
who found themselves under new suzerains as a result of the
treaty were extremely embittered. Some, bound to the Crown
by treaties of long standing and oaths of feudal allegiance, refused to recognize the lords now imposed upon them, and this
was true of the dependents of both kings.[14] Perhaps the most

---

[12] *Chronica monasterii de Melsa a fondatione usque ad annum 1396* (ed. E. A.
Bond, 3 vols., London, 1866–68), II, 29. Exactly the same sort of dissatisfaction
was expressed several centuries later by Froissart in regard to the disastrous Treaty
of Bretigny (1360). This reference is made by Choppin, *De domanio*, lib. II, tit. 1,
n. 8, and refers to Vol. I, cap. 490 (in the Luce ed. Vol. VI). The Treaty of
Bretigny may be read in E. Cosneau, *Les grands traités de la guerre de cent ans*
(Paris, 1889), pp. 44 *et seq.*

[13] Gervase of Canterbury, *Gesta regum continuata* in Vol. II of the *Historical
Works* (ed. W. Stubbs, 2 vols., London, 1879–80), II, 209-10. Rishanger expresses
disgust only with the forced nature of the treaty, Henry being obliged by home
troubles to give in to St. Louis: *Chronica* (ed. H. T. Riley, London, 1869), p. 123,
emphasizes the opposition of Montfort. All these chronicles referred to were written
in the late thirteenth century, and so may be regarded as contemporary opinion.
Other English comments in the same vein may be read in Gavrilovitch, *Etude*, p. 46.

[14] Several of the nobles whose lands were separated from the French crown as a
result of the treaty refused to allow masses sung in St. Louis' honor after his
canonization. And Joinville reports the bitter complaint of the nobles that Louis
had surrendered lands which had been won only with great effort by his father and

important of the nobles involved was the count of Perigord, whose ancestor had received from Philip Augustus, as we have seen, a pledge to keep the country forever under the Crown. Although the count at first renounced this privilege and took his oath to Edward, some years later he claimed the right to revert to his original status, and did so. Edward refused to recognize this second switch, but the Parlement of Paris sanctioned the count's action, presumably on the basis of the original pact between Count Archambaud and Philip Augustus.[15] Generally speaking, the French Crown did little to expedite the smooth effectuation of the agreement. In the French version of the treaty the lawyers agreed to the transfer of Perigord and other territories, but then inserted the saving clause: " sauves les choses qe li rois de France ne peut mettre hors de sa main par lettres de lui ou de ses anceisors." [16] However, several documents do survive to show us that a few French nobles did accept their new liege lord, and that when they did so they explicitly made a renunciation: " litteris, privilegiis et munimentis quae habunt a dicto Rege Francia et suis praedeccessoribus, continentia quod idem Rex non possit ipsum ponere extra manum suam." [17] Although, as evidenced in these French discussions, the idea of a ruler's obligations to his subjects is essentially feudal, it was to have important consequences with respect to the growth of the concept of national citizenship.

This concept developed slowly through the thirteenth century in discussions relating to the feudal problem: " Utrum dominus (rex) possit vasallum suum alii minori vel pari ipsius

---

grandfather. See Gavrilovitch, *Etude*, pp. 47-48, and Frantz Funck-Brentano, *Le moyen-âge* (Paris, 1922), p. 282.

[15] Gavrilovitch, *Etude*, pp. 77-80.

[16] *Layettes du trésor des chartes*, III, 411. Noteworthy too is the phraseology and implication of this escape clause. It would appear that the French lawyers had in mind, if not a specific rule, at least a general principle which could not be violated by the king in a treaty.

[17] *Foedera*, I, i, 425 and 426, both dated April, 1263. The first is that of Raymond, viscount of Touraine, the second that of a noble, Ponticus de Gordon.

vasallo delegare." [18] This is the statement of the problem formulated by Azo who answered in favor of the vassal, and based
his solution upon the constitution *Imperialem* of Barbarossa
and other passages in the civil law which in sum argued against
loss of dignity, reputation, and power in analogous situations.[19]
Accursius agreed with his master and was followed here by the
large majority of later jurists. Hostiensis and Innocent IV
stated a similar opinion in their commentaries on *Dilecti filii*
(*Decret. Greg. IX* 1, 33, 13), and so the canonist tradition developed identically.[20] True, there was constant discussion, and
some dissidents claimed that transfer of an unwilling vassal
might be made to another lord of higher authority, with a
theoretical benefit resulting to the vassal. Nevertheless, pre-
vailing opinion held against such transfer because of the significance attached to the vassal's own desire.[21] As Baldus later put
it, the special nature of the fief made it necessary for both
parties to agree to any change in the feudal contract.[22]

The opinions of Isernia indicate other views on the position
of the vassal which relate his alienation to the theory of the
public utility. The Sicilian jurist's views on this topic were
made in relation to the constitution *Imperialem* which had al-

---

[18] This is Azo's formulation of a question which concerned Philip Augustus, John,
and Arthur of Brittany: q. 13 in *Die Quaestiones des Azo* (ed. E. Landsberg, Freiburg
i. B., 1888), pp. 86 *et seq.* Not always, however, was Rex or Imperator specified,
and many discussions took in the problem of alienation to a "majori." On the
question of national citizenship, see the recent important article of Ernst Kantorowicz, "*Pro patria mori* in Medieval Political Thought," *A.H.R.*, LVI (1951), 472-92.
See also in this connection the article of Professor Strayer, "Defense of the Realm."

[19] Azo's references are spelled out in terms of modern citation on p. 87 of the
Landsberg edition. Another act of Frederick I bears mention: sec. 6 of the Treaty of
Roncaglia which forbids further subinfeudation, and prohibits a lord from trans-
ferring a vassal to another lord without the vassal's consent (*Constitutiones*, I, 248).

[20] Very probably it was the canonists who stressed the human element, emphasizing the rights of a free man. See the comments on X. 1, 33, 13 of Hostiensis, *Commentaria* (Venice, 1581), n. 3; Innocent IV, *Apparatus* (Venice, 1578); and Johannes
Andreae, *Commentaria* (Venice, 1581), n. 4.

[21] See, for example, Cynus, *Super codice* (Lyons, 1547), to C. 8, 41, 1 and
C. 5, 16, 26.

[22] *Consilia*, I, cons. 327, n. 1.

ready served a century as locus for similar comments.[23]    And what is important for our discussion is that he treats the alienation of royal lands, rights, and vassals all in the same discussion. If the vassal's alienation coincides with the best interests of the state as well as his own, fine; if not, then any such separation is invalid.    Then, to draw the network of concepts still closer, he cites *Intellecto* to show that all alienations harmful to royal dignity are without effect.    This is his extreme statement for the record, so to speak; moderation dictates his final opinion which is based upon the views of Innocent IV and Hostiensis, who sanctioned limited alienation in the interest of maintaining feudal society.    In effect, therefore, Isernia denies the alienation of vassals without their consent, while adding to the traditional justifying theories a criterion of public utility; and he simultaneously applies this criterion to the question always discussed in relation to *Intellecto,* that is, alienation of the principal foundations of majesty.[24]

Baldus was probably the first to go beyond Isernia's views, which represent what might be called the theoretical limit of the discussion in terms of feudalism.    Two ideas of his are important here.    The first is his statement that the king may not alienate " his people nor give them another king because a people is free despite its status under the king."    With this he underlines the idea that the rights of free people (and vassals) are outside the realm of commerce, and hence may not be alienated.[25]

More important for the present topic is the *consilium* in which he develops the idea of citizenship with regard to the nature of the individual and his status.    Having first posited such general principles as the need for mutual agreement between lord and vassal, the sanctity of the prince's word, and

[23] The general purport of Barbarossa's *Imperialem* was to forbid the alienation, by sale or any other means, of any fief or portion of a fief held from the emperor.

[24] *In feudorum,* II, 55, sec. 4, nn. 43-45.

[25] To *prooem. Digesti,* n. 18.

the prohibition of the alienation of unwilling vassals, he turns to the oath of allegiance. There are two types, he says, one the fealty of a feudal vassal, the other that of a person whose origin or domicile stamps him a citizen. Their difference is formal; they do not belong to the same species. And one sees this pragmatically, for according to Baldus, while the false vassal may lose his fief, theoretically the *raison d'être* of his relationship with his lord, the citizen can never lose his citizenship.[26] Here, applied to the people of the Italian city state, is the germ of the later idea of national citizenship. The nexus between ruler and ruled is no longer a personal and elaborate relationship of mutual dependency and respect. Rather it has become formally and legally an undeniable tie between the individual and the state, one end of which coheres to the individual despite his any action. Surely many social, political, and economic factors contributed to the appearance of this idea at the time of Baldus. It is suggested here that the legal background of the concept arose in the discussion of inalienability and is related to the wide contemporary mobilization of theories to protect the essential nature and rights of individuals and rulers. And the unity of the pattern of discussions centering about, or in relation to, the theory of inalienability is evident from Baldus' next statement, which refers to the emperor's responsibilities: he may not alienate the property of the Empire because he is not *dominus*, only *procurator maximus*.

After Baldus the question of vassals' alienations remained a live topic. A few jurists used a variant question to express their opinions on the Donation of Constantine: may a town be alienated without the consent of its citizens? Answering in the negative, they pointed out that since the legal donation of Rome would have required the consent of the people, Con-

---

[26] *Consilia*, I, cons. 327, nn. 3-7. See also his important remarks in *Consilia*, III, 159, n. 3: "... nam regnum continet in se non solum territorium ... sed etiam ipsos gentes regni quia ipsi populi collective regnum sunt et circumscripta obedientia populorum rex non posset dici regnare ...."

stantine must in fact have received such consent.[27]    So they
sanctioned the Donation, and from their assumption that Constantine did in fact receive the people's consent previous to his
transfer—one of the great events of Christian history—they
drew support for their view on the contemporary problem related to the theory of consent: they believed that the consent
of citizens should be sought when their interests were touched
in important matters of state.

Well into the sixteenth century French jurists continued to
relate these questions to contemporary affairs.    Their ideas were
not new; their purpose, the exaltation of the monarchy, was
not new either.    What perhaps was novel was their use of traditional legal principles in combination with history to support
claims of the state.    René Choppin, for example, while stating
that the king cannot alienate unwilling cities, refers to a letter
of the town of Uzès sent to the king in 1369.[28]    This plea referred to an ancient promise of the Crown never to separate the
town from its immediate jurisdiction—just that type of agreement we have repeatedly observed.    Another royalist writer,
following Baldus, Tartagnus, and Bartolus, denied the king the
right in question because he would thereby harm his successor
—again an example of reciprocal influence.[29]    It might well be
mentioned apropos this mutual dependence, that basic to the
requirement of consent before a noble or city might be alienated is the concept of *Quod omnes tangit* which, as we have
seen, is basic also to the theories of both renunciation and
alienation.

By the middle of the fourteenth century the political theo-

---

[27] Tartagnus, *Consiliorum voluminia quinque* (Venice, 1482), V, cons. 25.
Guy de la Pape, *Decisiones Gratianopolitanae* (Venice, 1558), decis. 239.    Also
interesting is decis. 560, which concerns the ability of a bishop to transfer his homage
without the consent of his city.    The answer is negative, and reference is again made
to Constantine, who acted *with* the consent of the Roman people.

[28] *De domanio Franciae* (4th ed., Frankfurt, 1701), lib. II, tit. 1.

[29] C. de Grassaille, *Regalium Franciae* (Paris, 1545), p. 27.

rists had identical thoughts on alienation without consent. Example may be given of Ockham who, denying the legality of the Donation of Constantine, claimed that without the tacit or expressed consent of all its people, the Roman Empire could not be divided or diminished.[30] Elsewhere he stated that while the Roman people may have been able, legally, to surrender all its rights as a people to the Papacy (through Constantine, of course) there remained certain rights which pertained to the Romans as individuals, and which, as individuals, they could not give up.[31] This is another influence of the complex of theories constituting the *Intellecto* tradition, and Ockham's repeated and accurate references to the legal texts document their importance for his thought.

This argument of Ockham's brings up one more relationship of the *Intellecto* theme to the main problems of medieval political thought: the question of the people's renunciation of its law-making powers to a higher authority. Medieval legal discussion of this issue—essentially a matter of pure theory since no real way was ever found in the Middle Ages to realize the effective participation of the " people " in government—began with the revival of Roman law studies in the late eleventh century. Irnerius took the position that the people through disuse had lost to the emperor the authority and privilege to make law. He stated, however, that the office imposed upon the ruler the obligation to care for his people as he would his own children.[32] Placentinus in a sense was harsher, for he made

---

[30] *Dialogus* 3, 2, 1, 31, in *Monarchia,* II, 901-2; and *Octo quaestiones* q. 8, cap. 3, *idem,* 384. For an identical rationalization of the Donation on grounds of consent, see Tholommeo de Lucca, *Determinatio compendiosa de jurisdictione imperii* (ed. M. Krammer, Hanover and Leipzig, 1909), p. 51.

[31] *Dialogus* 3, 2, 1, 30, in *Monarchia,* II, 902-1 (*sic*).

[32] *Summa codicis,* to C. 1, 14, 3 and his gloss to D. 1, 3, 32, reprinted by Savigny, *Geschichte,* IV, 459. I owe these references to A. J. Carlyle, "The Theory of the Source of Political Authority in the Medieval Civilians to the Time of Accursius," in *Mélanges Fitting,* I, 185-86. According to Carlyle, this view was also held by Placentinus and Rogerius.

the surrender by the people a definite act and at the same time
asserted the superiority of the written law and confirmed act
over custom.[33]  Against this position in the early glossator debate
stands that of Hugolinus, who conceived the emperor as *procurator ad hoc* to whom the people had merely delegated its
authority.  Later he was supported by Azo, who in addition
defended the people's right to recall its commission.[34]

In this tradition the various opinions were stated in interpretation of specific passages in the *Corpus,* and although the
legists were concerned to confirm the privileges to the Church
which were accorded by other titles in Justinian's books, they
never appealed to theological theories of society in their explanation of the source of power in the state.  It was the canonists as a group in the late twelfth century who introduced
new problems and new papalist solutions.  The question as they
saw it—and here the great papal ambitions of the period must
be remembered—was whether the emperor received his *iurisdictio* directly from God or through the agency of the pope.
Discussion was continuous from the Investiture controversy,
but it was only at the time of Huguccio that major theses were
developed in canonist legal writings.  In effect the canonists
by-passed the specific question of the people's action because
they were more concerned to prove that secular authority came
to the emperor through the agency of the pope than they were
about theories of popular sovereignty.  When they did comment on the question, however, the majority held that the people retained ultimate authority and could revoke it: another
theoretical limitation upon imperial power.  Against such a
view wrote Rufinus somewhat previous to the group of papal-
ists active towards the end of the century; in favor were

---

[33] *In codicis . . . libros IX summa* (Mainz, 1536), p. 6.

[34] Hugolinus, *Dist.* XXXIV, in *Dissensiones dominorum* (ed. G. Haenel, Leipzig,
1834), cited by Carlyle, "Theory of Political Authority," pp. 191-92.  Azo,
*Summa* (Lyons, 1533), to C. 1, 14, n. 8.  Bulgarus also supported this view.

Laurentius, Sylvester Hispanus, and Joannes Galensis.[35] Damasus held likewise, but believed too that the secular *iurisdictio* came directly from God.[36] Hostiensis, formalizing the pretensions of the great contemporary popes, discarded the issue altogether in his assertion of the immediate dependence of the emperor upon the pope for his authority.[37]

As a body, it was the post-glossators and commentators who discussed the people's renunciation in terms familiar to our theme, for they linked it to the debate over the legality of Constantine's Donation, with specific regard to the surrender of territory and privilege. Johannes Butrigarius (ca. 1274–1348), who finally accepted the Donation, at one time held that Constantine could have surrendered his authority over the western regions only into the hands of the Roman people. Considering the text upon which he made his comment—a law in the *Digest* which states that the emperor's deputy or a provincial governor does not lose his authority by relinquishing his office—Johannes may be interpreted as believing that any transfer of imperial power could originate only with the people, and that before a new delegation might be made, such authority had to be returned to them.[38]

Isernia was interested less in abstract political considerations than in exalting his king with the means at his command, legal theory. He quibbled on the Donation, saying that the gift was to God, not to the pope, and that the territory reverted to the

---

[35] For Rufinus, see Mochi-Onory, *Fonti canonistiche*, p. 193; for Laurentius and Johannes Galensis, *ibid.*, pp. 245, 246; and for Silvester, G. Post, "Some unpublished glosses," p. 414. In Silvester we find clearly expressed the notion that the secular *imperium* is God-created, while the individual emperor is people-elected.

[36] *Burchardica* (Lyons, 1566), reg. 127.

[37] *Summa* (Venice, 1574), to X. 3, 49. But a generation before Hostiensis, Goffredus de Trani discussed the ability of the people to revoke its grant of law-making power to the emperor (*Summa* [Venice, 1586], fol. 2v).

[38] *Additio* to D. 1, 18, 20 in *Corpus iuris civilis* (Venice, 1591). Baldus, in his commentary on the *prooem.* of the *Code*, n. 8, after mentioning that Butrigarius did hold such an opinion against the Donation, says "postea mutavit opinio et bene quia cum Papa sit superior . . . ."

Empire after the death of Sylvester.[39]  This view is a hedge also for the reason that Isernia elsewhere states that the king—already established as emperor within his own realm—being the object of the people's surrender of its rights, may not further separate the people from them.  Since cities, too, have sacrificed final authority over themselves to the king, he is supreme over both within his state.  However, given this exalted status, the ruler must never delegate power so as to lose its ultimate control.  Isernia bases this view upon the passage in the *Code* which states the people's surrender of its law-making ability.  And so, in distinguishing between *transferre* and *totaliter a se abdicare*, he forbids the latter mode of delegation because of the king's ultimate responsibility to his subjects.[40]

Baldus related the surrender of peoples' rights to another of the standard arguments against the Donation: the *reductio ad absurdam* that the Empire would soon be nought were each emperor permitted to grant away such great territories and rights.  The initial delegation of the people had constituted a certain *imperium* with definite limits and characteristics; were it to be divided its essential character would be lost.  And in so dividing the *imperium* the emperor would violate the condition of the state desired by those who had given him his office.[41]  The views of other jurists relegated the people to a lesser role in the formation of a constitution.  Lucas de Penna, for example, exalted the monarch in an absolutist sense, affirming that he held directly from God without the mediation of the people or of the pope.[42]  Johannes Faber achieved a compro-

[39] *In feudorum*, lib. I, tit. 1, n. 10.

[40] *Constitutionis regni utriusque Siciliae glossis* . . . (Lyons, 1559), col. 8 of *prooem*.  The passages in the *Digest* relating to the cession of the Roman people's rights are *D*. 1, 4, 1, and 1, 11, 1; and in the *Code*, 1, 17, 1, 7.

[41] *Super digestis* (Lyons, 1535–36), to *prooem*. n. 18.  For his opinion on the essential nature of the *imperium*, he cites *D*. 1, 5, 8, which protects the status of a child against forceful alteration of his legal position, and also *D*. 34, 3, 29, which refers to the indissoluble nature of a partnership.

[42] W. Ullman, *The Medieval Idea of Law: Lucas de Penna* (London, 1946), p. 51, cites Lucas' comment on *C*. 12, 35, 14, n. 9: sovereign rights are inseparable because

mise: temporal power does not come straight from God, but rather is directly conferred by the people with His permission.[43] And from this steady but inconclusive discussion in which it had been treated in relation to a good many of the principal issues of medieval public law, the question passed over into the books of the political theorists.

For Ockham, the source of the emperor's power is the people through whose action he is delegated his office.[44] And, as the people is the source of power, so too is it always a potential cause of deposition; an action always possible, but advisable only under extraordinary circumstances.[45] The emperor, therefore, has certain obligations to the people: he may never injure either the imperial dignity or the public welfare.[46] He is presumed to have certain rights in common with the people which he may not alienate. His subjects' consent is necessary for any transfer of land or prerogative, because ultimate authority, Ockham says, rests " apud universitatem mortalium." This appeal to the greatest possible number dovetails neatly with his claim that it was only when all the world had been united under the Roman Empire that the Roman people's rights became inalienable without universal consent. The reasoning here is analogous to the idea, embodied in the laws of the *Corpus iuris civilis,* that the emperor may not prejudice his equal, that is his successor: the Roman people may not prejudice future generations. It is only when all the people consent that public law may be abrogated, provided of course that the law in question is not at the same time divine or natural law. Here Ockham's analogue is the *privilegium fori* which the individual

---

they are " de regis ossibus inhaerentibus," and inalienable because held in trust " quorum omnium auctoritas et potestas est solis regibus et principibus a Deo concessa."

43 *In quattuor libros institutionum commentaria* (Venice, 1572), to *Inst.* 1, 2, n. 2.

44 *Breviloquium,* VI, c. 2; *Tractatus . . . matrimoniali* in *Opera politica* (ed. J. G. Sikes, Manchester, 1940), I, 283-84.

45 *Octo quaestiones,* p. 87. See also Lupold von Bebenberg, *Tractatus de iuribus regni et imperii* (Augsburg, 1603), p. 114.

46 *De imperatorum et pontificum potestate* (ed. K. Brampton, Oxford, 1927), pp. 35-36.

cleric may not renounce to the injury of the entire ecclesiastical community. The principle of *Quod omnes tangit* is specifically cited by Ockham at this point as his guiding concept.[47]

The intended emphasis in this discussion of the popular surrender of sovereignty to the emperor is upon the relationship of the *Intellecto* theme with one of the most fundamental theoretical issues of politics. Not only did the surrender of rights become an issue itself; it brought up for discussion subsidiary problems the solutions to which ultimately had to be accounted for in the treatment of the original issue. It is in this way that the theory of inalienability of sovereignty justifies its presence here, for the medieval jurists and theorists were often dependent on the criteria developed in relation to the *Intellecto* for their opinions as to the final source of authority in the state. In this way the question of the Donation involved several legists in a discussion of the people's rights, alienable and inalienable. From this problem it was but a step for Isernia to the next question, the ruler's responsibility to his people once it had granted him authority. Baldus went on and postulated for the people's surrender of rights a definite office which these rights constituted, an office endowed with specific powers which it was henceforth the ruler's duty to fulfill and preserve. And, as we have seen, the theorist Ockham, with his own axe to grind, stressed the ultimate rulership of the people, its rights in common with the emperor, and the need for its consent when common interests were at stake. In his formulation we have a full appreciation of the rich woven texture of medieval public law.

[47] *Dialogus* 3, 2, 1, 29, and 31, in *Monarchia*, II, 901-2.

# VII

## *The Continuity of Office and State*

CONTINUITY for the state was implied and sustained by the concept of the Crown, the restraining clause of the coronation oath, and the solutions offered to the question we have just discussed. It was all the more strongly developed as one of the theoretical supports of the monarchies in discussions concerning the relationship of the ruler both to the fisc or treasury of his realm, and to the obligations assumed by his predecessor on the throne. As we shall see, these matters were not treated within the purview of an academic private law. Rather, they were recognized for what they were, problems of deep constitutional importance, and they were seen, perhaps not as clearly as we see them today, to be questions of public law. As such they gained in significance because the king was involved, and simultaneously they reflected back upon the kingship theories exalting it. The theory of inalienability entered the picture because the same questions raised with respect to the ruler's prerogatives were raised with regard to the fisc as well. And the public utility, which had been established as final criterion by which the justice and legality of ecclesiastical, regal, and imperial alienations were measured, was discussed in terms of alienation, a ruler's obligations, and those of the fisc.

The Donation of Constantine again provided the link joining these related questions and theories. One very common argument against the Donation was based upon the impropriety of Constantine's action arising from his legal incapacity to injure his successor. The titles in the law books cited here by the

jurists were those which prohibited a Roman public official
from imposing his authority upon another of equal dignity and
rank.   Since, of course, one emperor was supposed to rule with
the same *imperium* as another, this protection easily was carried over the moment of succession by the legists and applied
to the status of two emperors, one living, the other deceased.
So, as the question of alienation was always linked to that of
the Donation, it was also discussed in terms of the emperor's
prejudice of his successor and the several questions arising from
this principle with which we are now concerned: the relationship of the fisc to the ruler's patrimony, prescription against
both these institutions, and the revocation of ill-advised
donations.

We must begin with the canonists, for the Church was
touched here on two points: oaths were involved; moreover,
the canonists were always concerned to express an opinion on
any issue related to the Donation.   With rare exception they
believed that the emperor's oath upon the gift did bind his successor for all time.[1]   Yet, qualifications were introduced early
to render the implications of such an injunction equitable.
Huguccio, referring to Louis the Pious' cession to the Roman
people of the right to elect the pope, stated that neither pope
nor emperor might surrender rights the loss of which would
injure his successors.[2]   Paulus Ungarus (d. ca. 1250) agreed,
asserting in the same breath that a bishop must continue the

---

[1] An exception I have noted is the early canonist Damasus who, in regard to the
question, " Quod Imperator non habet iurisdictionem a Papa," after opposing
citations *pro* and *contra*, states " Dicunt non nulli, Imperatorem habere gladium a
Papa, quia Constantinum Imperium reliqueret Romanae Ecclesiae ut . . . . Verius
tamen est quod a Deo habeat, quemadmodum dicit Augustinus . . . . Nec enim
apparet Papam imperium accepisse, neque Constantinus potuit successori suo praeiudi-
care " (*Burchardica* [Cologne, 1564], reg. 127).

[2] *Summa*, Vatican MS lat. 2280, fol. 65v, to *Dist.* LXIII, c. 30 (*Ego Ludovicus*)
ad vv. *electionem faciendi*: " sed nunquid haec renuntiatio potuit facere praeiudicium
successoribus, non videtur quia sicut factum papae non ligat successorem ita nec
factum imperatoris."

good works begun by his predecessor and that renunciations of rights should not be honored if fraudulently obtained.[3] And Johannes Teutonicus held much the same opinion: both pope and emperor may bind future rulers, but each should live and act in accordance with the best and established principles of conduct.[4] Later canonists sanctioned this view: Bartholomaeus Brixiensis (d. 1258), Hostiensis, and Panormitanus. With little variation they approved both the commitment and the safeguard against injurious actions.[5] In effect this was a translation into the terms of our immediate subject, the question of the force and permanence of a ruler's agreement, of the workable approach to feudal alienation which had been emphasized by Hostiensis and Innocent IV. Thus Durandus cites Johannes de Deo to the effect that alienations made for the founding of churches by one ruler may be revoked by another only if " Imperium vel Regnum vel Ducatus *enormiter laedantur*." [6] On the moral side, the canonists reasoned that the oath taken by a new authority on his accession to office effectively brought upon him the obligations of his predecessors.[7]

The teaching of the civilians offers much the same theory. From Azo on, emphasis is upon the ruler's living in accordance with the law. Yet, although not one of the legists suggested coercion, the force of tradition and moral suasion is at the same moment necessary and regarded as adequate restraint. Now, to bring out the problems in relation to which our present

[3] Vatican MS Borgh. 261, fol. 76v, gloss to *Comp. II.* 1, 15, 1 (*Sane dilecto filio: X.* 1, 9, 7).

[4] *Glossa ordinaria* (Venice, 1514), to *Ca.* XII, q. 2, c. 20 (*Non licet*) ad v. *Pape.* When Johannes and the others spoke of the ruler living according to law, they invariably referred to the *Lex regia, D.* 1, 4, 1, and also to *C.* 1, 14, 4, *Digna vox.*

[5] Bartholomaeus Brixiensis, *Glossa* to *Ca.* XII, q. 2, c. 20 (*Non licet*) (Mainz, 1472); Hostiensis, *Summa* (Venice, 1574), col. 1390, to *X.* 4, 17 (*Qui filii sint legitimi*); Panormitanus (Venice, 1578), to *X.* 2, 19, 1; 3, 13, 4.

[6] *Speculum iuris* (Venice, 1585), II, 677-78 (*De instrumentorum editione*), n. 11.

[7] *Super clementinis* (Lyons, 1520), fol. 28 (*De iureiurando*), nn. 11-12.

theme was discussed, we must treat several jurists in some detail, and follow the arguments as developed in relation to contemporary events.

What is at once striking is the frequency with which the theme " Par in parem non habet imperium " was discussed in relation to the law *Digna vox* (C. 1, 14, 4).[8] Azo, Cynus, Baldus, Albericus, all agreed in their commentaries upon this text that as a general rule the ruler should recognize the contracts and obligations of his predecessor—the inference being that legal actions of the ruler were to be recognized after his death.[9] Emphasis was on the legality of the acts, for there was equal sentiment that the illegal contracts and personal wicked-ness of former rulers were not to hurt the new one.[10] But besides *Digna vox,* other laws were chosen for the *locus ad quem* of a commentary. Bartolus, for example, related the whole problem to the Donation, and arranged all arguments which would favor the continuity of imperial obligations to support it. The contrary views which would have implied a break in imperial (and national) continuity, are those he rejects. This opposition to the Donation is common to other commentaries which discuss both sides of the question, and it is obvious that had the legists not given the Church special consideration they would have had to recognize that the emperor did in fact prejudice his successor. Bartolus' equivocation is very indicative of this dilemma, for, having discussed in the traditional

---

[8] The theory of *Digna vox* was fundamental to one main current of medieval political thought, what might be called the constitutional and legal emphasis. The principle stated was that the king should live according to, hence under, law.

[9] One explanation for the continuous treatment of this question is the fact that it had been developing as a school question, and as such had to be noticed by the professors. Cynus, *Lectura* (Frankfurt, 1578), to C. 1, 14, 4: " Ultimo sciendum quod Guido da Suzaria formavit hic questionem . . . ." See also Baldus, *Consilia,* III, cons. 371; Azo, *Summa* (Lyons, 1532), to C. 1, 14, n. 17; Accursius, *Glossa ordinaria,* to D. 36, 1, 13, 4; and Albericus, *Super codici* (Lyons, 1545), to C. 7, 37, 3, and C. 1, 14, 4.

[10] Oldradus, *Consilia* (Venice, 1570), cons. 94; Baldus, *Consilia* (Frankfurt, 1589), I, cons. 271.

manner the two sets of opposing arguments, he decides in favor of the Donation because he was then living in pro-papal territory. His phraseology indicates a consciousness of the whole play: " sed si quis vellet tenere opinionem quod non valuerit [the Donation] posset respondere ad contraria et probare opinionem per causam digna vox." In effect he tells the reader what his opinion might otherwise have been, and bases the rejected view upon a general theory of wise government buttressed by more specific arguments restricting the emperor's freedom of action.[11]

In the *consilia* of Baldus we come to grips with more contemporary problems of public law, and it should be emphasized, considering the lack of attention paid to the entire body of *consilia* literature, that questions of this type were presented for comment as well as those of more particular private law interest.[12] The most significant *consilium* for the present topic is that which concerns the plea of the great Genoese Spinola family against John I, king of Portugal, concerning one of their ships which had been captured by King Ferdinand before his death. A fight for the succession developed between Ferdinand's son-in-law, John I of Castile, and his natural brother, John. The latter succeeded finally in securing his position, and had himself elected king by the nobles. When asked for restitution of the captured Genoese goods he replied that he was an elected ruler, hence not bound by the observances of hereditary succession to acknowledge the obligations of his predecessor.

[11] Comment to the *prooem.* of the *Digest* in *Opera omnia* (Venice, 1596), nn. 13-14. He writes (sec. 14): " nos summus in terris amicis et ideo dico quod ista donatio valeat "; and in another passage: ". . . sed volens favere ecclesiae dico quod illa donatio valuit." Notice might be taken of his schematic Aristotelianism: he writes that both the Empire and the Church owe their authority directly to God who thus is the *causa efficiens*; so the Donation was valid because Constantine surrendered all to God's vicar, the pope. See also his comment on D. 43, 23, 3, nn. 1-5.

[12] I am at present engaged in a study of public law problems as developed in this literature, and have preferred here to limit my discussions of *consilia* to material pertinent to the theory of inalienability.

Baldus realized the full implications of the case and made his *responsum* the vehicle for his opinions on a whole range of connected ideas, all bearing ultimately on the growth of the national state.

Although a limited legal issue was involved, Baldus at the outset relates it to the familiar school question formulated by Guido da Suzaria: " utrum si Imperator ineat aliqua pacta cum aliqua civitate vel barone, teneatur ea observare tam ipse quam eius successores? " He then establishes the foundation for the rest of his discussion by affirming the immediate appropriateness and validity of such general principles as " grave est fidem fallere; naturalia iura suadent pacta servari; honestas ligat etiam principem; contractus principis est lex."

From these maxims it immediately follows that the king is indeed bound to honor the public obligations of his predecessor. The question is not of the means to the throne, hereditary succession or election, but rather of the permanence of the throne itself, or the Crown, and the responsibility of the ruler to maintain the honor of his kingdom. In this connection Baldus introduces one of the concepts we have emphasized, the emperor or king as temporary official, and his statement of the issue must be explained. His comment reads:

Rex potest obligare fiscum regni sui, non tantum quia est legitimus administrator, sed etiam quia habetur loco domini . . . dum tamen non faciat aliquem contractum per quem monarchia Regni et honor corone diminui possit ut . . . Intellecto . . . (et) Grandi . . . et hoc verum est, non solita faciendo sed etiam insolita aggrediendo. Quia regnum magis assimilatur dominio quam simplici regimini.[13]

Taken at face value, and interpreting " habetur loco domini " in the sense that the king is indeed held or considered

---

[13] *Consilia*, I, cons. 271, n. 3. Besides giving *Intellecto* as a reference here, he also refers to C. 7, 37, 3 which includes the classic statement of Justinian: " cum omnia principis esse intelligantur " which itself gave rise to much controversy, and besides was a favorite departure point for discussions of the Donation of Constantine and related problems.

to be *dominus,* this is a bald statement of the ruler's absolute
ownership of the kingdom. This idea, however, Baldus rejects
as did the great majority of civilians from the time the famous
question was asked of Bulgarus and Martinus by Frederick
Barbarossa. It is also at variance with his opinion in another
*consilium* in which he talks of the *tutela* of the kingdom. This
*consilium* is itself important for its denial to the kings of the
right to alienate in the manner of Constantine. Significantly,
Baldus does this on the basis of his denial to kings of the power
to prejudice their successors.[14] This comparison of *rex* with
*dominus* must be therefore an exaggeration made to emphasize
his point. But this was not an exaggeration without historical
causation, nor for that matter, historical effect. The medieval
lawyers to this moment had consciously developed a theory of
Crown in harmony with their theory of office. The universal
respect for law and tradition itself had emphasized the limitations upon the Crown. What this statement of Baldus does is
emphasize the powers inherent in the Crown's possessor, and in
the course of the next three hundred years this new element
was to prove historically most potent. Yet, despite this new
emphasis, Baldus continued to stress the traditional obligations
of kingship as developed by his predecessors and contemporaries, and by himself in other comments. Immediately after
his statement that the king " habetur loco domini," he specifically notes that he cannot engage himself so that the " honor
corone diminui possit," and gives as justification for this view
a reference to *Intellecto.* His immediate assimilation of such a
protected kingdom to a prince in the role of absolute *dominus*
—this is the novelty here.[15]

14 *Consilia,* III, cons. 159, n. 3. " Et haec vera sunt nisi Rex aliquid ordinaverit
in praeiudicium regni quia talis ordinatio ruit cum cessione, si laederit enormiter
ipsum regnum. quicquid dicitur de donatione Constantini quae fuit miraculosa, si
similes donationes fierent a regibus non ligarent successores, quibus Regni tutela non
dilapidatio est concessa."

15 It is interesting to note that when the great French royalist legists of the
seventeenth century treated this topic, they removed from the ruler *any* legal

That the novelty is a restrained one is evidenced by Baldus' other views in the Spinola *consilium*. Although the new king and the fisc are bound by previously made contracts, the ruler himself may not be touched, nor may his *dignitas* be affected, by the guilt of personal crimes attributable to his predecessor. A distinction is made between the king's private patrimony and the property of the fisc. Contracts made by the king in his private capacity do not bind the fisc, provided that he allows himself to be attacked under the law as he should. In other words, Baldus allows two obligations to stand from one reign to another: the contracts properly made by the king in his public capacity under the civil law, and those of the impersonal institutional fisc. And what is implied in addition is the responsibility of the ruler to honor the legitimate private commitments of his predecessor, a theme which he develops in other *consilia*.[16] Finally, we may note that Baldus was careful to include feudal relationships in his schema. The emperor, and inferentially the king, should be allowed to assign land and jurisdictional authority certain that his successor will recognize his grants and appointments.[17]

As the pro-papal legists used the idea that a ruler could bind his successor to support their approval of the Donation, and

---

obligation to honor the debts of his predecessors. (By that time other fundamental laws secured the theoretical continuity of the state, yet in this aspect the theorists did not bother to secure a full circle of protections.) The only obligation imposed upon the sovereign was a moral one. Nevertheless, rulers specifically were not supposed to alienate from the royal demesne, for the ruler is a tutor, etc. Here then we find the incompatibility of the concepts of the king as tutor and legally irresponsible autocrat (C. Le Bret, *De la souveraineté du roy* [Paris, 1632], pp. 621-24, and Charles Loyseau, *Des offices* [Paris, 1610], lib. II, cap. 2, n. 34).

[16] See, in addition, Vol. I, cons. 326, n. 10, where he speaks of the prince binding the fisc "de iure naturali"; and Vol. III, cons. 371.

[17] *Consilia*, I, cons. 333, n. 1. It should be noted that, like Bartolus, Baldus denies the ruler ability to prejudice and bind his successor in those passages in which he presents arguments against the legality of the Donation. See his comment on the *prooem.* of the *Digest*, n. 18, to the initial rubric *De novo codice componendo* of the *Code*; and to D. 1, 4, 1 (*Quod principi placuit* . . . ) where he would have to grant the ruler absolute freedom in order not to contradict himself.

from their acceptance of the Donation immediately applied this new authority to bolster their view of the successor's responsibility . . . so too did the imperial theorists use such a double *petitio principii* for their own purposes.  Ockham's view is best set forth in the final short summation of his political views written in 1347, the *De imperatorum et pontificum potestate*.  In the chapters wherein he is most concerned to exalt the Empire as against the Papacy, he states that the emperor may not transfer his authority so that his successors have less *imperium* than he.  His arguments are identical to those marshalled and then rejected by Bartolus, Baldus, and the others, with the difference that Ockham's emphasis is philosophical not legal.  How, he asks, can the new emperor be a *verus successor*, should his predecessor have surrendered integral rights of the *imperium* to the pope? [18]  Basic to this viewpoint are the assumptions that secular authority derives directly from God without papal intervention, and that this authority, the *imperium*, is definitely constituted with certain properties which make it what it is.  Given these assumptions, we see that Ockham's approach here is based upon that Aristotelian view of definition which we have already seen applied to the notion of office.

In that same *consilium* in which he discussed the responsibilities of a ruler to the obligations of his predecessors, Baldus pointed up the immediacy of the theory of inalienability to another contemporary dispute: the precise relationship of the ruler's private patrimony to the fisc.[19]  In distinguishing be-

---

[18] *De imperatorum* . . . (ed. K. Brampton, Oxford, 1927), pp. 32-36.  See also the treatise *An princeps* in Sikes, *Opera politica*, p. 263, where Ockham states that the pledges of predecessors should be strictly interpreted so that the least possible power is given to the pope; and the *Dialogus* 3, 2, 1, 18 in *Monarchia*, II, 886-87.  Also Lupold von Bebenberg, *Tractatus de iuribus regni* . . . , pp. 78-79; and John of Paris, *Tractatus de regia potestate et papali* in *Monarchia*, II, 140, both of whom were against both the Donation and the idea that a ruler could prejudice his successor.

[19] Still the most detailed account of the ancient and medieval ideas of the fisc is the article of F. E. Vassalli, "Concetto e natura del fisco," *Studi Senesi*, XXV

tween the two and asserting on the basis of *Intellecto* that the ruler might not make any contract "per quem monarchia Regni et honor corone diminui possit," he touched upon another of the conceptual interactions through which the *Intellecto* tradition contributed to the changing medieval theory of the state.[20] Baldus, however, was not the first to develop the connection; a traditional problem examined by all the glossators was the question: "Fiscus et respublica, an idem est?" and related discussions. The usual response that they were not, and that in addition to the Empire (which was the originally limited reference for *respublica*) every free city and kingdom which did not recognize a superior was itself a *respublica* and was entitled to a fisc of its own. In this vein wrote Isernia and Lucas de Penna, which is to be expected considering their antiimperial orientation; also Bartolus, who in every way tried his best to establish a reasonable relationship between the Empire and the many *de facto* polities which now confronted it.[21] Also in line with this realism were the writers who defined the fisc as the organ of the state which collected the taxes and disbursed monies for the maintenance of public affairs.[22]

---

(1908). More recent is Ernst Kantorowicz, "Christus-Fiscus," in *Synopsis: Festgabe für Alfred Weber* (Heidelberg, 1948). In his article Professor Kantorowicz emphasizes the unusual nature of the distinction between the office and person of a ruler in medieval thought, and also the importance for the idea of the fisc of the Romanocanonical notion of *persona ficta*. Vassalli concentrates upon the views of the civilians; their major tradition regarded the fisc as an organ of government of which the emperor or king was the administrator.

[20] *Consilia*, I, cons. 271, n. 3.

[21] Isernia, *Feudorum*, to *prooem.* (Naples, 1571), col. 15; Lucas, *Lectura* (Lyons, 1538), to C. 10, 10, 1; Bartolus, *Commentaria* (Venice, 1596), to C. 10, 1, nn. 3-5. On Bartolus, especially, but also for an introduction to this problem, see F. Ercole, *Da Bartolo all'Althusio* (Florence, 1932), pp. 76-78. The work of S. Woolf, *Bartolus de Sassoferrato* (Cambridge, 1913), is still fundamental for Bartolist political theory; and the author's principal topic is the legist's solution to this conflict between theory and reality.

[22] See Lucas, *Lectura* (Lyons, 1538), to C. 11, 58, 7: ". . . est sacus imperii, in quem omnes fructus redditusque et proventus rei publice ponebantur . . . . Nam fiscus est pars rei publice"; Baldus, *Consilia*, I, cons. 271, n. 2; Martinus Laudensis, *De fisco*, in *Tractatus universi juris*, XII, q. 141: "Bursa communis idem est quod

Having established a hierarchy of fiscs, the legists had then
to delineate the functional differences between the fisc and
patrimony.  We can best see how they did this by examining
the works of two differently oriented men: Baldus who followed his master, Bartolus, in supporting as far as he could the
traditional position of the emperor, and Petrus de Bellapertica
who worked for the Capetian court.

Baldus treats the fisc as merely part of the body politic, and
indeed refers to it as *Reipublicae anima.*  As such it is eternal,
and although it may be bound by the ruler, it may not be
harmed.[23]  It is here that he remarks that the king is perhaps
more than *administrator* and approaches *dominus.*  From this
juxtaposition of ideas we can see Baldus moving away from the
traditional idea of the ruler's guardianship and towards the
more modern concept of the absolute state.  A certain degree
of novelty is evident here, as has been suggested, for most of
his contemporaries; certainly the major antecedent tradition
strongly negated the concept of ruler as absolute *dominus,* and
just as firmly emphasized the special benefits to be accorded the
properties of an independent and impersonal fisc.[24]  This is
true not only of legal thought, but also of contemporary publicist writing.  Here the theory was that the fisc was distinct,
yet under the guardianship of the ruler who was bound to control it with utmost consideration for the welfare of his people.[25]

---

fiscus "; Jacobus Rebuffi, *Lectura super tribus ultimis libris codicis* (Turin, 1591),
to C. 10, 1, nn. 2-3; Albericus de Rosate, *Vocabularium iuris* (Venice, 1494):
" *Fiscus* . . . est saccus regius in quem reducuntur vel cui applicuntur bona banni-
torum vel praescriptorum . . . . vel est regii vel imperialis thesauri congregatio . . . ";
Paul de Castro, *Super codice* (Venice, 1550), to C. 2, 54, 4.

23 *Consilia,* I, cons. 271, n. 3. Here Baldus refers to *Intellecto* and to the decretal
*Grandi,* VI, 1, 8, 2 which provides that advisors be given to a rash ruler and which,
as we shall see, was important for other aspects of the theory of inalienability.

24 Accursius, *Glossa ordinaria,* to C. 7, 37, 3, ad vv. *omnia principis;* Cynus,
*Super codice* (Lyons, 1547), to C. 7, 38, 6; Lucas, *Lectura* (Lyons, 1538), to C.
11, 58, 7; Albericus, *Super codice* (Lyons, 1545), to C. 7, 37, 3, n. 25.

25 See John of Paris, *Tractatus de regia potestate et papali* in *Monarchia,* II, 140;
and Ockham, *Octo quaestiones* in *Monarchia,* II, 336.

Petrus' analysis is set forth in his commentary on the *pro-oemium* of the *Institutes,* and it stems directly from his discussion of the Donation of Constantine, the legal validity of which he rejects.[26] He does not, however, forbid all imperial alienation to the church, only such grand giving as might result in a veritable change in the nature of the state. Should the emperor wish to give, he may donate freely from the goods of his personal treasury, but not from the wealth of the fisc. Of the latter he is only *administrator,* hence without the absolute freedom conveyed by full *dominium.* Prescription may operate against the private patrimony which, however, received the same privileges as the fisc in this case. Nevertheless, not every possession and right of the fisc may be the object of prescription; public property is divided into two categories. The first of these consists in what we would broadly call public utilities—his example is a public street—and such public property may never be acquired by private persons. The second group, vaguer in outline, comprises properties which are not essentially concerned with the public utility but which touch it " per quandam consequentiam," and these may be lost by prescription over forty years. Petrus concludes his discussion by declaring that goods pertaining to the ruler *qua* ruler, that is, in his public capacity, may never be prescribed. In other words the public properties immediately subject to the ruler are approximated to the higher class of public goods, and are exceptionally protected.[27]

[26] In general, I tend to give greater weight to opinions expressed in commentaries on broadly theoretical passages than to those made in relation to a specific *lex*. It is difficult at times to distinguish between a writer's accurate *explication du texte* and his opinions as evidenced elsewhere in a theoretical observation. In their desire to be precise the legists often contradicted their basic positions in glosses to particular laws; in commentaries on *prooemia,* however, they were likely to indicate the basic texts and offer fundamental views.

[27] The argument may be followed in Bellapertica's *In libros institutionum . . . commentarii* (Lyons, 1536), to *prooem.,* nn. 11-16. See too his *Lectura . . . super prima parte codice* (Paris, 1519), to C. 4, 52, 2.

These opinions of Petrus introduce another topic which inspired important views on the question of the emperor's relation both to his own people and the independent monarchies: the question of prescription against the ruler and the fisc. As in other cases, there was no unanimity of opinion, and jurists of equal power were found on opposite sides. What is significant for us here, it must be stressed, is not so much the specific requirement of thirty, forty, or one hundred years, which varied according to circumstance, as the connection this particular problem had with the other elements which ultimately constituted a theory of inalienability.

In general, the legists allowed the operation of prescription against the fisc, at the same time following Justinian's law by demanding greater periods of time for its accomplishment than necessary against private individuals. Both Azo and Accursius permitted such action against the fisc, yet both asserted the precaution that properties in public use, secular as well as ecclesiastical, might not be lost to the state this way.[28] Johannes Faber based his opinion upon the degree of public importance of the thing in question, and was absolute in disallowing prescription of things whose loss would affect all the people.[29] Baldus allowed that *utilitas* of public goods might be prescribed, but never absolute *dominium*; and it should be noted, in line with our attempt to emphasize the influence of private law concepts upon public law, that in the same passage he denies prescription of both public properties and the liberty of a free man.[30] The Sicilian jurists allowed prescription against

---

[28] Azo, *Summa aurea* (Lyons, 1532), to C. 7, 37, 3, n. 2; C. 7, 37, 4.

[29] *In Institutionum* (Venice, 1572), to *Inst.* 2, 6, n. 5.

[30] *Commentaria . . . in feudorum*, n. 3; and to C. 6, 1, n. 30: " Solve quaedam non possunt alienari propter rem ipsam, ut homo liber, domus sacra, campus martius . . . via publica et similia, et ista praescribi non possunt." In his commentary on the *prooem.* to the *Code*, n. 10, Baldus uses a phrase which indicates the active nature of the discussion which centered about the Donation of Constantine and the issues of alienation and prescription which were discussed in connection with it. Speaking

the Empire for political reasons, for in this way they gave yet another legal justification for the independence of their kingdom from the Empire.[31]   But once the position of the kingdom had been established, the representative of the next generation of theorists was not so liberal.   Lucas de Penna absolutely condemned the prescription of *regalia*, the royal *iurisdictio*, or any aspect of the *merum et mistum imperium*.   Although for purposes of administration he had to allow delegation of authority, he was severe in adding that such delegations were *ad hoc* and might never be fully acquired.   Lucas believed that by any diminution of the royal *iurisdictio*, " disrumperetur nervus publice discipline et ideo reprobatur."   However, following the line developed by his predecessors, he allowed that those already in possession of the *imperium vel iurisdictionem* might aggrandize their powers.   This notion of public powers prescribing against public powers was meant of course to operate against the Empire to the ultimate benefit of the Sicilian kingdom.[32]

The canonist view on prescription against the prince and the public fisc was well summarized by Panormitanus, and is a mediate position.   *Merum et mistum imperium* may sometimes be won by prescription from the emperor, but only with his consent, and never with respect to aspects of his authority which pertain to him " in signum cuiusdam praerogativae," or " in signum supremae potestatis."   Given these conditions, which by the beginning of the fifteenth century were nebulous, Panormitanus allowed free kings to prescribe against the em-

---

at this point against the validity of the Donation, he says " quia dabo tibi duas rationes inconvincibiles quas nunquam audisti.   Primo ratio est quod illud quod non potest prescribi non potest alienari . . . ."

[31] Isernia, *prooem.* to *Constitutiones* (Venice, 1590), col. 19; *In feudorum* (Rome, 1634), p. 272.   Bartholomaeus da Capua also allowed a century to operate against the Empire in favor of the monarchies: cited in Gennaro Monti, *La dottrina antiimperiale*, II, 34, n. 6.

[32] *Lectura* (Lyons, 1538), to C. 12, 59, 8, nn. 3-6.

peror, but with the proviso that the king never be absolutely free of the traditional universal supremacy. Yet, he was quick to add that even the most intrinsically imperial prerogatives might be gained by prescription given papal intervention: " interveniente scientia papae." The political authority of the Papacy was enhanced yet another way: kings and free cities were allowed to acquire certain imperial powers by prescription with the emperor's knowledge (and implied tacit consent) and the approval of the Papacy. Moreover, declared Panormitanus, upon the death of the emperor, during the interregnum, all imperial properties and rights were to revert to the Papacy, against which prescription was ineffectual.[33]

In the fourteenth century, as might be expected, the publicists of the Empire were not as prone as were the legists to let fall one of the few remaining props of the imperial legal position. Ockham, for example, started from the position that true, hence legally valid, custom must be rational, and that any action against the ruler *ipso facto* would be to the contrary. Custom, and he included prescription under this rubric, must also enjoy the consent of the ruler if it is to have force. Moreover, in this instance the ruler was indeed *legibus solutus*.[34] For these reasons, Ockham argues, France was still *de jure* subject to the Empire, its claims to independence being negated by the fact of its unlawful separation from the Empire by means of violence.[35] And in another passage he remarks that no emperor ever made a law allowing prescription *totaliter* from the Empire, and that, therefore, no one acting in good faith can

33 Especially, *Lectura* (Venice, 1578), to X, 2, 2, 13, nn. 10-15; also to 4, 17, 13, nn. 10, 37; 3, 39, 10, n. 6; 2, 26, 14, n. 11. The consensus of canonist opinion allowed prescription against Church properties. See, for example, Panormitanus (1578), to X. 2, 2, 13, where he cites Innocent IV with whom " tenent moderni communiter hic." An opinion of Hostiensis indicates the restrictions placed upon such types of action against the Church: *Summa* (Venice, 1574), fol. 723, ad vv. *praescr. rerum immobilium.*
34 *Octo quaestiones*, III, 7 in *Monarchia*, II, 352.
35 *Octo quaestiones*, IV, 3 in *Monarchia*, II, 358.

ever hope legally and morally to separate himself from it.[36]
Almost exactly the same opinion was expressed by Lupold von
Bebenberg (d. 1363) who was most interested in defeating the
pretensions of the national monarchies to freedom from the
Empire. Although forced to recognize the *de facto* status of
the kingdoms, he nevertheless reserved for the emperor the
right to intervene in cases of the highest jurisdiction which
originally had been his exclusive province. And he too based
his view of the imprescriptability of the imperial *merum et
mistum imperium* upon the most fundamental ideas. Of these
the principal was that things in public use might not be lost
in this manner.[37]

[36] *Dialogus*, III, 2, 2, 5 in *Monarchia*, II, 905-6.
[37] *Tractatus de iuribus*, cap. 15, *passim*.

# VIII

## Revocation and Restraint
## on the Basis of Inalienability

THE REMEDIES AVAILABLE to the ruler when and where his
peculiar character was hurt must now be discussed. Having
treated questions which indicate the progress and direction
which the abstraction of protectionist sentiment took, we turn
to examine the efforts of medieval rulers to restore prejudicial
alienations of land and authority. It is most likely that the
need for such actions predated any theory of revocation, for
the tense struggle for supremacy implicit in feudalism always
provided good reason for the king or emperor to revoke or try
to revoke grants made by his predecessors. Although rulers
were in theory obliged to honor the deceased's commitments,
they were not always ready and willing to do this. Upon his
succession the new monarch found that he had a coterie to re-
ward; and there arose problems of usurped judicial or administrative authority, and of lands lost through false title, prescription, or usucaption. Long before Pope Honorius penned
*Intellecto* to the Hungarian king, therefore, medieval rulers
had ordered extensive examinations of charters to determine
which properties and rights might be recalled to the throne.[1]

1 William of Newburgh, *Historia rerum anglicarum*, in *Chronicles of the Reigns
of Stephen, Henry II, and Richard I* (ed. R. Howlett, 2 vols., London, 1884–85),
I, 103, referring to the year 1155 in which Henry II took back Crown lands lost
during the reign of Stephen. In 1205, John demanded an accounting of the improper alienations made since the days of Henry II: Pollock and Maitland, *History*,
I, 334-35. Ragewin tells us that in 1158 Frederick I induced his lawyers to inquire

After *Intellecto* was included in Gregory's compilation, writers had a focal point for their comments which in sum constituted a theory of revocation. The canonists drew no lengthy lessons for secular life, but stated and restated the Church's privileges of recall. Within the Church capitular consent was initially required for alienation, and when this was lacking revocation followed as a matter of course. What is most pertinent in the canonists' comments is the fact that they referred ultimately to the common good in their decisions on the revocability of donations.[2] Also, they were quite definite in disallowing imperial attempts to recall donations made to the Church.[3] The civilians, however, followed the *Intellecto* theory very carefully on the question of recall. Isernia mentioned Innocent IV's qualification, *grave*, when he stated that immoderate donations " in grave preiudicium coronae " must be recalled. Lucas de Penna, too, stressed the duty of the ruler to recall injurious gifts, and emphasized the obligation where the king had taken a coronation oath with the restraining clause. The moderate gift or delegation was necessary, he admits, but not gifts of powers and properties essential to the maintenance of government: " fiscalia et demanialia que sunt ad conservationem regie dignitatis et corone." And apart from the reliance upon canon law for his basic position, his opinion is interesting for its coordination, in relation to the subject of

---

" super justitia regni et de regalibus quae longo jam tempore seu temeritate prevalentium seu neglectu regum regno deperierant," his interest being his rights in " ducatus, marchias, comitatus, consulatus, monetas, teleonia, . . . omneque utilitatem ex decursu fluminum provenientem, nec terra tantum." He is cited by Georges Blondel, " Etude sur les droits régaliens," p. 241.

[2] For example, see Bartholomaeus Brixiensis, *Auree quaestiones dominicales ac veneriales* (Venice, 1508), fol. 18v, and also his gloss to the *Decretum* (Venice, 1477), to *Decret.* XII, q. 2, c. 39, ad vv. *non contulerit.*

[3] See the *Glossa ordinaria* on the *Decretum* (Venice, 1514), to *Dist.* LXIII, c. 30. Johannes Faber cited Hostiensis and Innocent IV to the same effect. See his comment on *C.* 1, 9, 5 (Lyons, 1594). That this injunction was at times observed is indicated by the action in 1219 of Frederick II in nullifying the alienation of church goods made by Archbishop Gerhard of Bremen (*Constitutiones*, II, 80).

revocation, of prince and prelate. Much as the ecclesiastic is bound by the limitations of his office, so too is the prince.[4] The emphasis once again is upon the primary importance of office as opposed to person, and intrinsic obligation as opposed to discretionary action.

The effect of such a theory upon day-to-day decisions of rulers is hard to determine, for, as has been suggested, motives for royal recall were always present. Nevertheless, what may be instructive is an examination of certain state documents which nullified existing titles and rights on the grounds that they were blemishes on the kingship. Our examples will be varied, for by the middle of the thirteenth century similarities are to be noticed in the documents of all the major states.

In 1226, the year of the *Compilatio quinta* in which *Intellecto* was included, Frederick II issued an important constitution censuring several cities and towns belonging to the counts of Provence and Forcalquier.[5] The towns had arrogated to themselves " iurisdictiones, potestates, consulatus, regimina et alia quedam statuta," and when reproached by the emperor they had declared that the counts had given them permission. To this Frederick replied that the counts could not infringe upon imperial prerogative; whereupon he revoked the usurped liberties. It is difficult to read a direct influence of *Intellecto* into this document which is simply an expression of the emperor's displeasure, and an example of his noted determination to maintain and increase the sum of imperial rights. He might, however, have remembered Innocent III's warning to his own advisors some twenty years before. More clear-cut in the his-

---

[4] Isernia, *Constitutiones* (Venice, 1590), fol. 210, to lib. III, tit. 4 (*Dignum*); Lucas de Penna, *Commentaria* (Lyons, 1538), to C. 11, 58, 7. We might also mention the comment of Bartolus upon D. 43, 23, 3, sec. *plane*, where he states that forced alienations made by a city under pressure of a tyrant, or the alienations of a prince " in magnum diminutionem iurisdictionis regalis . . . " cannot stand. Should the prince's gift be moderate, however, it is valid and must be honored by his successor.

[5] *Constitutiones* II, 140.

tory of the Empire is the *Sententia* of 1281, which declared
void all the alienations Richard of Cornwall had made without
the consent of the prince electors.[6]   Evident here, also, is the
influence of the Romano-canonical public law complex of
theories of which the *Intellecto* theme forms a part.

English documents present a similar problem of interpretation: the co-existence of a theory of inalienability and a socio-
political situation which made the quashing of alienations the
most likely thing in the world.   Given the danger of overesti-
mating the role of the *Intellecto* theory, and the state of the
sources, we cannot say for certain just when the English monarchy began to act with a definite theoretical principle in mind,
as opposed to an expedient immediate action, with regard to the
annulment of alienations.   In any event, it has been shown that
the *Intellecto* idea was known in England before 1266, the
date of the Dictum of Kenilworth.   This strong assertion of
royal authority concerns us because of its sixth article, which
demanded the return to the Crown unless held by proper war-
rant of all the pertinent things and rights of the monarchy:
" omnia loca, iura, res et alia ad coronam regiam pertinentia."
If it be remembered that the Dictum represented a full restora-
tion of the royal dignity, this provision may be taken as another indication of " the accepted doctrine of the royal duty to
maintain the liberties and resources of the Crown. . . ."[7]   A
decade later Edward I reaffirmed an identical royal intention,
and the *Quo warranto* proceedings over some twenty years give
further evidence that the king recognized a standing obligation
to maintain for the Crown its own.[8]   And, as is well known,

---

[6] *Constitutiones* III, i, 290.

[7] Powicke, *King Henry III*, II, 534.   The Dictum is printed in W. Stubbs, *Select Charters*, 407-11.

[8] *Statutes of the Realm*, I, 42-43.   The passage in question is section 4 of the Statute of Bigamy, 1276.   On the *quo warranto*, see Helen M. Cam, " *Quo Warranto* Proceedings."   Miss Cam notes that the writ was no invention of Edward, and that it had been used as early as the reign of Richard I.   Her interpretation of the writ's

Edward II in the Statute of York revoked the ordinances of 1308 because they limited the royal power " en blemissement de sa seynerie reale et encountre lestat de la Coronne." Here we have action to recover the intrinsic attributes of royal authority, not land or specific feudal rights. Edward was after the resumption of his full glory of majesty unfettered by the magnates' restraints.[9] These English statements indicate a royal consciousness of duty expressed in language which is ever more sophisticated, more replete with legal phraseology, and with words of considered constitutional significance. If nothing else, they show a very gradual movement towards action by principle; and historians who otherwise violently disagree are as one in praising the quality of the deliberations behind the Statute of York.[10]

If these English documents may be said to illustrate the constitutional aspect of revocation, a Spanish text will serve to illustrate the moral. In 1291 at the Cortes of Muntso, Alfonso II of Aragon issued a general cancellation of injurious donations, and in the preface to his order gave the reasons for his action which itself was unusual in that medieval rulers did not lightly break faith with their subjects.[11] The list is important,

---

use under Edward does not clash with our central thesis here, which is the strengthening of the kingship.

[9] For the statute itself, see *Statutes of the Realm*, I, 189. Professor Wilkinson gives a translation with commentary in his *Constitutional History*, II. I follow him in believing that the statute wiped out " every significant gain by the opposition since Edward II's accession to the throne." With regard to his comment that the interests of the king and Crown were identified to the hurt of the barons' picture of themselves as the Crown's special protectors, I might say that this view of Professor Wilkinson is not inimical to the theme I have been developing, for the king, having once achieved this identification of his own interests with those of the Crown, was able now to make resumptions of royal authority with all the more force and legitimacy.

[10] With the exception of Richardson who, as Professor Wilkinson has remarked, would deny to the statute any contemporary importance.

[11] *Ustages de Barcelona, El constitucions de Cataluña* (Barcelona, 1495), p. 147 (152). Compare the royal philosophy of 1291 with that of Peter of Aragon who, in 1204/5, borrowing 150,000 *solidi* from Raymond VI of Toulouse, renounced as

for he complains of the advantage taken of his youth by the nobles and their use of fraud, violence, and deceit. He now revokes the grants of his minority, and subjects all titles to his mature consideration. Nobles with proper charters will retain their holdings; those who presumed upon his innocence to despoil the kingdom must suffer under his general cassation. Maitland in a famous paper wrote of Edward II's lawyers equating *corona* and *ecclesia* and assigning to the former the protections specially granted the latter.[12] Here the Aragonese monarch equates *corona* and *minor* with the same purpose and by analogous reasoning; he grants the monarchy special protective privileges because of its indispensable function in society. It is rare that we have such a clear-cut example of the assimilation in public law of private law protection, for usually a legist or apologist would be the one to claim special safeguards for his king. In the present case it was the ruler himself, just passed into full estate, who was so conscious of the responsibilities of his office.

In theory the French rulers were equally solicitous for the improvement of their own position, but as the long series of their revocations indicates, there was little they could do but appeal with questionable practical effect to a fundamental law of the realm. In the fourteenth century, as we have seen, the kings repeatedly issued orders of revocation; and a specific clause was incorporated in a revised coronation oath in 1365. But actually the edicts and the new oath had little effect, as one more example will show. In a letter to the Chambre des Comptes, written in 1375, King Charles V describes the sale of Lavaur in the County of Toulouse by his brother. Although the king himself possessed all rights in the town, his brother

---

would any private citizen "... exceptionem non numerate pecunie opponere non possimus, imo illi specialiter renuntiamus; quam etiam pecuniam in utilitatem nostram versam esse recognoscimus"; in *Layettes du trésor des chartes*, I, 756.

[12] F. W. Maitland, "The Crown as Corporation," in *Selected Essays* (Cambridge, 1936), p. 106.

had prevailed upon the local royal officials to break their allegiance and countenance the sale which brought him some 5,500 pounds. Upon learning of the treachery, and after hearing the complaint of the municipal consuls that they had immemorially been in the royal demesne and wished to remain there, the king ruled that such an alienation of his rights was legally impossible, and revoked his brother's act.[13]

These examples indicate that rulers might take action on the basis of the theory of inalienability. The precise extent of *Intelecto's* direct influence will always be difficult to determine. We may assume on the basis of similar terminology that the decretal was certainly well known. But granting identical terminology, even the operating influence of a broad theory of inalienability of sovereignty, nevertheless it is logically possible only to suggest a presumed influence of theory upon practice. (Certainly the gaps between theory and practice are evident.) The view one will take upon this relationship will be determined, ultimately, by his opinion upon another basic problem of interpretation: the extent to which medieval men of theory in general effected constitutional change.

But theorists were not satisfied to provide only a basis for revocation. In a sense, they saw the problem before it began, and so developed a justification for restraint. Discussion of Innocent IV's decretal, *Grandi* (VI, 1, 8, 2), leads us to this new subject, the restraints upon a bad ruler suggested by legal theorists, and also to the set of problems linked to it. The Roman lawyers, especially those in the service of aggressive monarchies, had several important and contradictory texts to reconcile and discuss. One law, *Princeps legibus solutus est* (D. 1, 3, 31), seemingly freed the ruler from all legal restraint; while the title in the *Code, Digna vox,* imposed upon him a general obligation to live within the law, not only the *ius natu-*

---

13 Bibliothèque Nationale MS Nouv. Acq. Fran. 7420, fols. 6r-9v.

*rale* and the *ius gentium,* but also the private law of his own realm. Broadly speaking, the medieval Christian tradition favored the theory of *Digna vox,* and this emphasis gave rise to various views upon the regulation of irresponsible rulers. The civilians used as their text the aforementioned law of the *Code,* and the canonists found their favorite passage in *Grandi* which ultimately was incorporated by Boniface VIII in the *Sext.*

The statement of the case tells us of King Sancho II of Portugal, who ruled badly in every conceivable way. He neglected the welfare of his subjects; clerics, widows, and children went unprotected; churches, monasteries, and the nation's defenses fell in to disuse and ruin. After several complaints to Rome and the refusal of the king to reform, Innocent IV named as *curator* the king's brother, Alfonso, count of Boulogne.[14] A contemporary or near contemporary canonist, Bernardus Compostellanus, Jr., wanted the pope to depose the king altogether. He approved the choice of the ruler's brother as guardian, but would rather have seen a son legitimately upon the throne; or, had Portugal been an elective monarchy, the choice of a new ruler granted to the " people." And, in common with all the canonist commentators, he compares the action to be taken against the evil king with that demanded by canon law against one with similar evil qualities in ecclesiastical office.[15] Another churchman, Guido de Baysio, was careful to

---

[14] *VI,* 1, 8, 2. As far as I know, this decretal and the commentaries upon it have not received adequate attention from historians of political theory; a special study might be very rewarding. For the political background of Sancho's deposition see *C.M.H.,* VIII, 514-15. Portugal had been a papal fief for a century, which is the primary reason that the royal actions came under papal censure, ultimately provoking action. It is interesting to see that, during the pontificate of Innocent III, Alfonso II refused to carry out the terms of his father's will for the reason that to do so would have meant granting to his brothers and sisters Crown lands which he considered inalienable.

[15] Bernardus Compostellanus, Jr., *casus* to cap. *Grandi,* Vatican MS Pal. lat. 629, fol. 263r. For another example of the equation of lord and cleric, see Panormitanus (Venice, 1578), to X. 2, 2, 6, n. 2. Johannes Faber, too, would allow the kings to

point out that when the pope granted Alfonso *administrationem generalem et liberam regni* he did not mean to include authority to alienate against the best interests of the state. Should the king ever do this, his *curator* must revoke the donations, notwithstanding any pledge in the granting act. In other words the right acting *curator* must observe the obligations incumbent upon the right acting king.[16] At this point in his argument Guido refers directly to *Intellecto,* as does Johannes Andreae in his almost identical comment upon the same decretal. It is noteworthy, however, that both preserve for the ruler his normal role as giver—in moderation.

Sancho of Portugal presented an extreme case, in the sense that his ineptitude for rule was so acute, and perhaps more important, in that as a vassal he was legally subject to the pope in temporal affairs. Happily for the Papacy, the political situation on the peninsula at the time was such that the pope was able to exercise his feudal rights. Be that as it may, the decretal and its commentaries are significant in showing two things: that *Intellecto* was integrated with feudal law and practice and actually was used by the Papacy to buttress its political actions; and that here again the canonists, in developing theories and precedents in public law, emphasized the similar rôles and responsibilities of clerical and lay officials.

For their specific example of the restrictions placed upon medieval rulers, the legists often chose to discuss alienation of the *merum imperium.* And in relation to this question they developed a practical solution to the major problem created by a bald statement or interpretation of *Intellecto:* the problem of the relationship between the universal Empire of political theory and the evident reality of the many omnicompetent medieval states. As we might expect, with regard to the Do-

---

depose the emperor for "malam administrationem": *In codicem . . . annotationes* (Lyons, 1594), to C. 1, 14, 4 (*Digna vox*).

[16] *Rosarium seu in decretorum volumen commentaria* (Venice, 1577), to VI. 1, 8, 2.

nation of Constantine the canonists were agreed that the *merum imperium* might irretrievably be lost by the emperors.[17] With respect to lesser levels of authority, however, opinion was less unanimous. Jacobus de Arena believed that such high power could not be prescribed.[18] But the majority, according to Panormitanus, thought that it might be.[19] Yet, there must have been some doubt, for at one point Johannes Andreae, who is quoted by Petrus de Ancharano as believing that no prescription of any length of time would be efficacious,[20] raised a query. Having allowed prescription of *merum imperium* by the Church in the great donations of territory made by the emperors, he asks: "sed si talis donatio fiat, vel facta sit in laicum vel inferiorem ecclesiam. . . ?" And his reply indicates both the difficulty of his own and his fellows' position, and their attempt to save the status quo. He recognizes that the *imperium* may effectively pass from the emperor to a lesser authority, but declares: "licet transeat, tamen haeret ossibus imperii iure superioritatis."[21] In other words, in good canonist fashion he attempted to rationalize reality by allowing the legitimate use of necessary authority by lesser political bodies; and at the same moment he hoped to reaffirm the doctrinal concept of the universal secular Empire.

[17] Johannes Andreae, commentary upon the *Speculum iuris* of Guilelmus Durandus (Lyons, 1547), to tit. *De iurisdict. omni. iudic.* Approvingly he gives the opinion of Innocent IV: "Innoc. addebat quod in donatione facta ecclesiae Romanae per Ludo. et Ottonem et Const. de civitate Roma et adiacentibus, non fuit expressum merum et mistum imperium, tamen notorium est quod transivit et quod ecclesia Romana utitur illis . . . ." And in these donations "nulla ipsorum iurium adhaesio remanet penes donatorem vel imperium . . . ."

[18] Johannes Andreae reports the opinion of Jacobus de Arena in his *Commentaria* (Venice, 1581), to X. 2, 2, 13, n. 3: "an merum imperium sit praescriptibile . . . sed Jac. de Arena tenet quod non etiam tempus, cuius non extat memoria."

[19] *Lectura* (Lyons, 1547), to X. 2, 28, 55, n. 17.

[20] *Consilia* (Venice, 1585), cons. 142, n. 4. Petrus himself believed that ultimately *merum imperium* could be acquired by prescription. In passing he indicates the popularity of the problem: "antiqua est quaestio et disputa."

[21] See note 17 above. He also writes, giving various opinions on the prescription of *merum imperium*: "6° opinio habet quod merum imperium sic inhaeret ossibus Principis quod illud a se abdicare non potest . . . ."

Much the same was the task of the civilians, bound as they were to fill dead terms with new life. The early glossators, including Azo and Accursius, did not fully treat abdication of the *imperium,* yet it is clear that they recognized the necessity of its delegation. Roman provincial governors had enjoyed final judicial powers, and so the expository comments of the glossators implied that in their world lesser agencies than the emperor also exercised full powers. Placentinus went so far as to allow the emperor to permit the delegation of " potestatem condendi iura et interpretandi." [22] For this approach of the glossators there were several reasons. First, the lawyers of this period did not interpret contemporary society to the extent of their successors; by and large they kept closely to their texts. And second, the independence of the monarchies had only recently, comparatively speaking, become a problem for the legists; they had not yet followed through to the point of discussing all the legal conditions and consequences of the existence of the new political states.

But by the end of the thirteenth century the topic was no longer neglected. Very often, as in the case of Oldradus, the civilians joined the problem to that of the Donation of Constantine. Oldradus, having first discussed all the arguments pro and con, decided that the *merum imperium* was transferred with the territory included in the Donation. Princely munificence and liberality need know no restraint, and the statement of this concept was a frequently expressed argument: " magnificentia [principis] et liberalitas freno . . . non subiacet." More significant from the viewpoint of public law is his statement that the *imperium* must be available to a prince because of the exigencies of rule: ". . . merum imperium et mistum videntur adherere administrationi, quam quis ratione territorii habet. . . ." This is no more than a statement of the function

[22] *In codiciis . . . summa* (Mainz, 1536), to C. 1. ¹, 7.

of office and, as he is careful to point out, is well in line with canonical as well as civilian theory.[23]

Wilhelmus de Cuneo agreed;[24] Cynus allowed delegation of the *merum imperium* to the level of kingship, but prohibited further subdelegation.[25] Johannes Faber appears to have adopted similar views.[26] Isernia allowed the great nobles of the realm the *regalia,* provided they maintained and never alienated the king's rights. He realized that royal ability to endow counts and dukes with fiefs redounded to the prestige of the monarchy, and that such delegations did not lessen the honor of the realm or Crown. Moreover, thinking now of the actual social structure, the very possession of a fief stamped a man a noble, and so some means of investiture was essential to the system's perseverance.[27]

What these writers had in common was the idea of delegation; that is, they meant to provide the requisite judicial and administrative power for local government while at the same time retaining for the king ultimate exercise of his supreme authority. Fiscal privileges, wrote Lucas de Penna, may legitimately be granted to counts and to cities since such a delegation is necessary and would never result in " lasting damage to the Crown." However, having given such freedom to his subjects, the ruler must regard maladministration as *crimen laesae majestatis,* for the public welfare of the state was the basis for his original trust and grant. The ruler, in theory, was always to remain responsible for the *gubernatio* of the realm.[28] His

---

[23] *Consilia* (Venice, 1570), cons. 252, nn. 6-10. We may note that Oldradus cites Hostiensis on the validity of the Donation of Constantine, and his specific reference is to a statement of the bishop relating to the concept of ecclesiastical office.

[24] *Lectura super codicem* (Lyons, 1513), to C. 6, 61, 7.

[25] *Lectura* (Lyons, 1547), to C. 3, 4, 1.

[26] *In . . . libros institutionum . . . commentaria* (Venice, 1572), fol. 16v, ad v. *imperio.*

[27] *In usus feudorum* (Naples, 1571), to cap. *De his qui feudum dare possunt,* n. 10; *Constitutiones* (Lyons, 1560), to tit. *De iuribus rerum regalium.*

[28] *Lectura* (Lyons, 1586), to C. 12, 35, 14 and 12, 45, 1. See also his comments

trusteeship was "truly personal, indivisible, inalienable, and non-transferrable," and he might not even alienate authority to his wife, because his sovereign rights "inhered in his bones." [29]

For Baldus, too, the *imperium,* or rather the higher *iurisdictio,* is indivisible, for its character stems essentially from its philosophic unity. But whereas Lucas argued in favor of the Sicilian king, Baldus spoke for the emperor.[30] The emperor may not concede his supreme power to a private citizen, nor can he sell it, because the *imperium* is covered by public, not private law.[31] Baldus rejects the transfer of jurisdiction with territory, and specifies that its delegation to cities is merely provisionary. The cities may not sell or further alienate their privileges, and here Baldus singles out the power to tax because of its vital importance to the common welfare.[32]

In summation, we may say that the theory of delegation sanctioned by the anti-imperial theorists prevailed. It was well integrated with the civilian view of the national monarchies as

---

on *C.* 11, 29, 2, where he posits the need of special mention of the cession of full privileges in the charter.

[29] Ullman, *Medieval Idea of Law,* p. 51. Lucas lists the inalienable privileges in his commentary on *C.* 12, 21, 1, n. 18: "quae vero sunt regalia mere ut potestas condere leges . . . quae quidem non possunt cadere in privatum . . . quia ista velut regis ossibus inhearentibus nequererunt a potestate separari." Also, prescription of these major rights did not operate against the king: *C.* 12, 59, 8, n. 4: "contra principem in hoc (regalia) non curit praescriptio." But Lucas notes that both Cynus and Dynus disagree, *idem.*

[30] *Super* . . . digestis (Lyons, 1535–36), fol. 2v, n. 18.

[31] *Ibid.,* to *D.* 1, 12, 14, n. 6. But the emperor may, for the good of the realm, alienate and enfeoff, *salva maiestate imperii* . . . another recognition of the continued importance of feudal practice (*Consilia* I, cons. 333).

[32] *Ibid.,* to *D.* 1, 12, n. 2. See also his remarks upon *C.* 6, 14, 3, n. 34: "nam in eis (jurisdictionibus) semper auctoritas superioris reservatur et nisi eius auctoritate non potest exerceri, cum in eo resideat suprema potestas inseparabilis. Unde potest supprimere jurisdictionem aliorum, non solum singularum personarum sed etiam civitatum." See also his comment on the Peace of Constance in the *Extravagantes* to the *Liber feudorum,* fol. 125: "Imperator facit hanc pacem nomine sedis, non nomine proprio . . ."; and his remarks upon *C.* 7, 53, 5, n. 21. I have not attempted to discuss the views of S. Woolf, *Bartolus,* and J. N. Figgis, "Bartolus and the Development of European Political Ideas," *Trans. Roy. Hist. Society,* Vol. XIX (1905), New Series, pp. 147-69.

being merely *de facto* independent of the universal Empire, and it was based upon legal principle and experience. For the history of *Intellecto* it is important for the way it preserved for the king, or emperor, depending upon the theorist, his essential powers. Perhaps we may say that the theory of delegation was an answer to the absolute prohibition against alienating Crown rights. In this respect, like so many of the necessary modifications forced by politics and society, it was a salutary circumvention of the *Intellecto* theme. For had the theorists not developed such loopholes, the concept would have become brittle and eventually have been chipped away. Subtle legal quibbles and supple exceptions permitted to a great extent the by-passing of the rule. Yet the very fact that the rule remained an obstacle that could not frontally be assaulted indicates its strength.

In effect, the circumventions permitted the ruler a great latitude of legal as opposed to forced action. And the underlying reason for this was the decisive importance accorded the public utility. The assumption was that rulers always act in their own best interests, but now this assumption was formalized into public law of overriding importance. Thus, in times of national emergency the king theoretically could call upon the support of all his nobles, relying upon an allegiance to the *patria* which transcended all feudal relations.[33] His very infeudations were approved on the basis of their usefulness to the state and society . . . provided that the ruler always retained the theoretical power intact.[34] Even great gifts to family,

---

[33] Johannes Blanosc, *Tract. super feudis* in Calasso, *I glossatori*, p. 120: ". . . et ita rex vocat eos propter bona tocius patrie sive bonum publicum regni gallie cuius administrationem gerit, et ita isti tenentur pugnando pro patria talibus obedire preceptis, et ad hoc tenentur ex iure gentium." The feudal overlord might call upon his vassals " gratia private utilitatis," while the king relied upon ". . . publice utilitatis que preferenda est private . . . ."

[34] Isernia, *In feudorum* (Naples, 1571), to *De his qui feudorum dare possunt*, n. 10. This has been emphasized here as one of his important ideas. See also Baldus, *Consilia*, I, cons. 327, n. 6.

which at a moment of succession might weaken the state, were tolerated for their immediate advantage.[35]   And, although delegations of jurisdiction and proctorial mandates normally were conceived as lacking the power to alienate, special forms were invented to facilitate and give legitimacy to such actions.[36] Even the people, on a broad appeal to the principle of the public good, was able to sacrifice some of its rights.[37]

[35] Oldradus, cons. 94, n. 23.

[36] See the references cited by G. Post, "Plena Potestas," pp. 357-59. Also Isernia, *In feudorum* to *De prohib. feud. alien.*, n. 12.

[37] This is the substance of commentaries upon the decretal *Quanto*, X. 2, 24, 18. The king might devalue money of the realm with the consent of the people, *but* then it might not circulate outside the country's borders since the people can surrender only those rights touching it.   See the comments of Innocent IV and Johannes Andreae to this decretal.

# IX

## *Conclusion*

THE LEITMOTIV of inalienability might be traced further in its combinations with major medieval political ideas. To do this, however, would be to attempt here and now a broader approach to the entire literature of medieval political theory than has been planned. Yet, on the basis of the evidence presented, certain conclusions may be ventured relative to the *Intellecto* theme and its eventual significance. It has been a major point that this derives neither from a single crucial or dramatic event nor from a major treatise, but rather from the steady and varied employment of the idea on many occasions.

Given the universality of the canon and Roman law and the problem which the prohibitions on alienation sought to meet, it is no wonder that the adherents of the idea recognized no common allegiance. We have seen the concept used by Hohenstaufen emperors, and by Norman, French, Spanish, and English kings. Although the formulation of the idea was in the main the work of Italians, it soon had its protagonists among the publicists of every national state. Paradoxically, although these Italian jurists had so much to do with the concept, their peninsula profited little, and the German emperors whom they supported ultimately suffered as well.

Besides the ecumenical influence of the Roman and canon laws, our discussion has also shown some aspects of the process whereby the national states theoretically were freed from the Empire. Passages in Justinian's books which defined the exalted, unalterable position of the emperor were made the vehicles for special pleading by legists in royal service. These statists arrogated for their kings the perquisites of imperial status; and although the emperors never lacked formidable support, localist theory was aided to triumph by the facts of late medieval political and economic life.

Significantly, the course of legal doctrine saw the victory of concepts which stressed the individual's nature and value. So, in the development of the idea of privilege, the true condition of a person became the criterion by which his freedom to alienate was judged. Here important and congenial elements were the newly emphasized scholastic concepts of definition and teleology and the organic concept of society which stressed the proper function of every participating element. Because the woman and the child were *ipso facto* prey to their presumably more sophisticated environment they were owed special protection, as was the Church because of its peculiar and essential calling. And because the emperor, at first, and the kings, later, were regarded as fulfilling a unique role, they too had to be guarded for the ultimate well-being of all. What must be accented is the priority of influence: it was in relation to the common public good that rights were first called inalienable by the medieval theorists.

The public utility, the common good, these concepts were inextricably related to the *Intellecto* theme as they were to almost every other principle which promoted the growth of the national state. And as they were regarded as principles of public law to be acted upon and appealed to, so too was the theory of inalienability. On appeals to it kings and emperors recalled donations, popes quashed sacred oaths, and magnates rose in rebellion.

When we talk about the magnates' revolt or the theory of an office's duties, the Crown comes at once to mind. As a political symbol it antedates the strict formulation of the theory of inalienability; but once the latter manifested itself, the two concepts joined in immediate sympathy, for the idea of the Crown filled a natural want of the *Intellecto* theme. There had to be some reason why territories and rights could not be dissipated. The answer given was that it was not in the ruler's power to give what was only entrusted to him. And if he was merely a temporary administrator, the nation, or its symbol, the Crown, was the final and enduring residuum of essential rights. Aristotle enters here too, for a state as well as an individual has a conceptual *sine qua non*. Given this need and congruence, Crown, office, and inalienability reinforced each other in a common direction: towards the idea of a nation of independent sovereignty.

Besides its action at this high level, the theory of *Intellecto* was flexible enough to exert other influences. And as we have seen, through its intimate relationship to the public utility it aided in the definition of other medieval ideas: representation, responsibility, and consent; the proper conduct of a good king; the fisc and its privileges; the theory of oaths—to mention the more important. Basic to its influence upon these concepts, and indeed to its fundamental importance as an element of public law, were its flexibility and its harmony with contemporary ideas. Since the theory of inalienability of sovereignty developed against the background of an essentially feudal society, it had to come to terms with that surrounding reality. This it did by moderating the tone with which it proclaimed its prohibitions. Not all alienations or delegations of ruling authority were forbidden to the rulers of a state split into local units; only those which would substantially block the progress of the new social and political order. By accommodating their theory to the status quo, the legists and theorists were able to give it real force. The weary complaints and revocations of medieval rulers indicate a certain futility in the application of the principle. But they also indicate a faith in the righteousness of the claims which history ultimately justified.

# Bibliography

SEVERAL WORDS are necessary with regard to the organization of this bibliography. Since the research for this study was done in many libraries over several years, the author was forced to use various editions of the same work. Indeed, this practice was the rule, not the exception. For purposes of convenience and accuracy, therefore, references to the fifteenth or sixteenth century editions of most medieval authors will be made in the appropriate footnote, not here. For the sake of uniformity, medieval writers will be cited alphabetically under their given names; an attempt has been made to use the form of the medieval name most familiar to students of medieval political theory and legal history. Nevertheless, as will be seen in the footnotes, the spelling peculiar to the early edition will be maintained. Finally, documents relating to Aragon and Castile, and to the cities whose constitutions have been studied, will be found under the Anglicized name of the region or city. Because of the greater number of Imperial, French, and English sources, no attempt has been made to range these under a national rubric.

## PRIMARY SOURCES

Abbas Antiquus. Lectura aurea super quinque libris decretalium.
Accursius. Glossa ordinaria.
Aegidius Romanus. De regimine principum. Rome, 1607.
———— De renunciatione pape, in Bibliotheca maxima pontifica, ed. J. T. Roccaberti. Vol. II. Rome, 1695.
Albericus de Rosate. Prima et secunda super codice commentarium iuris.
———— Vocabularium iuris.

Alvarus Pelagius. Speculum regum. Vatican MS lat. 1477, in Unbekannte kirchenpolitische Streitschriften, ed. R. Scholz. Vol. II. Rome, 1914.

Andrea de Isernia. Constitutiones regni utriusque Siciliae glossis ordinariis commentariisque.

———— In usus feudorum commentaria.

Antonius de Butrio. Super primo decretalium.

Antonius de Rosellis. Monarchia sive de potestate imperatoris et papae, in M. Goldast, Monarchia, Vol. I.

Aragon. Cortes de los antiquos reinos de Aragon y de Valencia y principado de Cataluña. Madrid, 1896 *et seq.*

Azo. Quaestiones, ed. E. Landsberg. Freiburg i. B., 1888.

———— Summa aurea.

Baldus de Ubaldis. Opera omnia.

Barcelona. Ustages de Barcelona el constituciones de Cataluña. Barcelona, 1495.

Baronius-Theiner. Annales ecclesiastici. Vol. XXIII. Bar-le-Duc, 1871.

Bartholomaeus Brixiensis. Auree quaestiones dominicales ac veneriales nec non brocarda.

———— Decretum cum glossis.

Bartolus de Saxoferrato. Opera omnia.

Bernardus Bottoni. Casus longi super decretales.

———— Glossa in libros decretalium.

Bernardus Compostellanus, Jr. Apparatus in decretales Innocentii IV. Vatican MS Pal. lat. 629.

Bernardus Papiensis. Summa decretalium, ed. E. A. T. Laspeyres. Ratisbon, 1861.

Bracton. De legibus et consuetudinibus Angliae, ed. G. E. Woodbine. 4 vols. New Haven, 1915–42.

Britton, ed. and trans. M. Nichols. 2 vols. Oxford, 1865.

Bologna. Statuti del popolo di Bologna del secolo XIII, ed. A. Gaudenzi. Bologna, 1888.

———— Statuti di Bologna dell'anno 1288, ed. G. Fasoli and P. Sella. 2 vols. Vatican City, 1937–39.

Boniface VIII. Les registres de B. VIII, ed. A. Thomas. Paris, 1884 *et seq.*

Calendar of Close Rolls. Edward I, 1272–79. London, 1900.

Los Castigos e documentos del Rey Don Sancho, in Bibliotheca de autores españoles. Vol. LI. Madrid, 1891.

Choppin, René. De domanio Franciae. 4th ed. Frankfurt, 1701.

Chronica monasterii de Melsa a fondatione usque ad annum 1396, ed. E. A. Bond. 3 vols. London, 1866–68.

Chronicles of the Reigns of Edward I and Edward II, ed. W. Stubbs. 2 vols. London, 1882.

Cosneau, E., ed. Les grands traités de la guerre de cent ans. Paris, 1889.

Cynus (Cino da Pistoia). Super codice et digesto veteri lectura.

Damasus. Burchardica, sive regulae canonicae.

Dante Alighieri. De monarchia libri tres.

Dumoulin, Charles. Opera omnia.

Dupuy, Pierre. Histoire du differand d'entre Pape Boniface VIII et Philippe le Bel, Roy de France.

Dynus de Mugello. Commentaria in regulas juris pontifici.

Engelbert von Admont. De ortu et fine romani imperii liber, in M. Goldast, Politica imperialia. Frankfort, 1614.

Especulo, in Opusculos legales del rey Alfonso el Sabio. 2 vols. Madrid, 1836.

Exceptiones Petri, ed. H. Fitting. Halle, 1876.

Fleta, ed. J. Selden. 2d ed. London, 1685.

Florence. I più antiche frammento del constituto fiorentino, in Publicazioni del R. instituto de studi superiori di Firenze, ed. G. Rondini. Florence, 1895.

Foedera, ed. T. Rymer. 2d ed. 4 vols. in 7. London, 1816–69.

Genoa. Liber iurium reipublicae Januensium, in Monumenta historiae patriae, ed. H. Ruoffio. Vol. VII. Turin, 1854.

Gerald of Wales. De principis instructione liber, in Opera, ed. J. S. Brewer. 8 vols. London, 1861–91.

Gervase of Canterbury. Historical Works, ed. W. Stubbs. 2 vols. London, 1879–80.

Godefroy, Théodore. Le cérémonial français. 2 vols. Paris, 1649.

Godefroid de Fontaines. Quodlibeta. Vatican MS lat. 1032.

Goffredus de Trani. Summa super titulos decretalium.

Goldast, Melchior. De monarchia sive romani imperii sive tractatus de jurisdictione imperiali. 3 vols. Hanover and Frankfurt, 1611–14.

Goldast, Melchior. Politica imperialia. Frankfurt, 1614.

Grassaille, Charles de. Regalium Franciae libri duo.

Guido de Baysio. Rosarium seu in decretorum volumen commentaria.

Guilhelmus de Cuneo. Lectura super codicem.

Guilhelmus Durandus. Speculum iuris.

Guilhelmus de Ockham. Breviloquium de potestate papae, ed. L. Baudry. Paris, 1937.

———— Consultatio de causa matrimoniali, ed. H. S. Offler, in Guillelmi de Ockham opera politica, ed. J. G. Sikes. Vol. I. Manchester, 1940.

———— Dialogus, in M. Goldast, Monarchia. Vol. II.

———— De imperatorum et pontificum potestate, ed. K. Brampton. Oxford, 1927.

———— Opus nonaginta dierum, in M. Goldast, Monarchia. Vol. II.

Hermanus de Schildiz. Contra hereticos negantes emunitatem et iurisdictionem sancte ecclesie, in Unbekannte kirchenpolitische Streitschriften, ed. R. Scholz. Vol. II. Rome, 1914.

Hostiensis. In primum . . . quintum decretalium librum commentaria.

———— Summa aurea.

Hotman, François. Consilia.

———— Controversia successionis regiae.

Hugolinus. Dissensiones dominorum, ed. G. Haenel. Leipzig, 1834.

Huguccio. Summa. Vatican MS lat. 2280.

Huillard-Bréholles, J. L. A. Historia diplomatica Frederici Secundi sive constitutiones, privilegis mandata . . . et documenta varia. 7 vols. in 12. Paris, 1852–59.

Innocent III. Opera omnia, in *M.P.L.* Vols. CCXIV–CCXVII.

Innocent IV. In quinque libros decretalium commentaria.

Irnerius. Summa codices, ed. H. Fitting. Berlin, 1894.

Jacobus de Albenga. Apparatus ad compilationem V. Brit. Mus. MS Royal 11. C. VII.

Jacobus Rebuffi. Lectura super tribus ultimis libris codicis.

Johannes Andreae. In primum . . . quintum librum decretalium novella commentaria.

———— Glossa ad librum sextum.

Johannes Andreae. Apparatus in constitutiones clementinas.

Johannes Blanchus (Blanosc). Epitome feudorum, in Tractatus universi juris. Vol. X, i.

———— Tractatus super feudis et homagiis, in *Nouv. rev. hist. de droit fran. et étranger*, ed. Archer. Vol. XXX, 1906.

Johannes Faber. In codicem Justiniani annotationes.

———— In quatuor libros institutionum commentaria.

Johannes Monachus. In sextum librum decretalium commentaria.

Johannes Parisiensis. Tractatus de regia potestate et papali, in M. Goldast, Monarchia, Vol. II.

Johannes de Terra Rubea (Jean de Terre Rouge). Controversia successionis regiae, in F. Hotman, Disputatio de controversia regiae. Geneva, 1586.

Johannes Teutonicus. Glossa ordinaria ad decretum. Vatican MS lat. 1367 (and editions cited in notes).

———— Apparatus ad compilitionem III. Vatican MS Chis. E. VII. 207.

Johannes de Viterbo. Liber de regimine civitatum, in Biblioteca juridica medii aevi, ed. G. Salvemini. Vol. III. Bologna, 1901.

Layettes du trésor des chartes, ed. J. Teulet and others. 5 vols. Paris, 1863–1909.

Lebret, Cardin. De la souveraineté du roy. Paris, 1632.

Le Caron, Charondas. Glosse à la somme rurale. Paris, 1611.

Liber censuum de l'église romaine, ed. P. Fabre. Paris, 1889–1910.

Lieberman, F., ed. Die Gesetze der Angelsachsen. 3 vols. Halle, 1903–16.

Loyseau, Charles. Des seigneuries. Paris, 1600.

Lucas de Penna. Lectura . . . super tribus libris codicis.

Luchaire, A. Etudes sur les actes de Louis VII. Paris, 1888.

Lunig, Johann. Codex Italiae diplomaticus. 4 vols. Frankfurt and Leipzig, 1725–35.

Lupold von Bebenburg. Tractatus de iuribus regni et imperii romanorum. Augsburg, 1603.

Mansi, I. D. Sacrorum conciliorum nova et amplissima collectio. 31 vols. Florence, 1759–98.

Marinus de Carimanico. Prooemium . . . ad constitutiones regni utriusque Siciliae.

Marsilius of Padua. Defensor pacis, ed. R. Scholz. Hanover, 1932.

Martinus Laudensis. De fisco, in Tractatus universi juris, Vol. XII.

Matthew Paris. Chronica majora, ed. H. R. Luard. 7 vols. London, 1872–93.

Modena. (Statuta) Respublica Mutinensis, ed. E. Vicini. Milan, 1929.

Monumenta Germaniae historica. Legum. Sectio IV. Constitutiones et acta publica imperatorum et regum. Hanover, 1893 *et seq.*

——— Libelli de lite imperatorum et pontificum. 3 vols. Hanover, 1891–97.

Nice. Statuti Niciae, in Monumenta historiae patriae, ed. A. Silopis. Vol. II. Turin, 1831.

Nicholas Trivet. Annales, ed. T. Hog. London, 1845.

Oldradus de Ponte. Consilia.

Ordonnances des rois de France de la troisième race. 21 vols. Paris, 1723–1849.

Padua. Statuti del commune di Padova dal secolo XII all'anno 1285, ed. A. Gloria. Padova, 1873.

Panormitanus. Opera omnia.

Pape, Guy de la. Decisiones Gratianapolitanae.

Paucapalea. Summa, ed. F. v. Schulte. Giessen, 1890.

Paulus de Castro. Super codici. Pars I, II.

——— Super digesto veteri.

Paulus Ungarus. Notabilia. Vatican MS Borgh. 261.

Petrus de Ancharano. Consilia sive juris responsa.

——— Super clementinis.

Petrus de Bellapertica. Lectura . . . super prima parte codice.

——— In libros institutionum.

Philippe Auguste. Catalogue des actes, ed. L. Delisle. Paris, 1856.

——— Recueil des actes de P.A. Roi de France, ed. C. Petit-Dutaillis and J. Morncat. 2 vols. Paris, 1943.

Philippe de Mézières. Somnium viridarii, in M. Goldast, Monarchia. Vol. I.

Philippus de Leyden. De cura reipublicae et sorte principantis, ed. R. Fruin and P. C. Molhuysen. The Hague, 1915.

Pierre d'Auvergne. Quodlibeta. Vatican MS lat. 932.

Pierre Dubois. De recuperatione terrae sanctae, ed. C. Langlois. Paris, 1891.

Pisa. Statuti inediti della città di Pisa dal XII al XIV secolo, ed. F. Bonaini. 3 vols. Florence, 1854–70.

Placentinus. In codicis . . . summa.

—— In summam institutionum.

Recueil général des anciennes lois françaises, ed. F. Isambert. 29 vols. Paris, 1821–33.

Rishanger. Chronica, ed. H. T. Riley. London, 1869.

Rufinus. Summa, ed. F. v. Schulte. Giessen, 1891.

Scholz, Richard, ed. Unbekannte kirchenpolitische Streitschriften aus der Zeit Ludwigs von Bayern. 2 vols. Rome, 1911–14.

Secretum secretorum, in Opera hactenus inedita Rogerii Baconi, Fasc. V., ed. R. Steele. Oxford, 1920.

Selden, John. Ad fletam dissertatio, ed. and trans. D. Ogg. Cambridge, 1925.

Siena. Il constituto del commune di Siena dell'anno 1262, ed. L. Zdekauer. Milan, 1897.

—— Il costituto del commune di Siena volgarizzato nel MCCCIX-MCCCX, ed. A. Lisini. 2 vols. Siena, 1903.

Siete partidas, ed. A. de San Martin, in Los codigos españoles concordados y anotados. 2d ed. 12 vols. Madrid, 1872.

Socinus. Consilia.

Statutes of the Realm. 9 vols. in 10. London, 1810–28.

Stephen of Tournai. Summa, ed. F. v. Schulte. Giessen, 1891.

Stubbs, William. Select Charters, ed. H. W. C. Davis. 9th ed. Oxford, 1913.

Summa Reginensis. Vatican MS Reg. lat. 1061.

Tancred. Glossae ad compilationes I, II, III. Vatican MS lat. 1377.

Tanursi, Gaetano. Allegazione istorico-critico-diplomatico-legale . . . concernante i diritti incontrastibili del Papa sulla città, e stato di Avignono . . . Rome, 1792.

Tartagnus. Consiliorum volumina quinque.

Tholommeus de Lucca. Determinatio compendiosa de jurisdictione imperii, ed. M. Krammer. Hanover and Leipzig, 1909.

Tractatus universi juris. 18 vols. Venice, 1584–86.

Ursins, Juvenal des. Histoire de Charles VI Roy de France, ed. D. Godefroy. Paris, 1653.

Verona. Gli statuti veronesi del 1276 colle correzioni e le aggiunte fino al 1323, ed. G. Sandri. Venice, 1940.

Vincentius Hispanus. Apparatus ad compilationem III. Vatican MS lat. 1378.

Walter of Heminghburgh. Chronicon . . . de gestis regum Angliae, ed. H. C. Hamilton. 2 vols. London, 1848–49.

William of Newburgh. Historia rerum Anglicarum, ed. R. Howlett. 2 vols. London, 1884–85.

## SECONDARY SOURCES

Andrieu, Michel. Le pontifical romain au moyen-âge. 3 vols. Vatican City, 1938–40.

Arquillière, H. X. "L'appel au concile sous Philippe le Bel et la genèse des théories conciliares," *Revue des questions historiques,* XLV (1911), 23-55.

Barraclough, Geoffrey. The Origins of Modern Germany. Oxford, 1947.

Bayley, Charles C. The Formation of the German College of Electors in the Mid-Thirteenth Century. Toronto, 1949.

Bémont, Charles. Chartes des libertés anglaises (1100–1305). Paris, 1892.

Berges, Wilhelm. Die Fürstenspiegel des hohen und späten Mittelalters. Stuttgart, 1952.

Blondel, Georges. "Etude sur les droits régaliens et la constitution de Roncaglia," in Mélanges Paul Fabre. Paris, 1902.

Born, Lester K. "The Perfect Prince: a Study in Thirteenth and Fourteenth Century Ideals," *Speculum,* III (1928), 470 *et seq.*

Brachmann, Albert. "The Beginnings of the National State in Medieval Germany and the Norman Monarchies," in Medieval Germany, ed. and trans. G. Barraclough. Oxford, 1948.

Brandi, Brando. Notizie intorno a Guillelmo de Cunio. Le sue opere e il suo insegnamento a Tolosa. Rome, 1892.

Brandileone, F. Il diritto romano nelle leggi normanne e sveve del regno di Sicilia. Turin, 1884.

Buckland, W. W. A Textbook of Roman Law from Augustus to Justinian. 2d ed. Cambridge, 1932.

Calasso, F. I glossatori e la teoria della sovranità. 2d ed. Milan, 1951.

Cam, Helen M. "The *Quo Warranto* Proceedings Under Edward I," *History*, XI (1927), 143-48.

Carlyle, A. J. "The Theory of the Source of Political Authority in the Medieval Civilians to the Time of Accursius," in Mélanges Fitting. Vol. I. Montpellier, 1906.

Carlyle, Alexander J., and Robert W. Carlyle. A History of Medieval Political Theory in the West. 6 vols. Edinburgh, 1903–36.

Chalandon, Ferdinand. Histoire de la domination normande en Italie et en Sicile. 2 vols. Paris, 1907.

Chénon, E. "Le droit romain à la Curia Regis de Philippe Auguste à Philippe le Bel," in Mélanges Fitting. Vol. I. Montpellier, 1906.

Chevallier, Samuel. Le pouvoir royal français à la fin du XIII<sup>e</sup> siècle: Les droits régaliens. Laval, 1930.

Chrimes, S. An Introduction to the Administrative History of Medieval England. Oxford, 1952.

Cleary, Joseph. Canonical Limitations on the Alienation of Church Property. Washington, 1936.

Coville, Alfred. L'ordonnance cabochiènne (26–7 mai, 1413). Paris, 1891.

David, M. "Le serment du sacre du IX<sup>e</sup> au XV<sup>e</sup> siècle. Contributions à l'étude des limites juridiques de la souveraineté," *Revue du moyen-âge latin*, VI (1950), 5-272.

———— La souveraineté et les limites juridiques du pouvoir monarchique du IX<sup>e</sup> au XV<sup>e</sup> siècle. Paris, 1954.

Davis, Gifford. "The Incipient Sentiment in Medieval Castile: The Patrimonial Real," *Speculum*, XII (1937), 351-58.

Denholm-Young, N. "Who Wrote *Fleta?*" *E. H. R.*, LVIII (1943), 1-12.

Denifle, Heinrich. "Die Denkschriften der Colonna gegen Bonifaz VIII und der Cardinale gegen die Colonna," *Archiv für Literatur- und Kirchengeschichte des Mittelalters*, V (1889), 493-530.

Devic, C., and J. Vaisette. Histoire générale de Languedoc. 15 vols. Paris, 1872-93.

Dickinson, John. "The Medieval Concept of Kingship and Some of Its Limitations as Developed in the *Policraticus* of John of Salisbury," *Speculum*, I (1926), 308-37.

Dopsch, Alfons. The Economic and Social Foundations of European Civilization. London, 1937.

Dupont-Ferrier, Gustave. "Ou en était la formation de l'unité française aux XVᵉ et XVIᵉ siècles?" *Journal des savants* (1941), 10-24, 54-64, 106-19.

Entreves, A. P. d'. Dante as a Political Thinker. Oxford, 1952.

Ercole, Francesco. Da Bartolo all'Althusio. Florence, 1932.

———— Dal commune al principato. Florence, 1929.

Eschmann, T. "A Thomistic Glossary on the Principle of the Preeminence of a Common Good," *Medieval Studies*, V (1943), 123-66.

Esmein, Adhémar. Cours élémentaire d'histoire de droit français. 9th ed. Paris, 1908.

———— "L'inalienabilité du domaine de la couronne devant les Etats Généraux du XVIᵉ siècle," in Festschrift für Otto v. Gierke. Weimar, 1911.

———— "La maxime *Princeps legibus solutus est* dans l'ancien droit public français," in Essays in Legal History, ed. P. Vinogradoff. Oxford, 1913.

———— "Le serment promissoire dans le droit canonique," *Nouv. rev. hist. de droit fran. et etranger*, XII (1888), 248-77, 311-52.

Figgis, J. N. "Bartolus and the Development of European Political Ideas," *Transactions of the Royal Historical Society*, XIX (1905), 147-69.

———— Studies of Political Thought from Gerson to Grotius 1414–1625. 2d ed. Cambridge, 1931.

———— The Divine Right of Kings. 2d ed. London, 1922.

Fliche, A. "Les théories germaniques de la souveraineté," *Revue historique*, CXXV (1917), 1-67.

Fournier, Paul. "La 'Monarchia' de Dante et l'opinion française," in Bulletin du jubilé du Comité franc. cath. pour la célébration du VIᵉ centenaire de la mort de D.A., Fasc. III. Paris, 1921.

Funck-Brentano, F. Le moyen-âge. Paris, 1922.

Galbraith, V. H.   Studies in the Public Records.   London, 1948.

Gallet, Léon.   Les traités de pariage dans la France féodale.   Paris, 1935.

Ganshof, François.   Feudalism.   London, 1952.

Gavrilovitch, Michel.   Etude sur le Traité de Paris de 1259.   Paris, 1899.

Génestal, R.   Le *Privilegium fori* en France du décret de Gratien à la fin du XIVe siècle.   2 vols.   Paris, 1925–31.

Gierke, Otto von.   Johannes Althusius.   New York, 1939.

——— Political Theories of the Middle Age.   Cambridge, 1938.

Gilmore, Myron P.   Argument from Roman Law in Political Thought 1200–1600.   Cambridge, 1941.

Glorieux, P.   Le littérature quodlibetique de 1260 à 1330.   2 vols.   Le Salchoir-Paris, 1925–35.

Grabmann, M.   "Studien über den Einfluss der aristotelischen Philosophie auf die mittelalterlichen Theorien über das Verhaltnis von Staat und Kirchen," *S. B. der Bayer. Akad. der Wissen.*   (1934), Heft 2.

Hamman, Adelbert.   La doctrine de l'église et de l'état chez Occam: étude sur le *Breviloquium*.   Paris, 1942.

Hartung, Fritz.   "Die Krone als Symbol der monarchischen Herrschaft im ausgehenden Mittelalter," *Abhandlungen der Preussische Akademie, Phil.-hist. Klasse.*   XIII (1940–41).

Haskins, C. H.   "England and Sicily in the Twelfth Century," *E.H.R.*, XXVI (1911), 433-47, 641-65.

Haskins, G.   "The Doncaster Petition," *E.H.R.*, LIII (1938), 478-85.

Hefele, C. J., and H. Leclercq.   Histoire des conciles.   10 vols.   Paris, 1907–38.

Hinojosa, Eduardo de.   "La reception du droit romain en Catalogne," in Mélanges Fitting.   Vol. II.   Montpellier, 1908.

Hoyt, R. S.   The Royal Demesne in English Constitutional History: 1066–1272.   Ithaca, 1950.

Jones, J. Walter.   "Cino da Pistoia," in Essays in Honor of Roscoe Pound.   New York, 1947.

Kantorowicz, Ernst.   "Christus-Fiscus," in Synopsis: Festgabe für Alfred Weber.   Heidelberg, 1948.

Kantorowicz, Ernst. "Inalienability: A Note on Canonical Practice and the English Coronation Oath in the Thirteenth Century," *Speculum*, XXIX (1954), 488-502.

———— *"Pro Patria Mori* in Medieval Political Thought," *A.H.R.*, LVI (1951), 472-92.

Kerckhove, M. van de. "La notion de jurisdiction dans la doctrine des decretistes et des decretalistes de Gratien (1140) à Bernard de Bottoni (1250)," *Etudes franciscaines*, XLIX (1937), 420-55.

Kern, Fritz. Kingship and Law in the Middle Ages. Oxford, 1948.

Koeppler, H. "Frederick Barbarossa and the Schools of Bologna," *E.H.R.*, LIV (1939), 577-607.

Kuttner, Stephan. "Die Novellen Papst Innozenz IV," *Zeitschrift der Savigny-Stiftung, Kan. Abt.*, XXVI (1937), 436-70.

———— Repertorium der Kanonistik (1140–1234). Vatican City, 1937.

Kuttner, S., and S. Rathbone. "Anglo-Norman Canonists of the Twelfth Century," *Traditio*, VII (1949–51), 279-358.

Kuttner, S., and B. Smalley. "The 'Glossa ordinaria' to the Gregorian Decretals," *E.H.R.*, LX (1945), 97-105.

Ladner, Gerhart B. "Aspects of Medieval Thought on Church and State," *Review of Politics*, IX (1947), 403-22.

Lagarde, Georges de. La naissance de l'esprit laïque au declin du moyen-âge. Le bilan du XIIIᵉ siècle. Paris, 1934.

La Mantia, Vito. Cenni storici su le fonti del diritto greco-romano e le assise e leggi dei re di Sicilia. Palermo, 1887.

Lapsley, Gaillard. "Bracton and the Authorship of the *Addicio de Cartis*," *E.H.R.*, LXII (1947), 1-19.

———— "Interpretation of the Statute of York, 1322," in Crown, Community, and Parliament in the Later Middle Ages. Oxford, 1951.

Leclercq, J. "La renonciation de Celestine V et l'opinion théologique en France du vivant de Boniface VIII," *Revue d'histoire de l'église de France*, XXV (1939), 183-92.

Lemaire, André. Les lois fondamentales de la monarchie française. Paris, 1907.

Luchaire, Achille. Louis VII, Philippe-Auguste, Louis VIII (1137–1226). Paris, 1902.

McIlwain, C. H. Constitutionalism: Ancient and Modern. Ithaca, 1947.

—— Constitutionalism and the Changing World. Cambridge, 1939.

—— The Growth of Political Thought in the West. New York, 1932.

Maitland, F. W. "The Crown as Corporation," in Selected Essays. Cambridge, 1936.

Martin, Victor. "Comment s'est formée la doctrine de la superiorité du concile sur le pape: I. La tradition canonique avant le grand schisme d'occident," *Revue des sciences religieuses*, XVIII (1937), 121-43.

—— Les origines du gallicanisme. 2 vols. Paris, 1939.

Mélanges Fitting. 2 vols. Montpellier, 1906–8.

Meynial, Edouard. "Des renonciations au moyen-âge et dans nôtre ancien droit," *Nouv. rev. hist. de droit fran. et étranger*, XXIV–XXVI (1900–1902).

Minguijón, Salvador. Historia del derecho español. 3d ed. Madrid-Barcelona, 1943.

Mochi-Onory, Sergio. Fonti canonistiche dell'idea moderna dello stato. Milan, 1951.

Mols, Roger. "Celestine V," *Dictionnaire d'histoire et de géographie ecclésiastique*, Fasc. LXVII (Paris, 1950).

Monti, Gennaro. "Intorno a Marino da Caramanico e alla formula *Rex est imperator in suo regno*," in Anuali del seminario giuridico della Università di Bari (1933).

—— "La dottrina anti-imperiale degli Angioini di Napoli . . . , i loro vicariati imperiali e Bartolomeo da Capua," in Studi di storia e diritto in onore di A. Solmi. Vol. II. Milan, 1941.

—— "L'influenza francese sul diritto publico del Regno Angioino di Napoli," *Riv. stor. dir. ital.*, XI (1938), 556-59.

Nardi, Bruno. "La Donatio Constantini e Dante," in Nel mondo di Dante. Rome, 1944.

Newman, W. M. Le domaine royal sous les premiers capétiens (987-1180). Paris, 1937.

Oliger, P. L. "Petri Johannis Olivi De renuntiatione Papae Coelestini

V, Quaestio e epistola," *Archivum franciscanum historicum,* XI
(1918), 309-73.

Olivier-Martin, F.   Histoire du droit français des origines à la revolution.   Montchrestien, 1948, 1951.

———— L'assemblée de Vincennes de 1329 et ses consequences.
Etude sur les conflits entre la jurisdiction laïque et la jurisdiction
ecclésiastique au XIV^e siècle, in Travaux juridiques et économi-
ques de l'Université de Rennes.   Rennes, 1909.

Pange, Jean de.   Le roi très chrétien.   Paris, 1949.

Petit-Dutaillis, Charles.   Etude sur la vie et le regne de Louis VIII
(1187–1226).   Paris, 1894.

Pollock, F., and F. W. Maitland.   The History of English Law before
the Time of Edward I.   2 vols.   2d ed., Cambridge and Boston,
1905.

Post, Gaines.   "Plena Potestas and Consent in Medieval Assemblies
(1150–1325)," *Traditio,* I (1943), 355-408.

———— "A Romano-Canonical Maxim, 'Quod Omnes Tangit,' in
Bracton," *Traditio,* IV (1946), 197-251.

———— "The Theory of Public Law and the State in the Thirteenth
Century," *Seminar,* VI (1948), 42-59.

———— "Some Unpublished Glosses (ca. 1210–1214) on the Translatio Imperii and the Two Swords," *Archiv für katholisches
Kirchenrecht,* CXVII (1937), 403-18.

Powicke, Maurice.   King Henry III and the Lord Edward.   2 vols.
Oxford, 1947.

Prestage, Edgar.   "Portugal in the Middle Ages," in Cambridge
Medieval History.   Vol. VIII.   Cambridge, 1936.

Richardson, H. G.   "The English Coronation Oath," *Speculum,*
XXIV (1949), 44-75.

———— "Studies in Bracton," *Traditio,* VI (1948), 61-104.

Rivière, J.   Le problème de l'église et de l'état au temps de Philippe
le Bel.   Louvain and Paris, 1926.

Sarti, M.   De claris archgymnasii Bononiensis professoribus a saeculo
XI usque ad saeculum XIV.   2 vols.   2d ed.   Bologna, 1888–96.

Savigny, Friedrich C. von.   Geschichte des römischen Rechts im Mittelalter.   6 vols.   2d ed.   Heidelberg, 1834–51.

Schulte, Johann F. von. Geschichte der Quellen und Literatur des canonischen Rechts. 3 vols. Stuttgart, 1875–80.

Schulz, Fritz. "Bracton on Kingship," *E.H.R.*, LX (1945), 136–76.

Strayer, Joseph R. "Defense of the Realm and Royal Power in France," in Studi in onore di Gino Luzzatto. Vol. I. Milan, 1950.

——— "The Laicization of French and English Society in the Thirteenth Century," *Speculum*, XV (1940), 76–86.

Tamassia, Nino. Baldo, studiato nelle sue opere. Perugia, 1900.

Tangl, Michael. Die päpstlichen Kanzleiordnungen von 1200–1500. Innsbruck, 1894.

Tierney, Brian. "Ockham, Conciliar Theory and the Canonists," *Journal of the History of Ideas*, XV (1954), 40-70.

Tout, T. F. The Place of the Reign of Edward II in English History. 2d ed. Manchester, 1936.

Ullman, Walter. "The Development of the Medieval Idea of Sovereignty," *E.H.R.*, LXIV (1949), 1-34.

——— "A Medieval Document on Papal Theories of Government. Rex Pacificus," *E.H.R.*, LXI (1946), 180-201.

——— The Medieval Idea of Law: Lucas da Penna. London, 1946.

——— Medieval Papalism. London, 1949.

Van Hove, A. Prolegomena ad codicem iuris canonici. Malines and Rome, 1945.

Vassalli, F. E. "Concetto e natura del fisco," in Studi Senesi. Turin, 1908.

Viollet, Paul. Histoire des institutions politiques et administratives de la France. 3 vols. Paris, 1890–1903.

Ward, P. L. "The Coronation Ceremony in Medieval England," *Speculum*, XIV (1939), 160-78.

——— "An Early Version of the Anglo-Saxon Coronation Ceremony," *E.H.R.*, LVII (1942), 345-61.

Wilkinson, Bertie. The Constitutional History of Medieval England 1216–1399. 2 vols. London, 1948–52.

Woolf, C. Sidney. Bartolus de Sassoferrato. His Position in the History of Medieval Political Thought. Cambridge, 1913.

# Index